Visionary Fictions

Edward J. Ahearn

Visionary Fictions ✍

Apocalyptic Writing from Blake to the Modern Age

Yale University Press   New Haven and London

Designed by Rebecca Gibb.
Set in Fournier type by Northeastern Graphic Services, Inc., Hackensack, New Jersey.
Printed in the United States of America by BookCrafters, Inc., Chelsea, Michigan.

Library of Congress Cataloging-in-Publication Data
Ahearn, Edward J.
Visionary fictions : apocalyptic writing from Blake to the modern
age / Edward J. Ahearn.
p. cm.
Includes bibliographical references and index.
ISBN 0-300-06536-1
1. Literature, Modern—History and criticism. 2. Apocalyptic
literature—History and criticism. 3. Apocalypse in literature.
4. Visions in literature. 5. Prophecies in literature.
6. Millennialism in literature. 7. End of the world in literature.
I. Title.
PN701.A34 1996
809'.9338—dc20   95-46640
                                                      CIP
A catalogue record for this book is available from the British Library.

The paper in this book meets the guidelines for permanence and durability of the Committee on Production Guidelines for Book Longevity of the Council on Library Resources.

10 9 8 7 6 5 4 3 2 1

For my brothers
Jack, Jim, Harry, and Bill

contents

Acknowledgments ✍

This book is the product of longstanding interests — no, passions and furies — and is reflective of an American career in teaching and scholarship in the second half of the twentieth century. These interests were kindled in graduate studies in comparative literature at Yale with one of the founders of American comparatism, the late René Wellek, who along with many others had been displaced from Europe by the greatest horror of our era. They resurfaced in 1976 when I was a reader for a fine doctoral thesis by Stephen Coon on several of the writers treated here, were nourished by the contributions of other Brown University students in courses that I subsequently taught, and came to written expression in a year-long sabbatical. For that leave I am grateful to Thomas Anton, then dean of the faculty, with whom I have since had the pleasure of team-teaching. Colleagues and friends at Brown and elsewhere, particularly Arnold Weinstein, Albert Cook, Michel-André Bossy, Bill Crossgrove, Priscilla Parkhurst Ferguson, and most of all Ross Chambers, have encouraged and advised me on the project. I have profited from ideas and suggestions for bibliography and revision from Larry Porter, Kay Goodman, Virginia Hules, and anonymous readers for Yale University Press. I am grateful for substantial research on bibliography and translations by William Shotwell, Laura Pirott-Quintero, Mona Delgado, and especially Ellen Douglass, not to mention the computer expertise of Shem Garlock and my colleague and dear friend Dore Levy, and the editorial assistance of Jane Hedges, Cynthia Wells, and Jane Zanichkowsky. For help with the illustrations I thank Mark McMorris, and most of all Mme. Arlette Souhami of the Galerie Dionne and Roland and Edith Flak of the Galerie Flak, both in Paris. I am grateful to Brown University for aid in the reproduction of these illustrations. As always, I dedicate this book to members of my family, of whose goodness and courage I am constantly aware. The most important of them is my wife, *la merveille*, that most loving, strong, imaginative, and visionary of women, Michèle Respaut.

Introduction ꙮ

I dislike introductions but find them inescapable, if informational and pertinent yet concise. Here goes. In the past I have written books centered on Arthur Rimbaud and Karl Marx, hence on efforts to explode both our customary ways of perceiving things and the very bases of our socioeconomic-political system.[1] There is a hint of this dual thrust in my current title and subtitle. There is inevitably also a hint of the debate about the relation between action in history and transformations of consciousness that runs from Marx and Engels's *German Ideology* to André Breton's surrealist manifestos and beyond. Both poles of what is clearly an unacceptable dichotomy, between the "mental" and the "material," are implicit, though with varying emphases, in the writers whom I group here under the related rubric *Visionary Fictions*.

The writers are William Blake (1757–1827), Novalis (Friedrich von Hardenberg, 1772–1801), Gérard de Nerval (Gérard Labrunie, 1808–55), le comte de Lautréamont (Isidore Ducasse, 1846–70), André Breton (1896–1966), and Louis Aragon (1897–1982), and the contemporary authors William Burroughs (1914–), Monique Wittig (1935–), and Jamaica Kincaid (1949–) — the last also a pseudonym. My argument essentially is that these writers constitute a very persistent tradition of visionary and apocalyptic writing, only partially recognized by scholars and critics, that

1

is closely related to the upheaval and trauma of the French Revolution and to succeeding horrendous events in world history.

Apocalypse of course means the violent end of the world and the coming of the Last Judgment, as mystically described in the biblical book of John of Patmos, and many have viewed events from the French Revolution to the nuclear age in apocalyptic terms. We shall see that a number of our works have apocalyptic elements, whereas some are "millennial" in projecting a final or at least a thousand-year-long period of universal peace. Although I occasionally use the word *utopian* to describe some of them in relation to various hopeful tendencies or endings, none of the works is utopian in the formal sense (seen from Plato to More or Bacon or nineteenth-century reformers) of imagining the workings of an ideal society.[2] But all involve a radical transformation of how we perceive the world, with inevitable implications for our judgment on the state of society; hence all are what I call visionary fictions.

Fictions may seem to privilege excessively the formal or "merely" aesthetic, which would be strange considering what I have already written here. But it has been argued that works of literature, far from being entirely imaginary, may not only "reflect" reality but may contribute to "constructing" the reality experienced by their readers. All of my authors would agree with this argument; indeed, most of them assert it expressly. A striking example is Blake, who, we shall find, shows us a horrible vision of sexuality by descending *into* the Bible and emerging from the experience clutching a body that turns out to be a book of philosophy by Aristotle!

More specifically, *fictions* is meant to draw attention to the ways in which our visionary works, though mostly written in prose, subvert the increasingly dominant form of the realistic novel. Blake seems to have largely ignored the long history of novelistic writing in eighteenth- and early nineteenth-century England. As we shall see, although producing works that are in appearance novelistic, Novalis and Nerval developed sophisticated theories of antirealistic, mystical forms of expression. And from Lautréamont on, the rest of our writers by practice (and in most cases by explicit assertion) massively burlesque, satirize, and in every imaginable way undermine the hegemony of the novel.

Despite the myriad permutations of that genre, it has been intriguingly argued that its ascendancy is related to the development of the societal system as we know it and that novelistic form corresponds to, even "enforces," the parameters of temporal and spatial, personal and societal experience that we normally take to be "real."

Although classic proponents of this view include Ian Watt and Lucien Goldmann, I refer particularly to Roland Barthes, who attacks the nineteenth-century novel for creating a false "proprietary consciousness," for supporting what he calls the "totalitarian ideology of the referent." We glimpse salient features of "poststructuralist" thought that have recently come under violent criticism — the instability, even fictionality, of the human self or subject, the attack on referentiality, on literature as providing an image of life, in the interest of an unencumbered *écriture*. After all, Barthes's essay is entitled "To Write: An Intransitive Verb?"[3] The question of poststructuralist notions of "writing" in relation to our visionary authors will recur. As already indicated, however, the authors to be treated here are not Marcel Proust or Alain Robbe-Grillet but a series of writers who challenge our sense of self and reality in more harrowing and exalting ways, through a variety of kinds of writing that constitute what I call visionary (and in one case antivisionary) textualities.

Visionary, then. A favorite word of Blake, later used in a somewhat similar way by Aragon, it indicates the superior, "fourfold" vision that Blake claims to possess, in opposition to the "Single vision" of "Newtons sleep," which we have in our ordinary states of consciousness.[4] That is, the writers I study vehemently claim that the world as we perceive it is an impoverished and dull thing, fundamentally delusory, and that they can put us in touch with a reality far more exciting, even "infinite."

Despite our workaday habits, we know that in at least one fundamental way they are right. From philosophy since Berkeley and Kant (once again, that is, in the most recent history of philosophy, not to speak of many religious traditions), in the wake of the discoveries of science, we know that our vision of our selves, of our bodies, of others, and of the external world and the universe is a limited, even a fabricated one. We have the organs to perceive the world in a certain way and have gone through an infant process of "primal construction of the world," and had we not those organs, and that process, we would not be able so to perceive the world.[5] Telescopes and microscopes enable us to see other "realities." But Blake is right in asserting that such instruments only change the "ratio" of our organs to the objects perceived and hence produce a vision no more real than the first one.[6] In the perspective of molecular biology and subatomic physics, and cosmic time, too, how puny our "realities" seem. Such an insight produced the famous expression of anguish in Blaise Pascal's *Pensées*, an anguish that persists but also incites to exaltation in figures like Blake and Novalis and Gérard de Nerval and Jamaica Kincaid.

As the references to Pascal, Kant, Blake, and current but historically knowledgeable neural science suggest, visionary writing involves substantial knowledge of and complex relations with science, philosophy, and religion. Excessive rationalism in the first two is a target, but the knowledge of bodily organs and of cosmic processes and the idealist tradition in philosophy nonetheless are positively exploited in works from romantics to surrealists and William Burroughs and beyond. What is more, scientific experimentation has demonstrated the objectively different forms of cerebral activity associated with various "altered states of consciousness," whether related to drugs, forms of mental illness, artistic experience, trances and ecstatic states induced by meditation, or other phenomena.[7]

Although it is not my goal to repeat well-known intellectual history,[8] it will be useful to sketch a few arguments here in preparation for future chapters. First, regarding "idealist" philosophy, one recalls famous justifications of creative imagination. Samuel Taylor Coleridge in *Biographia Literaria* (1815) summarizes the history of Western philosophy in terms of materialist and idealist tendencies, drawing on Kant and emphasizing the idealist tactic of supposing mind to be the primordial reality on the way to proposing his theory of "primary" imagination. Charles Baudelaire produces similar formulations in the *Salon* of 1859, arguing that the imagination (we would probably say our neural system) *creates* the world.

More extreme idealist positions on the priority of mind in constructing our view of reality are adopted by the visionary writers. Blake uses the arguments of Bishop Berkeley, Novalis the absolute idealism of Fichte to formulate his doctrine of imagination as "magic idealism." One of the ingredients in the justification of the notion of surrealism is the reference by Aragon and Breton to Berkeley, Kant, Hegel, and others. And sophisticated epistemological arguments are adduced or implied to validate the impossible or absurd visions shown us by Lautréamont, Burroughs, and Wittig. Indeed, the surreal, which projects a reality beyond the distinction of real from unreal, corresponds to what I call the "antivisionary" in Lautréamont, a form of writing causing us to *see* what is simultaneously claimed to be outrageously *impossible*. But such claims for the reality of what can be imagined come early, from Blake and the supposedly insane Nerval: "Everything possible to be believ'd is an image of truth"; "I do not think that human imagination has invented anything which is not true either in this world or in others, and I could not doubt what I had so clearly *seen* myself."

Like many leading intellectuals, our visionary writers were interested in the debates carried on throughout the seventeenth, eighteenth, and nineteenth centuries by scientists, philosophers, and writers concerning the brain, our sense organs, and our acts of perception.[9] There was also of course growing speculation about and keen interest in the structure and evolution of the earth. Novalis, who was a student of mining and geology, combined his literary-philosophical pursuits with scientific and mathematical studies, and it is clear that Blake and a number of the others have had similar encyclopedic projects. Recurrent motifs will show us individuals carried off on space- and time-transforming terrestrial and cosmic voyages as well as analogies between the structure of the brain and of the earth. These are enacted as visions and dreams in Blake, Novalis, Nerval, and Kincaid, presented as the result of drug use in Burroughs.

As for religion, many of the sources of the writing studied here are found in religious myth, and undoubtedly the overall impact of some of our works is deeply religious. Yet it would be hard to imagine more vicious attacks on religion and morality than what is found in many a passage by Blake, Lautréamont, Breton, Aragon, and Burroughs. This is a paradox that we will need to try to grasp: Why is the modern, post–French Revolution, visionary tradition so consistently subversive of religion, so frequently sacrilegious?

Another paradox concerns the human self, existing *as* body or *in* the body? The body and its organs provide access to all experience, but as is clear from everything above, the body-self in this literature is radically exposed to annihilation and transfiguration. Ecstatic apocalypses may be sublime or sordid, with intervening degrees of anguish and destruction. The early Blake, we shall see, tells us the key is an "improvement of sensual enjoyment," Burroughs that "we see God through our assholes in the flash bulb of orgasm."

But various critics have characterized a somewhat later Blake, and Burroughs as well, as "gnostic" in their distrust of the body. *Gnostic,* deriving from a Greek word for knowledge, generally refers to early Christian dualistic sects that condemned the material world and claimed mystical knowledge of divine things, often associated with another Greek word for knowledge, *sophia.* An exalted form of the gnostic involving an idealized view of women, of a female figure sometimes referred to as Sophie, is visible in Novalis, Nerval, and Breton, whereas the mistrust of the body does at various points characterize Blake and Burroughs. Still the body remains in both of the latter the means of access to the visionary, so I avoid that sense of *gnostic* in discussing them.

Nonetheless, in them various "perversions" come to the fore, if I may risk such phrases in this context, and sadism, masochism, homosexuality, multisexuality, and varying degrees of misogyny are significant in virtually all the writers, sometimes very disturbingly so. The marquis de Sade, although highly transgressive and relevant for many passages we shall encounter, is not in my terms visionary, so he will be mentioned only in passing regarding Lautréamont and Breton. Similarly the *Faust* of Goethe, one of a number of German texts translated by Nerval, plays only a muted role in that writer's *Aurélia* and later in Breton. Multiple and "perverse" sexuality is related, finally, to a myth current in many sources and traditions of a lost primal unity, expressed in sexual terms in the figure of the Androgyne. Beginning with critical debates about the erotic in Blake's *Milton* and pursuing the theme through assorted marriages, couplings, and conflicts in our other texts, including the homosexual in Lautréamont, Burroughs, and Wittig, we shall try to see to what extent visionary sexuality strives for that enlarged and rediscovered Being.

It becomes ever clearer, however, that this counterliterature is, in the arena of sexuality, no counterliterature at all but an increasingly sexist form of obsessive male writing, calling for a female response. My chapter on Monique Wittig and Jamaica Kincaid, although an incomplete coda, is in no way tokenist but rather is an unapologetic effort at providing at least a partial response, one from which sadistic and destructive features are also not absent.

Erotic energy may be a constant, but there are other visionary states, experiences, means, and tactics that we will encounter. These include prophetic vision, dream, myth and legend, hallucination and insanity, automatic writing, trance, and drugs. The last is persistent in a related group, from Samuel Taylor Coleridge to Rimbaud and beyond. But among our writers it is important only in Burroughs, where the example of Coleridge's poem "Kubla Khan" will be relevant. In *Le paysan de Paris* Aragon uses the motif humorously, and in *Les Guérillères* Wittig gives it a largely symbolic role, although she also highlights collective, sex-induced trance.

We will also encounter a strange array of kinds of writing, from Klingsohr's tale in Novalis's *Heinrich von Ofterdingen* to the "antivisionary" exploits of Lautréamont's *Les chants de Maldoror*. There will be fragmentary forms of expression as well as pronouncements in the form of proverbs, aphorisms, manifestos. At other times the convention of journal notation will register strange or impossible events. As mentioned, criticism of the novel, and outrageous spoofs of its typical forms, are increasingly prevalent. There will be mystical visions and magical flights, voyages that end in recurrently recognizable natural, architectural, or urban scenes, but also abrupt transitions, impossible combinations, juxtapositions of the beautiful and the absurd. This list will be illustrated in detail in each writer, with certain family resemblances but also extraordinary individual creativity visible.

The sources of our visionary writers are exceptionally various, not to say contradictory. Biblical and nonbiblical, they tend toward syncretist unity in Blake, Novalis, and Nerval and make their influence felt in serious or parodic form in many another writer, although much less in the women, who are bent on liberating themselves from male-dominated traditions. I make no claim to expert learning in these mystic sciences, usually grouped under the heading of the "esoteric." I will therefore not write extensively here about them, particularly since there is an abundant scholarly literature, both older and recent, on them. In any event, this book is not a source study; I am interested in attracting the reader to the wonders, and possibly the trauma, to be experienced in the modern, post–French Revolution writers I treat. But for the sake of clarity, I will sketch here some important sources and terms, citing the scholarly works that I have found most useful.[10]

As indicated already, the Bible has a large importance, in Blake the Old Testament prophets, the Apocalypse, and an extremely subversive view of Jesus. The Jesus of Nerval's *Aurélia* is only apparently more orthodox, playing as we shall see a most destructive role. The Song of Songs is relevant for Novalis and Nerval, and that work and Genesis are taken over for feminist goals in books by Wittig. The sacrilege and parody we encounter already in Blake are massively augmented in Lautréamont, the surrealists, and Burroughs. In Jamaica Kincaid, religion, but voodoo or obeah religion, makes an enormous visionary contribution.

Not unrelated are various mystics, in the background earlier Catholics like Eckehart, John of the Cross, and Theresa of Avila as well as Renaissance believers in the new science such as Giordano Bruno, burned at the stake for his acceptance of Copernican theories. Later Protestant mystical writers, notably Jacob Boehme and Emmanuel Swedenborg, are important for Blake, Novalis, and Nerval. Then there are the occult, or hermetic, traditions. *Hermetic* means "obscure" when said, for instance, of a Mallarmé sonnet, but it is also related to the secret doctrines organized under the patronage of the priest or divinity Hermes Trismegistus. Nerval's sonnet collection *Les chimères* is hermetic in both senses, and another of Wittig's feminist appropriations is to have men praise woman as "tristmegista." Our visionary writers refer as well to the alchemist Paracelsus, to the Jewish Cabala (mystic interpretations of biblical texts influenced by the Neoplatonism of Alexandria), and to the ideas of the German Rosicrucians. Readers who plowed through the preceding note on scholarly source studies may enjoy this one on the American novelist E. L. Doctorow.[11]

Interest in these various strands of religious and occult doctrines grew greatly in Europe on the eve of the French Revolution, and at the same time there was a widespread tendency toward syncretic amalgamation of myths from around the world, with an emphasis on their origin in the Middle East and the Orient. This was a repetition of a much older version of the importance of the East for the origins of humanity, dating back to Plato's *Timaeus*, in which the Egyptian priest of Saïs recounts the Atlantis myth and with it the myth of the lost Golden Age, one or both of which are used by Blake, Novalis, Nerval and, with some disclaimers, Breton. In the romantic period an important compilation was Georg Friedrich Creuzer's *Symbolik und Mythologie der alten Völker, besonders der Griechen* (1810–12), which was widely translated and disseminated. This was one of Nerval's sources and seems to have been read, but humorously dismissed, by Aragon. Blake probably didn't use it, but he developed his own amalgamation of myths from many regions, again with the characteristic emphasis on the East: "The philosophy of the east taught the first principles of human perception."

This Orientalism, to make use of an argument from Edward Said,[12] is a significant element of the visionary tradition, as we will see in studying not only Blake but Novalis and Nerval. It finds its place in Lautréamont's parodies and reappears in sordid form, somewhat lightly in the surrealists, shockingly in Burroughs's *Naked Lunch*.

I will return to the issue of Orientalism. For the moment I want to make clear that, having provided the above summary information about sources, terms, and scholarship, I shall hereafter use words like *millennial, gnostic, hermetic,* and *cabalistic* in their normally accepted designations. In contrast, although much of the recurrent imagery that we will encounter may strike one as "archetypal," I rarely use that word, wishing to avoid Jungian universalist suggestions, although Northrup Frye's notion of the literary archetype is relevant.[13] These last references will allow me here further to delineate the nature of the visionary and to suggest the contribution the present book makes to existing studies of this tradition.

One cannot dismiss Jung without thinking of Freud, who in the case of Breton becomes a "source" or justification of the surreal, notably for what his writing about dreams and the unconscious reveals about the limits of our waking sense of "reality." Indeed, I myself use such arguments from Freud, in relation to surrealism, to explain the oneiric power of "antivisionary" writing by Lautréamont. Freud showed little enthusiasm, but to Breton psychoanalysis could appear to provide "scientific" confirmation, akin to earlier debates about perception and the external world, of the human subject's literally creative power.

Further, Freud has a bearing on a literary trend that is closely related to but not identical with the visionary, namely, the fantastic. Among studies of that widespread nineteenth- and twentieth-century current of writing, Todorov's point, that the fantastic suddenly, perhaps momentarily, unsettles our apparently stable sense of the real, signals the difference.[14] In contrast, the visionary writers tend to want to make "the real" go away altogether; their onslaught is far more total. And Freud's classic work on the fantastic, "The 'Uncanny,'"[15] indicates his deep-seated "disagreement" with the fantastic and, a fortiori, with the visionary. For he concludes that

the fantastic represents a recrudescence of primitive wishful reality thinking, in which desire seems able to transform reality. There is a significant
difference in degree between the fantastic and the visionary; despite the appeal of Freud's writing on dreams and the unconscious, between the visionary and the Freud of the reality principle there is total opposition.

The other use of *archetypal*, Frye's, reminds us that, regarding literary
history, the visionary tradition is a highly self-conscious one. Blake, Novalis, and Nerval did not know one another's work, but each had read essentially the same books and been influenced by the same traditions, the ones
sketched above. Lautréamont and the surrealists display a high degree of
awareness of their predecessors, at least of the French and the Germans.
Burroughs clearly knows Rimbaud and the surrealists and English romantic writers, explicitly Coleridge and implicitly Blake. Older and more recent scholarship recognizes this affiliation of religious and occult writings,
Blake, Novalis, Nerval, and the surrealists, particularly Breton. And scholarship on Burroughs is conscious of his associations with visionary, surrealist, and drug currents. But there has been little sense of this long tradition
as a whole, of this remarkable phenomenon of visionary writing persisting
from the French Revolution into the present day, in texts by women as well
as men.

In addition to whatever interest my readings of individual works may
hold, this larger overall view is what the current book has to offer to the
reader willing to be persuaded by the analyses in succeeding chapters. But
also another important thing: the striking connection between these texts
and what my subtitle calls the modern age, namely postrevolutionary, modern, history in the larger sense.

Indeed our works illustrate the complex relation between revolution and
writing, history and apocalypse that constantly looms. Blake apocalyptically, Novalis in millennial fashion, as well as Nerval and Lautréamont,
write in direct response to the upheavals of the French Revolution and its
nineteenth-century sequels. Nerval, supposedly apolitical, clearly signals
the anguish of the failed revolutions of 1830 and 1848 and the Crimean War,
whereas Lautréamont's *Maldoror* is eerily predictive of the class war that
ended in the destruction of the Commune in 1871. In this perspective the
French Revolution, with its successes and horrors, itself seems a gigantic
"visionary fiction,"[16] engendering apocalyptic and millennial expectations
together with destruction and slaughter.

The Orientalism mentioned earlier returns in the broader picture of
world history evoked by Novalis and Nerval. The East is the source of
mystic knowledge in both *Heinrich von Ofterdingen* and *Aurélia*. But the
nuptial conclusion of the former is preceded by a severe critique of Europe's

role in the Crusades. And one instance of Nerval's anguished consciousness of the bloodiness of human history is again the warfare between Europeans and Arabs. The theme reappears in outrageously antic form in Burroughs's *Naked Lunch*.

In Aragon, Breton, and Burroughs visionary writing has as its backdrop the horrors of twentieth-century history. As we shall see, the surrealists, and Wittig too, write in periods of renewed revolutionary expectation and deception. Nor is this history lacking in Kincaid, although she and Wittig tend to highlight the dimension of sexual politics. The historical and political may be flagrant, as in Blake and Breton, or covert and guarded, as in Nerval and Lautréamont, but throughout we will not miss it.

Although in their responses to history the majority of our writers are explicitly or implicitly on the side of revolution, even when they are not their writing tends to be subversive. This is already apparent in comments on religion and sexuality. Taken together, the texts to be studied here constitute a corrosive onslaught against our entire "reality system" and the institutions and values that support it. These include religion and church, including the divinity, moral values extending to reversal of conceptions of good and evil, governments and national myths, sexuality and family, the solidity of the external world, the stability and permanence of the self, of *ourselves*.

Inevitably a question insinuates itself: Why this protracted literature of visionary subversion? How does the ambiguously religious challenge to our sense of reality relate to vigorous or muted protest against the sociopolitical and, integrally, personal-sexual order? Each chapter will provide some insight into this question, and by the end a larger perspective should emerge.

This last remark exemplifies my organizational strategy. Having sketched backgrounds and themes here, I will use Blake to flesh them out, in some sense providing an inventory of visionary motifs and issues. The succeeding chapters are chronological in order — Novalis, Nerval, Lautréamont, Breton and Aragon, Burroughs, Wittig and Kincaid — and will display a variety of changes rung on that "inventory." In each case one or more major works will be chosen for close study, but in each case too a framing background context will be furnished, with considerable detail provided in the notes. Despite the complex and overlapping range of features in each writer, from chapter to chapter insight will, I hope, be cumulative, with the last two chapters already drawing issues together in preparation for the conclusion.

The use of the word *inventory* above points to a paradox, a danger I want to avoid, that of academic literary criticism on such exuberant writing.

From Blake's broadsides and the ridiculous but dangerous figure of the Scribe in Klingsohr's tale to Aragon's attacks on critics, these writers resist perhaps even more than others the desiccating touch of "criticism." On the other hand, their work demonstrably involves much intellectual work, encyclopedic knowledge, analytic and synthesizing qualities, and high degrees of rational as well as other kinds of intelligence. Nonetheless, although a lot of what follows involves interpretative "analysis," much also takes the form of summary, paraphrase, explanation, and quotation.

In this respect my goal is to introduce the nonspecialist reader to the pleasures, the exaltation, but often also the dread and disgust of forms of writing that dare to challenge our assumptions about reality and much of the underpinning of those assumptions, from religion and morality to family and sexuality and the forms of society. As has been suggested regarding the "antivisionary" in Lautréamont, these texts, despite various largely rhetorical disclaimers, display an extraordinary confidence in their ability to make us experience what we think to be impossible. The reader is insistently engaged, sometimes almost to the point of violation. Blake and Aragon harangue us, Lautréamont tries to kiss us through the page (!), to paralyze and cretinize us; like "The Ancient Mariner" Burroughs wants to mesmerize us.

Another fundamental question therefore emerges: Why are we (if we are — obviously I am) attracted to these writings? But that is a way of expressing a further question: How have these works, produced as an "esoteric" counterliterature, attained and maintained over time a large readership? Further, as I will suggest for the surrealists and Burroughs (but the remark is perhaps also relevant for Kincaid), does success in attracting the doubting reader, do popularity and even bestsellership threaten the visionary enterprise itself?

Despite the scope of this book, which interprets a persistent tradition rather than "defining" a "genre," I am aware of what is left out. Blake, Novalis, Nerval, to a lesser degree Breton and Aragon, are among our great poets, yet I treat closely only the brief poems by the first two that are incorporated in *The Marriage of Heaven and Hell* and *Heinrich von Ofterdingen*.[17] Mention of these titles indicates another principle of selectivity. In the interest of reaching a readership other than that made up of academics and adepts, I have chosen classic and in most cases relatively accessible texts. Hence Blake's *Marriage* and Breton's *Nadja*, rather than *Milton* and *Arcane 17*, but in both instances I have felt it necessary to expand succinctly from the earlier text to the later one. As for the vast corpus of surrealist works, and the considerable body of female utopian writing, these can only be suggested by the pairing of Breton and Aragon, Wittig and Kincaid. Inevita-

introduction

11

bly, too, I have not been able to address the visionary as a multimedia phenomenon, from Blake's engravings, the magic book in which Heinrich von Ofterdingen reads, and the composite compositions of Nerval's protagonist to the variety of surrealist productions in numerous media, not to speak of the importance of film for Burroughs. I hope that the illustrations compensate, partially but strikingly, for that. Chosen with care, they resonate with (or against) single authors but also with all the writers treated, and with one another. They too demonstrate the persistence of the visionary impulse into the present day.

For foreign-language works I give translations (specifying when my own hand is involved), except in a few cases in which the passage is virtually translated in the commentary or where the English is cognate. All italicized words are in the original. In spite of my claim not to be the sort of critic Aragon attacks, I provide as well substantial summaries of the scholarship on my writers. Much of it is fine, some Scribe-like, but all of it pales before the visionary works, as inevitably does my own, even devoted as it is to revealing their stunning flights and voids and transfigurations.

An Anatomy of the Visionary ❧
Blake's *Marriage of Heaven and Hell*

In spite of Blake's striking individuality, there is nothing surprising about studying *The Marriage of Heaven and Hell* at the outset of this book. But just about everything in this work, as in the rest of Blake's production, *is* surprising.

Born in 1757, this self-educated writer and artist spent most of the seventy years of his life in isolation. A dissenter in religion[1] and prorepublican in politics in a country that had recently lost its American colonies and was in conflict with revolutionary France, Blake also signaled his opposition to the new industrial order by refusing to have his works printed; he illustrated and etched each individual copy of his major productions. These include poetry, notably *Songs of Innocence and Experience*, as well as manuscript poems and letters containing poems, various prose manifestos, and longer and shorter "prophetic books" written in unrhymed verse and dramatizing cosmic and mythological themes and events. Antirationalist and indiscriminately anti-Enlightenment, as suggested in the manuscript poem beginning, "Mock on Mock on Voltaire Rousseau," Blake railed against the precepts of neoclassical art in marginalia to the works of Sir Joshua Reynolds.

Instead his models and sources include the Bible, notably Old Testament prophetic books, John's Apocalypse, and Jesus reinterpreted in a subversive, the traditional would say sacrilegious, way, as well as Dante, Shakespeare, and Milton, the last in quite conflicted ways. Blake read Boehme and Swedenborg in English translation, attended meetings of the Swedenborg society in London, and critically annotated some of his works as well.

Blake also drew on idealist philosophy, chiefly that of Bishop Berkeley, to refute Lockean positions about the priority of sense and the passivity of mind and to express extreme visionary positions that will find echoes or opposition in writers from Novalis to the surrealists: "The desire of Man being Infinite the possession is Infinite & himself Infinite"; "Forms must be apprehended by Sense or the Eye of Imagination"; "Man is All Imagination God is Man & exists in us & we in him."[2] Indeed, claiming that imagination and poetry are at the source of all religion and knowledge, Blake anticipates the syncretism of later writers in combining elements from Eastern religions, Scandinavian myth, conceptions of Druidic practice, and much else. The words of one of his own mythological personages justify this syncretism: "I must Create a System or be enslav'd by another Mans."[3]

As stressed in the introduction and as implied above, the amalgamation of prophetic religious and literary forms, Protestant mysticism, idealist philosophy, infinite desire and imagination, and diverse mythic traditions promotes not only spiritual illumination but acute historical, in Blake's case revolutionary, consciousness. As we shall see, *The Marriage of Heaven and Hell* is written in immediate response to the French Revolution and inaugurates a series of visionary works that are produced in counterpoint to that upheaval and subsequent ones extending from the nineteenth century into our own period.

The earliest in date of the texts to be treated in this book (1790–1793),[4] the *Marriage* is for Blake relatively accessible, certainly much more so than the long *Jerusalem* and even the shorter, very beautiful *Milton*. But for the sake of completeness and of issues relevant throughout this book, a sketch of selected features of the latter will nonetheless be in order. The *Marriage*'s ambiguous, even parodic, roots in earlier prophetic literature, notably the Bible and some Protestant forms of mysticism (Swedenborg, Boehme) are noticeable, but so also is its reference to nonbiblical traditions.[5] It antedates the dominance of the realist novel form in the nineteenth century and presents the reader with an array of nonnovelistic, and sometimes dismaying, modes of writing, in addition to enigmatic and discomforting ideas.

Major "thematic" concerns apparent in the visionary tradition are nonetheless formulated in the *Marriage*, albeit with a particular vigor. These include the visionary itself, as experience and as variety of modes of expression; a provocative treatment of the body and sexuality; a reversal of moral values that is related to a pervasive nineteenth-century satanism but that also has the very disturbing seriousness of, and eighty years' advance on,

Nietzsche's philosophy; and a related and very violent attack on established religion. Blake, in his belief in the visionary and the infinite, is nonetheless a profoundly religious writer. We will see to what extent these emphases are echoed, or contradicted, in succeeding writers. In Blake, as in a number of the others, such features are linked to an apocalyptic vision of history, a societal-political critique that in Blake's case is unreservedly revolutionary. Indeed, as opposed to the anguish, pain, or doubt that characterizes some later writers, the *Marriage* displays an exuberance that is bound to have an effect on the reader.

As suggested, therefore, the *Marriage* is a heteroclite combination of literary modes.[6] It opens with an "Argument" that takes the form not of philosophical or legal prose but of an enigmatic poem; it closes with a song and a chorus. In between we hear "The voice of the Devil" and various other imposing pronouncements. The narrator presents us with a series of "Proverbs of Hell," which he has collected in order to illustrate "Infernal wisdom." And, although Swedenborg is criticized, Dante, Shakespeare, Boehme, and Paracelsus being preferred, a form derived from Swedenborg, that of the "Memorable Fancy," is used to narrate supernatural encounters. Despite this formal complexity and Blake's insistence on the contrariness, as we shall see, of truth, the themes enumerated above are framed with startling clarity. In pursuing them we shall also be able to note some of the typical tactics of visionary writing in their Blakean vehemence.

First, then, the *Marriage* enunciates a major theme of the tradition, namely that, beyond the impoverished or illusory sensations we take to be normal, there is *really* a world of infinite perception. Somewhat as in Novalis and Nerval, this takes the form of the myth of a primitive enlarged consciousness that has in the course of history been lost. Hence in the *Marriage* our senses are said to be only "the chief inlets of Soul in this age," so that perhaps the bird we perceive is actually "an immense world of delight, clos'd by [our] senses five" (34–35). This is the trace in the *Marriage* of the myth in Blake's shorter and longer prophetic books of the disintegration of the original human being into deluded consciousness, sexual division, nationhood, and international war.

Vico-like, but with a revolutionary difference,[7] Blake thus derives all organized religion, as abstract system, from the animating imagination of the "ancient Poets," who perceived vaster realities through "their enlarged & numerous senses" (38). Figures from a later historical time, the prophets Isaiah and Ezekiel, dine with Blake in the immediately following "Memorable Fancy" (38–39). Isaiah asserts that his "senses discover'd the infinite in every thing," while Ezekiel explains that all religions originally derived from the "philosophy of the east," which "taught the first principles of human perception," hence again making "Poetic Genius" the source of religion. In response to Blake's questions about his ascetic practices, he answers that they derived from his "desire of raising other men into a perception of the infinite." In keeping with the syncretism characteristic of other writers in this tradition, Blake has Ezekiel indicate that in this he is no different from the Greek Diogenes and from currently living "North American tribes."

Hence is rapidly sketched a version of an original fullness of consciousness as opposed to our shrunken contemporary perceptions, with a universal sense of visionary initiatives and tactics at various times and places in human history. In plate 14 this philosophy becomes apocalyptic. The speaker asserts that the "ancient tradition" prophesying the end of the world is true: "the whole creation will be consumed, and appear infinite and holy whereas it now appears finite & corrupt." Whereas currently "man has closed himself up, till he sees all things thro' narrow chinks of his cavern," instead, in the celebrated lines, "if the doors of perception were cleansed every thing would appear to man as it is: infinite." Here Blake's view of the unrestrained body, presented earlier in the work, again finds expression: "This will come to pass by an improvement of sensual enjoyment"; "But first the notion that man has a body distinct from his soul, is to be expunged; this I shall do, by printing in the infernal method, by corrosives, which in Hell are salutary and medicinal, melting apparent surfaces away, and displaying the infinite which was hid."

By thus referring to the effect of his practice of etching his works, Blake opens for us the possibility of analyzing the forms of his writing. At the same time, the allusion to the body points us to his revaluing of values and his attack on conventional religion, features prominent in him and resonant for all of our writers.

It is indeed early on in the *Marriage*, in the plates (3–6) immediately following "The Argument," to which we will return, that Blake inverts received values in relation to the body. In contrast to the opposition held by "the religious" between good and evil, the speaker proclaims that "Without Contraries is no progression"; not only attraction, reason, and love, but also repulsion, energy, and hate, are "necessary to Human existence." Although the balance is immediately tipped against the traditional values, with good defined as passive and obedient and evil as "the active springing from Energy," we should retain the centrality of contrariness in Blake's view. Both sides of any opposition are necessary, which, of course, militates against a univocal reading of any portion, let alone the whole, of the *Marriage* itself. There may be something of a contradiction, rather than a contrary, between this conclusion and the assertiveness of other passages.

Nonetheless, the principle of the contraries adds an additional unsettling note to the challenging of fundamental values.

And that challenge is quickly restated in the assertion that all "Bibles or sacred codes" (another syncretist formula) are the source of errors concerning the separation of body and soul, the evil of energy as deriving exclusively from the body, and the eternal punishment God inflicts on man. Against these, the "following Contraries" are said to be "True," and immediately the ambiguity noted above is apparent: there is no separation between body and soul; yet "Energy is the only life and is from the Body," reason being the "outward circumference of Energy"; and, finally, the stunningly and simply beautiful "Energy is Eternal Delight."

This antidualistic revalorizing of the body, seen by some as at variance with the later prophetic works,[8] and the attack on repressive religion and reason, leads to a revision of Old and New Testaments. In brief scope, expanded later in *Milton*, Milton's Messiah is identified with Job's Satan, since in the devil's "account" it was the Messiah who fell. Needless to say, this also subverts the depiction of Satan and the Last Judgment in John's Apocalypse. Jesus prays to his father to send "the comforter or Desire that Reason may have Ideas to build on," and Milton is famously claimed to be "of the Devils party without knowing it." Later, in the last "Memorable Fancy," Jesus is presented as having acted "from impulse: not from rules" and as being virtuous despite having broken all ten commandments.

Elsewhere in the *Marriage* Blake asserts that "all deities reside in the human breast" and that "God only Acts & Is, in existing beings or Men" (38, 40). This magnification of the human anticipates Nietzsche, but one would not consider Blake an atheist like Nietzsche. Yet his equation of restraint with weakness, as in "Those who restrain desire, do so because theirs is weak enough to be restrained," is close to the latter's *Genealogy of Morals*. Moreover, Blake's rejection of the God who torments "Man in Eternity for following his Energies" (34) could well explain that most vehement of attacks on the divinity, contemporaneous with Nietzsche's beginnings, *Les chants de Maldoror*.

In addition to such pronouncements, rendered to some extent ambiguous by the principle of contraries, Blake pursues these themes through the "Proverbs of Hell" and certain of the "Memorable Fancies." The first exploit the formal qualities of proverbs, moralizing generalities on the scope of human life, replete with imperatives and references to the seasons and other phases of existence.

Some of them in fact sound not infernal but rather like "ordinary" proverbs: "In seed time learn, in harvest teach, in winter enjoy"; "The busy bee has no time for sorrow"; "Think in the morning, Act in the noon, Eat in the evening, Sleep in the night." But one might interpret these as playing an ironic role, particularly since others like them intrude slight imbalances of symmetry or suggestion: "The bird a nest, the spider a web, man friendship"; "As the plow follows words, so God rewards prayers." Given Blake's dislike of restraining structures, are we comfortable with the analogy between friendship and the web of the spider? What is the precise link between the verbal expressions of words and prayers and between plowing and divine rewards? Plowing is an immemorially positive function, producing the harvest mentioned in a proverb already cited, the first of the "Proverbs of Hell" in fact. But we have also read another, "The cut worm forgives the plow," which justifies the apparently legitimate suffering imposed on a supposedly inferior order of life by this human-divine activity.

Other "simple" proverbs exemplify the not-simple principle of contraries already discussed: "Joys impregnate. Sorrows bring forth"; "Damn. braces: Bless relaxes"; "Prayers plow not! Praises reap not!"; "Joys laugh not! Sorrows weep not!" The first of these four states a commonplace complementary relation between opposites, not incompatible with Blake's contraries. The second plays with a similar contrast, that between restraining and relaxing activities, but it can be read in at least two ways, due to the subtle grammatical imbalance of its parallelisms. *Damn* can be an imperative, producing a typically Blakean rejection of constriction, here in clothing. But this structure in the second half turns *relaxes* into a noun, as if there were some comfortable item of dress called by that name. That half reads more naturally as an infinitive expression: to bless, or the act of blessing, brings relaxation. Then why not read the first half that way? To damn, to curse something, is a bracing activity. The last two proverbs go beyond such subtleties and achieve not contraries but contradiction. We encountered earlier a parallelism between plowing and prayers. Here that reciprocity is denied: prayers don't plow, any more than praises reap. Beyond this deconstruction of the conventional analogy, there is denial, stated absolutely, of what we take to be fundamental meaning: "Joys laugh not! Sorrows weep not!" But this last must be associated with the earlier contrary-dialectical proverb: "Excess of sorrow laughs. Excess of joy weeps."

So the "simple" Proverbs of Hell produce ambiguity and contradiction. But, as was the case earlier, this does not prevent Blake from also framing striking, and sometimes disturbing, formulations of his favorite themes. Among a number on energy and excess: "The road of excess leads to the palace of wisdom"; "You never know what is enough unless you know what is more than enough," which is related to the concluding "Enough! or Too much"; "Exuberance is Beauty."

And a few on the body, desire, joy: "He who desires but acts not, breeds pestilence"; "The lust of the goat is the bounty of God"; "The nakedness of woman is the work of God"; "The soul of sweet delight. can never be defil'd" (keep in mind Blake's refusal to admit a distinction between body and soul). The last two contrast with the shame in the presence of nudity expressed in the Apocalypse as in other biblical texts. The next to last, setting female nakedness amid animals expressive of divine qualities, might provide reason to recall the sexism of some of Blake's symbolism. This is not necessarily the case here, since many animals have a highly positive function in Blake's symbolism, but we also recall that elsewhere female nature opposes male prophetic imagination.[9]

Nonetheless, in another proverb there is not sexism but sex, sex appropriately related to other bodily-spiritual features: "The head Sublime, the heart Pathos, the genitals Beauty, the hands & feet Proportion." Here the sexual is given its rightful place, not overemphasized; related to sublimity, pathos, and proportion, but in no way hidden. How much healthier indeed would people have been then, would we be now, if beauty were so matter-of-factly identified with the genital organs.

Other proverbs exemplify Blake's reversal of values and pursue the attack on religion. Of the first, consider "Prudence is a rich ugly old maid courted by Incapacity"; "Shame is Prides cloke." Similarly, not only are lust and nakedness divine; so also are the "pride of the peacock" and the "wrath of the lion." The sources of the virtues that are here overturned again come in for attack: "Prisons are built with stones of Law, Brothels with bricks of Religion" (which is close to "London" in *Songs of Experience*); and "As the catterpiller chooses the fairest leaves to lay her eggs on, so the priest lays his curse on the fairest joys" (which recalls "The Garden of Love," in the same collection).

These infernal proverbs are shocking indeed for anyone devoted to religion and to the ethical system it espouses, hardly less shocking, as suggested earlier, than anything in Nietzsche or Lautréamont. But there are a few other proverbs that are perhaps even more disturbing, regardless of our degree of religious adherence: "Drive your cart and your plow over the bones of the dead"; "A dead. body revenges not injuries"; "Sooner murder an infant in its cradle than nurse unacted desires." These are troubling because of the possible atmosphere of murder, or at least an apparent indifference to human death, that they suggest. The second is literally true, but is it also an incitement to murder? Following the first, when we plow (plowing again), do we in some literal sense violate the dead — inevitably? As for the last, it utters the horrible phrase, "murder an infant in its cradle," as well as transposing the nursing of children to our nurturing of repressed desire. Relevant for issues such as birth control and abortion then and now, this proverb does not in fact urge us to murder children. Instead its logic is that restraining desire is even worse than murdering them, a very large and disturbing claim. And its form ("Sooner murder . . .") is that of an invitation to an action.

The "Memorable Fancies," which introduce prophets, angels, and devils and hence propose supernatural experiences as well as debate on religious questions, are generally more genial, in fact full of humor. But the fourth and longest of these (41–42), although funny, also leads to an unsettling vision. It illustrates as well the *Marriage*'s parodic relation to the Apocalypse.

In this passage an angel shows Blake the eternal suffering in hell that supposedly awaits him: "he took me thro' a stable & thro' a church & down into the church vault at the end of which was a mill: thro' the mill we went, and came to a cave. down the winding cavern we groped our tedious way till a void boundless [. . .] appeared." The description of hell that now unfolds echoes the Apocalypse in its motifs of black sun, monstrous animal shapes, fire, and blood. But the writing is overblown and ironic, most blatantly in the description of the leviathan that this hell also contains: "his forehead was divided into streaks of green & purple like those on a tygers forehead: soon we saw his mouth & red gills hang just above the raging foam tinging the black deep with beams of blood, advancing toward us with all the fury of a spiritual existence." Moreover, when the angel departs, the vision disappears, the horrific scene having been the product of his "metaphysics."

Blake now takes the angel by force and flies through the night until he is "above the earths shadow," whereupon he flings himself and the angel into "the body of the sun," clothes himself in white, grasps Swedenborg's books, passes the planets, and leaps into the "void, between saturn & the fixed stars." There the stable and church reappear. At the altar Blake opens the Bible — "and lo! it was a deep pit, into which I descended driving the Angel before me, soon we saw seven houses of brick, one we enter'd; in it were a number of monkeys." Wrestling with angels, cosmic flights, stables and mills and churches and pits, the symbolism of sacred numbers, the displacements to other realms afforded by ascensions and descents — some of these familiar biblical motifs[10] will variously serve the visionary or antivisionary writing of Nerval and Lautréamont, as we shall see. The effect here is very different from that of reading the Bible, however, for once descended into that book, Blake and the reader encounter something hideous:

monkeys, baboons, & all of that species chaind by the middle, grinning and snatching at one another, but witheld by the shortness of their chains: however I saw that they sometimes grew numerous, and then the weak

were caught by the strong and with a grinning aspect, first coupled with
& then devourd, by plucking off first one limb and then another till the
body was left a helpless trunk. this after grinning & kissing it with seeming fondness they devourd too; and here & there I saw one savourily
picking the flesh off of his own tail; as the stench terribly annoyd us both
we went into the mill, & I in my hand brought the skeleton of a body,
which in the mill was Aristotles Analytics. (40)

This is a powerful attack on what Blake presents as a very destructive
form of religion. For it is the Bible that contains this view of the simian, how
close to human, body. The degraded animality, the stench, sex as rape and
devouring: this is the real hell that, according to Blake, such religion contains. This combination of visionary tactics of writing in the service of condemnation of unhealthy religion, and grotesque depiction of the body, will
not be encountered again until we treat *Les chants de Maldoror*.

This intensely realized scene, from which we want to escape along with
Blake and the angel, is contained in a book, the Bible. At the outset, despite,
or because of, his criticism of Swedenborg, that writer's productions are involved. And at the end, typically expressive of Blake's critique of the alli-
ance of abstract reason and repressive religion, Aristotle's *Analytics* are all
that remain of the experience. Another "Memorable Fancy" instead positively valorizes the visions contained in other books:

I was in a Printing house in Hell & saw the method in which knowledge
   is transmitted from generation to generation.
In the first chamber was a Dragon-Man, clearing away the rubbish from a
   cave's mouth; within, a number of Dragons were hollowing the cave,
In the second chamber was a Viper folding round the rock & the cave,
   and others adorning it with gold silver and precious stones.
In the third chamber was an Eagle with wings and feathers of air, he
   caused the inside of the cave to be infinite, around were numbers of
   Eagle like men, who built palaces in the immense cliffs.
In the fourth chamber were Lions of flaming fire raging around & melting
   the metals into living fluids.
In the fifth chamber were Unnam'd forms, which cast the metals into the
   expanse.
There they were reciev'd by Men who occupied the sixth chamber, and
   took the forms of books & were arranged in libraries. (40)

The opening paragraph and the sixth chamber evoke the same thing:
how knowledge was and to a great extent still is transmitted, namely,

through the writing and reading of books. Pace Derrida, maybe a certain civilization of the book is also, in a far more invigorating sense, a civilization of the text.[11] Between the opening and the closing paragraphs, the writing communicates first an enormous expansion, then a condensation — all that proliferation in chambers one through five reduced to books arranged in libraries. The point is that the process can be reversed: when we read, we can experience all that is expressed in the preceding chambers.

The division into chambers allows another set of visionary progressions having to do with the beings, substances, activities, and results of each room. The creatures evoked have biblical and Blakean resonances, usually relating human beings not to apes but to reptiles with a bad biblical history, vipers and dragons, and nobler beings celebrated both in the Bible and in some Proverbs of Hell other than those quoted by me. The progression itself is meaningful — dragons, vipers, eagles, lions, men. So also is the succession of activities, substances, and accomplishments: clearing away and hollowing out; enfolding and adorning with precious metals and jewels; creating an *interior infinity* having the vastness of the air; raging in flames, thus melting metals into "living fluids." A process of clearing away, followed by embellishing, gives way to an immaterial opening to infinity. Then rage, so recurrent in Blake, melts solid substance into fluid and *living* forms. Beyond that, the agents in the fifth chamber can only be grasped as "Unnam'd forms" who cast the molten metals into the expanse. That, according to Blake, is what a book worthy of its name is. Think about it when next you take one out — if you do — from a library.

My last sentence is a pale echo of another essential aspect of Blake's writing, his assertiveness (some might say his arrogance) and his domination of the reader through a series of orders, questions, counsels: "How do you know but ev'ry Bird . . . ?"; "see Isaiah xxxiv & xxxv Chap." (which we will shortly do).[12] Even "Sooner murder an infant . . ."! Occasionally he gives us advice that we realize he has all along been following: "Always be ready to speak your mind, and a base man will avoid you"; "He who has sufferd you to impose on him, knows you"; "Listen to the fools reproach! it is a kingly title!"

Blake, or his narrative persona (the two are difficult to separate, as we shall find too for Nerval, Lautréamont, and Burroughs) indeed exudes an utter self-confidence. There is one exception, a response to Ezekiel's statement that all have been submitted to the Jewish religion, that is, the one Blake attacks throughout: "I heard this with some wonder, & must confess my own conviction." Elsewhere he without hesitation demolishes the "Errors" of "All Bibles or sacred codes," rewrites both Bible and Milton, condemns Swedenborg, locates the divinity in human beings, and predicts the

Apocalypse ("as I have heard from Hell"). Having overpowered the angel in the "Memorable Fancy" studied earlier, concluding that "Opposition is true Friendship," in the last of these pieces he disputes with another angel, who is consumed in flames, arising as Elijah. Blake adds:

Note. This Angel, who is now become a Devil, is my particular friend;
    we often read the Bible together in its infernal or diabolical sense
    which the world shall have if they behave well.
I have also The Bible of Hell: which the world shall have whether they
    will or no.

One Law for the Lion & Ox is Oppression (44)

Without excluding readerly resistance, we may ask, Why is all of this appealing? I think it is so to the extent that we accept the truthfulness of Blake's message, enjoy his humorous presentation of supernatural beings and fantastic transformations, recognize the germ of a community in his friendship with the angel, sympathize with his rebellion against authority, and admire the power and wit of his actions and words. We will see that Lautréamont and Burroughs force us to ask such questions in more unsettling ways.

Beyond these speculations, Blake formulates a number of propositions, highly debatable to the "nonvisionary" mind, that is, you and me in our ordinary mood, which in some sense provide a litmus test, a standard to which his own writing must adhere in order to succeed. We saw that in his encounter with the prophets he himself experiences some wonder. He asks them "how they dared so roundly to assert. that God spake to them; and whether they did not think at the time, that they would be misunderstood, & so be the cause of imposition." Here Blake himself questions the audacity of prophetic writing and raises the possibility of misunderstanding and delusion (note "imposition") in its audience. Isaiah responds by implicitly questioning the concept of God, since he perceived not God but "the infinite in every thing." He adds, "As I was [. . .] perswaded [. . .] that the voice of honest indignation is the voice of God, I cared not for consequences but wrote." Once again infinite perception, and indignation, against religious and social evil are central to visionary writing.

When Blake questions Isaiah's reliance on "firm perswasion," the prophet refers to ages when imagination was strong enough to move mountains, adding that "many are not capable of a firm perswasion of any thing." Imagination as powerful enough to transform what we take to be real? This is hard to swallow, but Isaiah suggests that the fault is in us. Some of Blake's proverbs state matters in equally risky and challenging ways. "Every thing possible to be believ'd is an image of truth" seems impossibly large in scope, making belief, not proof, crucial. But there is the mitigating *"image* of truth." Further, an earlier proverb is relevant and persuasive: "What is now proved was once, only imagin'd." Together with "Where man is not nature is barren," this statement formulates an epistemology of creative and transforming consciousness at the base of Blake's endeavor.[13]

But the penultimate proverb, "Truth can never be told so as to be understood, and not be believ'd," ups the ante. According to this, truth *inevitably* produces belief if "told so as to be understood." Beyond the complexity of the contraries and the subtleties of the proverbs, Blake believes in the possibility of provoking belief. By all the means that we have been analyzing, in *The Marriage of Heaven and Hell* he handsomely carries off that *défi.*

If the *Marriage* is emblematic in pursuing the visionary to the point of explicitly formulating its goals and risks, it is also exemplary in situating such writing in a complex relationship with history. The history we have encountered in the work is prophetic and apocalyptic, as in the "ancient tradition that the world will be consumed in fire at the end of six thousand years." Elsewhere Blake gives us a mythical, in part nonbiblical version of the origin and evolution of the world: "The Giants who formed this world into its sensual existence and now seem to live in it in chains; are in truth. the causes of its life & the sources of all activity, but the chains are, the cunning of weak and tame minds. which have power to resist energy. according to the proverb, the weak in courage is strong in cunning."

Here Blake quotes one of the Proverbs of Hell, emphasizing the astonishing argument that the supposedly mythical giants *in fact* animate all life but that they are enchained by the cunning of individual (many, but still individual) minds. This is a startling convergence of mythic temporality, conceived as real, and individual existence, and it leads to a division of all human beings into two types: the prolific and the devouring. The biblical is introduced when Jesus' separating activity is used to counter the delusive effort of religion to reconcile these two classes.

This passage and much else that we have studied may be used to show the elusive poetic "Argument" at the opening as another version of human history:

> Rintrah roars & shakes his fires in the burdend air;
> Hungry clouds swag on the deep.
>
> Once meek, and in a perilous path,
> The just man kept his course along

The vale of death.
Roses are planted where thorns grow.
And on the barren heath
Sing the honey bees.

Then the perilous path was planted:
And a river and a spring
On every cliff and tomb;
And on the bleached bones
Red clay brought forth.

Till the villain left the paths of ease,
To walk in perilous paths, and drive
The just man into barren climes.

Now the sneaking serpent walks
In mild humility.
And the just man rages in the wilds
Where lions roam.

Rintrah roars & shakes his fires in the burdend air;
Hungry clouds swag on the deep. (33)

One of the many enigmas here is that the first word is a name that we do not recognize, and its reappearance in the refrain hardly brings clarification, at least on the first reading. Among other works in which he is mentioned, Rintrah appears more extensively in *Milton* (1804–8), with the same function, however: that of raging about. He is a figure of the poet's invention who we may say here represents prophetic anger, and his fires and storms recall numerous passages in the Bible.

We can relate Rintrah's anger to the interaction between the just man and the villain, retrospectively illuminated by the subsequent contrasting of good and evil and prolific and devouring. The relationship is elaborated in spatial and temporal terms. Originally meek, the just man inhabits the perilous path along the vale of death; but when the perilous path is planted, the villain, previously in the paths of ease, drives the just man into barren climes. Here the villain resembles the hypocritically good as later described ("the sneaking serpent walks / In mild humility"), and the just man, no longer meek, like Rintrah "rages in the wilds," associated with lions, those other figures of prophetic wrath. Seen in the light of this analysis, the refrain takes on a lot more meaning, particularly since the progression outlined here is emphasized by the temporal notations in the opening words of the strophes: "Once," "Then," "Till," "Now." "The Argument" is a miniature emblem of human history, in which the hypocritical good have come to a position of such power that both human and supernatural figures react with rage. We may wonder, Is it different now?

As suggested above, the symbolism is not only temporal but spatial. The danger and awareness of death that surround the just man are represented as a path, whereas the villain's paths are easy ones; when the perilous paths get planted, he moves in there too. As with the references to plowing and harvests, the central element here is the interaction of nature, barren without human intervention, according to Blake in the Proverbs, and agriculture. Hence these few lines evoke the immemorial evolution of human society, with echoes of the creation story in Genesis: "And on the bleached bones / Red clay brought forth." In this connection lines 6–8 are marvelous:

> Roses are planted where thorns grow.
> And on the barren heath
> Sing the honey bees.

These beautifully simple verses contain disjunctions and ambiguities that make them at the same time wonderfully rich, with suggestions of satisfaction and pain, good and evil. First, the roses "are planted": the word *planted* suggests that they do not grow naturally, but the passive construction minimizes human agency. Roses *and* their thorns, together traditionally symbolic of beauty and pain, are here disconnected, as if the thorns grow separately. According to this, nature is indeed improved by the act of planting. There are similar subtleties in the lines concerning the bees. If the heath is barren, what are they doing there? Whereas bee stings hurt and may kill, here only positive features, their song and their honey, are mentioned. Most important, whereas the past tense is used to evoke ancient phases of human development, the song of the honey bees is in the present tense, like the last stanza and the refrain. Subtly, "The Argument" violates linear time and puts the present of 1790–93, and our time, in touch with prehistory. Profundity of Blake!

The prose that follows the verse "Argument," that may be thought to be part of it, that is certainly related to it, and that introduces Blake's "Contraries," opens as follows:

> As a new heaven is begun, and it is now thirty-three years since its advent; the Eternal Hell revives. And lo! Swedenborg is the Angel sitting at the tomb; his writings are the linen clothes folded up. Now is the domination of Edom, & the return of Adam into Paradise; see Isaiah xxxiv & xxxv Chap.

As is characteristic of the Christian tradition, Old and New Testaments are conflated: Jesus' resurrection, Isaiah's prophecies. There is a Blakean and perhaps sacrilegious twist, relating sacred history to his own period and life, with the reference to the beginning of the new heaven thirty-three years ago. Blake started etching the work in 1790, and since he was born in 1757 this would give him Jesus' traditional age.[14]

As we have seen, Blake later dines with Isaiah and Ezekiel. From their writings we may retain the following essential features: the prophet transported in spirit (mainly Ezekiel); Yahweh's condemnation of the sins of Jerusalem; lamentations over the destruction of Jerusalem by its several enemy states and Yahweh's revenge against these states; and the anticipated celebration of the New Jerusalem, to be rebuilt by its enemies, bejewelled and radiant, exercising political and spiritual hegemony. The New Jerusalem and the messianic and apocalyptic suggestions of the Old Testament books are turned into a vision of the end of the world in the Apocalypse. But we have seen Blake's (in part) parodic relation to that work in the *Marriage*, and here he gives us instead a reference to Isaiah's description of the destruction of Edom (representative of Israel's enemies) and the flowering of the promised land.

The motifs of desert and water in that projective passage, so relevant still in our own world, again reflect on "The Argument," just as the reconciliation of wolf and lamb elsewhere in Isaiah (11:6) will be echoed at the end of the *Marriage*. And the symbolism of a corrupt Jerusalem and a transcendent New Jerusalem, although absent from the *Marriage*, appears extensively elsewhere in Blake, from "London"[15] to *Jerusalem*, not to speak of *Milton*.

As mentioned at the outset, the *Marriage* ends with "A Song of Liberty," a transparent revolutionary allegory, followed by a "Chorus." The latter reemphasizes themes of sexuality and religion, attacking the "Priests of the Raven" and the "pale religious letchery" that calls virginity that which "wishes but acts not!" So strong in Blake, as later in Rimbaud and the surrealists, is the resistance to religious morality and the stress on the liberation of sexual desire, so direct his sense of the link between that kind of freedom and the liberty sought by political and military revolution, the subjects of "A Song of Liberty."

This "song" is a rudimentary version of elements of Blake's early prophetic books, notably *America* (1793) and *Europe* (1794). Revolutionary events and their impact in England and America are evoked ("Albions coast is sick silent; the American meadows faint!"), followed by references to France, Spain, and Rome. These events promise universal enlightenment: "Look up! look up! O citizen of London. enlarge thy countenance; O Jew, leave counting gold! return to thy oil and wine; O African! black

African! (go. winged thought widen his forehead.)" No one would claim that Blake has freed *himself* of religious and racial stereotypes, but the global scope is typical, as is the reaction against money, shared by figures as diametrically opposed as Burke and Marx. For the smokescreen tactic that identifies worship of money with being Jewish, see Marx's "On the Jewish Question."

Amid the generalized historical references there is the nucleus of Blake's early mythical symbolism: an "Eternal Female," an aged and jealous king who like the Old Testament divinity "promulgates his ten commandments," and a fiery and howling "new born terror," who stamps the commandments to dust, crying "Empire is no more! and now the lion & wolf shall cease." These figures are later called Enitharmon, Urizen, and Orc, and they project not only political but also familial conflict.[16] Revolutionary violence thus is confidently seen as destroying the bonds of repressive religion, family, and empire, with the reference to lions and wolves, recalling the Bible, implying a definitive end to human strife.

Written in the immediate wake of revolution in France, at the same time that Edmund Burke was composing his perceptive negative view of the revolution, the "Song" is more single-mindedly optimistic even than reactions expressed by other poets, the early Wordsworth for example. In particular there is no expressed concern about the problems inherent in a program of revolutionary violence.[17] Although Blake's ideas about revolution and apocalypse certainly evolved, it nonetheless is worth noting that "The Everlasting Gospel," parts of which may have been written as late as 1818,[18] proposes the same view of Jesus as the *Marriage*. That is, there is a significant continuity of position with regard to the relations between humanity, divinity, and ethical behavior throughout Blake's career. It is also worth summarizing selected major features of *Milton*, begun in 1804, in the interest of accuracy and completeness for Blake and of relevance for later writers.

Milton is every bit as visionary and apocalyptic as the *Marriage*. At the end of the later work we realize that its complex and difficult symbolism culminates in an out-of-body experience like those of the Old Testament prophets and John. Blake writes that he "fell outstretched upon the path / A moment, & [his] soul returnd into its mortal state," as he awakens in his garden in the company of his wife (II, 42, ll. 25–28). Before that, the speaker/Blake is initially less obstreperous than in the *Marriage*, in the face of what seems to be a more traditionally conceived divinity:

O how can I with my gross tongue that cleaveth to the dust,
Tell of the Four-fold Man, in starry numbers fitly orderd

Or how can I with my cold hand of clay! But thou O Lord
Do with me as thou wilt! for I am nothing, and vanity.

(I, 20, ll. 15–18)

Milton, as is made clear in the preface and throughout, differs from the *Marriage* in being very little parodic of "the Sublime of the Bible" (I, 1), and not only Milton but John and Swedenborg are given their due (I, 22, ll. 46–50; II, 40, ll. 21–22). Blake's recurrent figure of prophetic imagination, the "Shadowy Prophet" Los, enters his soul, however, whereupon he takes on the fury of the earlier work: "His terrors now posses'd me whole! I arose in fury & strength" (I, 22, ll. 14–15) (see fig. 1). Moreover, although the relationship between the "Lord" and the "Four-Fold Man" is not specified here, elsewhere it is not at all the traditional divinity but still, as in the *Marriage*, the human that is to be adored: "the Eternal Great Humanity, / To whom be Glory & Dominion Evermore Amen" (II, 30, ll. 15–16).

The "Great Humanity" or "Four-Fold Man" is typical of Blake's mature system, succeeding the binary contraries of *The Marriage of Heaven and Hell* as well as the triadic group glimpsed at the end of that work and active in family themes in *Songs of Innocence and Experience* and some of the shorter prophetic books. But just as the marriage metaphor implies an ultimate union or reconciliation, the major action of *Milton* is similar in involving the reunification of the single great human being, fallen into individual and sexual division according to a myth that some critics have called Neoplatonic or Gnostic.[19]

These terms, which I think misleading, derive from the myth of fall and reunification on the one hand and the negative depiction of the body and sexuality in the fallen state on the other. Near the end indeed it is said that Jesus is to purge with fire the "Sexual Garments, the Abomination of Desolation" (II, 41, ll. 25–28). Yet from early on we have been told that the "Human Imagination" is the "Divine Body of the Lord Jesus" (I, 3, ll. 3–4), so there is a persistence of the *Marriage*'s refusal to separate mental and bodily principles as well as human and divine principles. In feminine Beulah, the closest of *Milton*'s four regions to Eternity, where that divine body is to be found, soft sexuality has a positive role but is also called a delusion (I, 2, ll. 1–5). And without question the original fall involves not only the closing in of the senses as in the *Marriage*, but the division between the sexes as well (I, 3).

Bisexual confusions and homosexual tendencies contribute further to the corruption of the fully human as presented in Satan's attraction to Palamabron (I, 12). The fault there is that of a woman (Leutha), and despite courageous and self-sacrificing acts by some female personages, feminist crit-

1 William Blake, illustrating passage from *Milton*, copy D, I, 22, ll. 14-15. Library of Congress.

ics are persuasive in seeing women in the work as on the whole either destructive or submissive. But the harlot "which John in Patmos saw" in *Milton* is not female but hermaphroditic, "A Female hidden in a Male, Religion hidden in War, / Namd Moral Virtue" (II, 40, 20–22). Similarly, the most generous act of self-sacrifice is that of Milton, who returns to his earthly condition — a "mournful form double; hermaphroditic: male & female / In one wonderful body" (I, 14, ll. 37–38). Rather than being primarily misogynous, Blake has an acute sense of the hermaphroditic aspect of sexuality. Or, in formulations by Alicia Ostriker that are richly relevant not only for Blake but for our later writers, his writing displays both "anti-patriarchal and proto-feminist sensibility" and "its opposite, a homocentric gynophobia in which heterosexual love means human destruction."[20]

There are also several powerful sequences on sadistic and masochistic pleasure, including one early on in which females prepare victims and males dance "the dance of tears & pain" and human beings are "shut in narrow doleful form," their voices bringing forth only "Moral Virtue the cruel Virgin Babylon" (I, 5, 15–27). Just as Blake makes the harlot bisexual, here where we would traditionally expect to find the Whore of Babylon we encounter instead virginity and morality, the targets in the *Marriage*. We might conclude that in *Milton* hermaphroditic and sadomasochistic features complicate the repressed sexuality criticized in the early work.

And if the sexual is threefold and the fully human fourfold, (I, 4, l. 5), and if Eternity seems not fully androgynous but fundamentally male, the body nonetheless plays a major role in *Milton* as well as in the *Marriage*'s "improvement of sensual enjoyment." Many passages appeal to our bodily organs as capable of perceiving beauty in the tiniest of natural objects, and many explanations are given us about the nature of "visionary" time and space (two examples among many are I, 29, ll. 17–21; II, 31, ll. 46 ff.), most magnificently perhaps when Milton descends, entering Blake's foot:

And all this Vegetable World appeard on my left Foot,
As a bright sandal formd immortal of precious stones &
                gold:
I stooped down & bound it on to walk forward thro'
                Eternity.
                    (I, 21, ll. 12–14)

I hope that this brief excursion on myth, sexuality, and vision in *Milton* will give an adequate sense of the differences and continuities between *The Marriage of Heaven and Hell* and Blake's later work. I have also stressed features that will be seen to be relevant for later writers, concerning not only the relationship between our "Vegetable World" and "Eternity" but also the link between that relationship and the experience(s) of sexuality. Sacrifice of the female on the one hand and anguished male sexuality in connection with religion on the other characterize the visionary conclusions of

Heinrich von Ofterdingen and *Aurélia*, and a markedly sexist kind of love is central to the surrealist enterprise. As for the horrendous content and tone of *Les chants de Maldoror* and *Naked Lunch*, not to speak of the antimale violence in Wittig and Kincaid, perhaps in a Blakean perspective they reflect the sadistic and hermaphroditic features of unredeemed sexuality glimpsed in the *Marriage* and developed in *Milton*.

The view that religion, morality, and virtue are part of the system of *war*, themes also important in our later writers, persists, as the discussion above indicates, from the *Marriage* to *Milton*. The fall in the latter involves not only individuality and sexuality but the strife of nationhood and war: "Los lamented over Satan, who triumphant divided the Nations" (I, 10, l. 21). Thus Milton's goal in redescending to earth is not only to further the resurrection of the sleeping body from "corruptibility" but to crush the nations' "pomp / Of warlike selfhood" — where warfare and alienated selfhood are equated (I, 14, ll. 14–18). And when he enters Blake's foot, "a black cloud redounding spread over Europe" (I, 15, l. 50). This is the same revolutionary destruction as in the "Song," which in *Milton* is accompanied by extensive harvest imagery leading to the concluding line, "To go forth to the Great Harvest & Vintage of the Nations." Urban symbolism is equally in evidence, as the "spiritual Four-fold London eternal" is related to specific districts in historical London (I, 6, ll. 1 ff.).

The traditional symbolism, and Blake's own (including that of the visionary city of Golgonooza), as in the *Marriage*, do not obscure the political point:

> The Wine-press on the Rhine groans loud, but all its central
> > beams
> Act more terrific in the central Cities of the Nations
> Where Human Thought is crushd beneath the iron hand of
> > Power.
> There Los puts all into the Press, the Opressor & the
> > Opressed
> Together, ripe for the Harvest & Vintage & ready for the
> > Loom.
> > (I, 25, ll. 3–7)

Indeed, in a movingly idealistic preface, Blake awaits the coming of a "New Age" and urges the "Young Men of the New Age" to fight against the hirelings in army, government, and university, "who would if they could, for ever depress Mental & prolong Corporeal War." Not military violence, now, but militant intelligence and art. Before closing the preface with a quote from Numbers (11:29) — "Would to God that all the Lords people were Prophets" — Blake includes a short poem, the last strophe of which will serve as a conclusion to this study of the poet who at the outset of our tradition most clearly links visionary writing to the political struggle for liberation:

I will not cease from Mental Fight,
Nor shall my Sword sleep in my hand:
Till we have built Jerusalem,
In Englands green & pleasant Land.

The Visionary and the Millennial ✍
Novalis's *Heinrich von Ofterdingen*

As opposed to the exuberant Blake, for the English-speaking reader Novalis may unfairly suffer from the image of the ethereal romantic poet, as exemplified by Heinrich von Ofterdingen's quest for the blue flower, a certain stylistic lushness, and the themes of idealized love and tragic death. Not usually considered revolutionary, in other writing Novalis celebrated medieval Europe and Christian, specifically Marian, religion, subtly noted the contradictions of the French Revolution while praising (although not without ambiguity) the present and future promise of monarchy in Prussia, and wrote intensely of the nature that Blake so high-handedly dismissed. Finally, *Heinrich von Ofterdingen*, published posthumously and in incomplete form in 1802, with its structure of travel, education, and love for its young poet figure, could look like a quite linear version of what it is called, a novel.[1]

The portrait sketched above is simplistic. *Heinrich* exposes us to an array of strange experiences, contains familial-sexual and historical themes that can hardly leave us at ease, and submits us to considerable textual violence. A work in which the visionary tends to millennial resolutions, Novalis's novel is a *Marriage* provocative in different ways than Blake's.

This is not surprising in that *Heinrich*, and Novalis's entire production — including unfinished prose works, poetry, notably the beautiful *Hymnen an die Nacht*, myriad fragments and aphorisms, only a portion of which were published during his short lifetime, letters — are all expressive of a totalizing intellectual and creative enterprise that is every bit as reflective of the historical and spiritual aftermath of the French Revolution as Blake's work.

There was as yet no unified German state or national consciousness, little resistance to the French before Napoleon's defeat of the Prussians at Jena in 1806, and no active revolutionary movement before the middle of the nineteenth century. But many in the intellectual elite, including Kant, Goethe, a number of younger romantics, and other less well-known individuals, such as the father of Karl Marx, thought of the revolution and of subsequent French influence as decisively progressive. Unlike Blake, the young Novalis was part of a highly talented and self-conscious group including Ludwig Tieck and Friedrich Schlegel that was linked (in ways reminding us of the French surrealists) by a sense of magical encounters and early deaths, notably those of his beloved Sophie von Kuhn and then of the poet himself.

In an important exchange of letters, Novalis described to Friedrich Schlegel his project of producing a new Bible, a magical book that would encyclopedically encompass every realm of knowledge and creation, from religion to literature to science. In his exalted but historically acute response Schlegel stressed the need to link history and praxis to philosophy and religion and argued that in the postrevolutionary period there was the possibility in such a Bible of a new revelation, a new "Evangelium." Although formulated by Schlegel, this idealistic and optimistic view of the historical circumstances was shared by Novalis and accords with the millennial accents of his *Heinrich*. In his letter Schlegel goes on to report that Tieck is studying Boehme, to wonder if the now-classical Goethe can be reconciled with the extreme idealist philosopher Fichte, and to indicate that he does not yet know much about Franz von Baader (1765–1842), about whom Novalis is so enthusiastic.[2]

I sketch the contents of these letters, only two among many, to indicate the intellectual ferment from which *Heinrich* emerged and also to suggest the range of the sources that contribute to Novalis's speculations. At Tieck's suggestion he read Boehme, who mystically reinforced Fichte's insistence on the absolute priority of mind before sense experience, leading to Novalis's conception of "magic idealism," according to which our imagination animates the world. The exchange of letters occurred while Novalis was a student at the school of mining in Freiburg. The reference to Baader, a mining engineer and physicist of visionary leanings, reminds us that Novalis studied extensively in mathematics and numerous sciences in an attempt to unify science and religion. Like Blake and Nerval he was fascinated by analogies between the structure of the human organism and that of the terrestrial globe.[3] An even more important teacher at the mining school was Abraham Gottlob Werner (1750–1815), a geologist of European reputation whose explanations of the origins of the world are now little heeded. We shall see that Heinrich encounters a miner-sage named Werner and that mining allows a glimpse of prehistoric and primeval realities.[4]

Finally, to round out this glimpse of the many strands of conception and imagination that contribute to Novalis's visionary aspirations, we must mention the intensive reflections on literary form by the group of young writers to which he belonged. Goethe's *Wilhelm Meisters Wanderjahre* (1796) had established the model of the novel of formation as a journey. But Novalis appreciated in it other qualities, asserting at one point that as the geology of Werner situated the center of gravity of the earth near Fez in Morocco, so Goethe's novel revealed that the intellectual center of gravity was now to be found among the German states. The comment indicates not only the limitations of Werner's science but also the union of science and literature that Novalis and his friends sought, as well as their historical idealism, not to mention the familiar fascination with the Middle East. Elsewhere Novalis was critical of *Wilhelm Meister*,[5] and his *Heinrich* is a voyage not of social adaptation but of spiritual initiation. As already suggested, much attention was also given by Novalis and his friends to fragmentary forms of writing, although the incomplete form of *Heinrich* is due primarily to the premature death of its author. Most important, the widespread attention to folk tales or fairy tales (*Märchen*), with their magical, fantastic, dreamlike, and supernatural effects, and Novalis's interest in dreams themselves contribute to the visionary qualities of *Heinrich von Ofterdingen*.

By virtue of its medieval setting (the title character and his mentor, Klingsohr, have the names of semilegendary thirteenth-century poet figures),[6] seemingly removed from modern conditions of reality, and by virtue of its apparent simplicity of form, *Heinrich* evokes exalted experiences that hardly appear to touch, let alone trouble, the lives that we think we now lead. Novalis's versions of visionary experiences and forms are there in crystal clarity. First there is dream, most of all Heinrich's initial one, with its sexual dimension and terrestrial voyages and his sight of the famous blue flower. Then also tale and myth, particularly in the stories of Arion and Atlantis, as well as recurrent encounters with aged wise men including the miner, Sylvester, count von Hohenzollern, not to speak of exploits of warfare in the castle of the Crusader. Finally, the fairy tale related by Klingsohr at the end of the first part concludes with a millennial allegory of universal love and harmony.

Such experiences and themes are set within a firm if also, as we shall see, complex structure. As suggested above, travel from paternal authority, Eisenach, a feudal city that was the site of legendary poetic contests, and the north to grandfather, the south, and the commercial center Augsburg, where Heinrich nonetheless encounters the poet Klingsohr, underlies the evolution. On the whole, the interspersed poems further the movement. Chapter 5, together with chapter 9 by far the longest, is capital, in that there Heinrich encounters two sages, experiences prehistoric nature, and in a mystic book recognizes himself and others in past ages and in the future. The narrator then explains that Heinrich's voyage is ended, and he himself recognizes that it is appropriate that he encounter Mathilde only now (94, 105). His poetic formation under the direction of Klingsohr corresponds to another ingredient of the manuscript from chapter 5. As Klingsohr also summarizes it, his journey has exposed him to the "romantic Orient," that is, the Middle East, which is the country of poetry, and to war, nature, and history (111). Beyond poetry, there is love, which comes rapidly, soon to be followed by marriage. Then Klingsohr's tale caps the whole.

But the thematic and formal violence of that tale, the death of Mathilde and the saddened maturation of Heinrich in the *interval* before the beginning of the second part, and the fact that that part is a fragment, consisting of a single chapter — all of these make Novalis's romantic novel considerably less simple and stable than it first appears.[7]

Before Klingsohr's discombobulating and dreamlike tale, the reader has been exposed to an array of mystic sights and flights. The first is dream,[8] in fact the double dream of Heinrich and his father in the opening chapter. The father is generally skeptical of inspiration, and this is true of his current attitude toward dreams: "The times are past when divine apparitions appeared in dreams, and we cannot and will not fathom the state of mind of those chosen men the Bible speaks of. The nature of dreams as well as of the world of men must have been different in those days" (18). Although he has Sylvester discuss poetry and the Bible in the second part, Novalis is not very biblical. From his friend Tieck's and his own notes for the second part we know that a vast syncretism — Persian legend, Greek, Oriental, biblical, Christian, Scandinavian, and Indian myth — was intended.[9]

But the initial effective tactic is the involvement of the reader in Heinrich's dream, which is provoked by the visitor's stories, discourse hence preceding vision. The dream begins with terrestrial voyages involving immeasurable distances, wild regions, oceans and strange creatures, many kinds of people in different circumstances, captivity and the heights of experience, death and rebirth. (See fig. 2.) The dream affording dismaying excursions by the individual self in geological and evolutionary time and space: this is a recurrent

2 Roberto Matta, *Au Temps des graines*, D 95/13, 1995. © 1996 Artists Rights Society (ARS), New York/ADAGP, Paris.

motif, encountered in somewhat different form in Blake, later in *Aurélia*, parodically in *Les chants de Maldoror*, in stunningly devastating passages in Jamaica Kincaid. As in Nerval and the surrealists too, love is haunted by loss, as the dreamer is eternally separated from his loved one.

But at dawn the movement becomes calmer, the images clearer. There is a progression through heightened natural scenery ("dark forest," "rocky gorge," mountain slope, meadow, then a crag with an opening and a passage leading to a cave lit by a mysteriously glowing fountain), as well as an emphasis on arduous movement, climbing, arrival. This sequence subsequently produces a satisfying libidinal experience leading to the vision of the blue flower, which harbors a face, later to be recognized as that of Mathilde. The lush language — "bright light," "mighty beam of light," "countless mistlike sparks" — again will find echoes, with characteristic differences, in Nerval and Kincaid. Their passages too stress the dazzlingly visual nature of the experience, strangely luminous and utterly silent. Here "Not the faintest sound was to be heard; a holy stillness enveloped the glorious spectacle." So already there are two characteristic, one might say archetypal, visionary motifs or landscapes: the terrestrial voyage through prehistoric time and space and the heightened natural scenery of mountain, gorge, and silently luminous pool.

But the visual in the second scene leads to the tactile and erotic. Typical of Novalis, the sexual vocabulary makes this a kind of visionary wet dream (an overwhelming longing, disrobing and bathing, words like "Verlangen," "Wollust," "überströmte sein Inneres," the waves as breasts and as girls "embodying themselves" against the bather). Significantly, Heinrich's desire is unsatisfied — he is awakened by the voice of his mother.

The father's youthful dream was similar. Provoked by discussion in Italy with a sage (the very same Sylvester from the second part) as well as by wine, it first carries us across views of the German countryside, then through a staircase into a mountain, where an old man and a carving of a girl and passageways and flowers lead to unfettered visionary language and cosmic flight. The father awakes "stirred by violent love" and soon returns to Germany to marry Heinrich's mother. As in Heinrich's dream, this passage takes the reader on a magical trip but includes as well a familiar and satisfying male sexuality.

There are no other such dreams in the novel, although the motif of the death of the beloved recurs as Heinrich dreams of Mathilde's death and promise of their reunion in the afterlife. He awakes unable to recall a magical word he had learned (106). Instead the supernal inspirations come through encounters and discourses. The merchants' description of ancient poetry contains the elements of the work's first dreams: deep caverns, ancient and future times, countless people and marvelous regions, strange occurrences, a language both alien and magical (31–32). On the next page the merchants derive all of human culture from the early poets, but without the vehement critique of religion met in Blake. Similarly the princess in the Atlantis chapter learns of the "history of the primal world," and her lover charms the king and his court with a poem about the origins of the constellations and earthly orders, the original golden age succeeded by epochs of barbarous conflict, and the promised "rejuvenation of nature, and the return of an everlasting golden age" (43, 48). We recognize not just the successful love story here but also how both it and the golden age theme are distanced from us. For in the last lines of the chapter we learn that all that we have read took place in the legendary Atlantis: "No one knows what became of that country. Only in legends are we told that floods took mighty Atlantis from the sight of men" (52).

The mining chapter brings us more direct, but still tantalizing, contact with the primeval, as Heinrich and the others view the fossilized remains of prehistoric animals. The hermit count recognizes the structural similarity between cosmic and earthly geological processes and calls the miners "astrologers in reverse" ("verkehrte Astrologen," 86). He also believes that nature is becoming milder, drawing closer to human beings. A less positive note is that his mystic manuscript is missing its ending. Again chapter 5 epitomizes the whole. This recalls a late discussion (chapter 8) in which Heinrich tells Mathilde that nature is not yet ripe, that vision is an eternal idea, a part of the unknown holy world: "das Bild ist ein ewiges Urbild, ein Teil der unbekannten heiligen Welt" (118). The myth of primal origins and return in Novalis again recalls Nerval, since there seems always a gap between us and the higher world. We are far from Blake's confidence: "this I shall do by [. . .] melting apparent surfaces away, and displaying the infinite which was hid." Rather one thinks of the first of the *Pollens*: "Wir suchen überall das Unbedingte, und finden immer nur Dinge."[10]

But this is to neglect Klingsohr's tale, discombobulating and dreamlike, as I have said, in its mixture of strange characters and actions, abrupt and unexplained shifts, absurdly comic notes, and attention to the body and sex, including desire, repression, infidelity, incest, ecstasy, decrepitude, and death. It is also to neglect its author, a figure whose name has a medieval and even an Islamic connection, the masterful and Goethe-like poet who in previous chapters has explained to Heinrich the superiority of poetic intelligence both to phenomenal nature and to subjective emotion.[11]

Something of the latter themes is suggested within his tale by the contrast between Fable's wonderful writing and the mechanical and defective writing practiced by the Scribe. One wants to avoid sounding like him. He has to tickle his own ribs in order to laugh, and, in a lighter version of Blake's roaring attack on rationalism, when Sophie's magic liquid touches him he drapes it around his shoulders in the form of numbers and geometric figures. Yet we must account for the *different* and powerful mode of writing embodied in the tale. Is it visionary, is it the language capable of rendering present the primal world? We recall that like Goethe's famous tale of 1795, it is an *art form* resembling popular tales (*Märchen*) such as those collected by Goethe and Herder in the belief that they perpetuated primeval expression, a belief shared by the merchants (32). Perhaps in its self-consciousness it is not visionary, but it *is* not only different but *powerful*, in that after the brief introduction to chapter 9 it installs itself for twenty-five pages or so as the conclusion to that chapter and indeed to the first part.[12]

In the tale characters both familiar and unfamiliar circulate in a number of realms, something like five, Scribe help us! In the first we meet a king whose name is the Greek word for a constellation, Arcturus, and later we encounter other constellations, called not only Perseus but also Phoenix. Arcturus inhabits a metallic and frozen city with his daughter, first unnamed, then called Freya after the Scandinavian fertility goddess. After a distanced but electrically sexual contact with Freya, an aged warrior (is he Perseus, later?) hurls his sword into the world so that the place of *peace* will be known.

In another realm, ambiguously related to the first only by the link "At this time," we encounter a larger cast of characters: an unnamed father and mother, the Scribe, the godlike woman who we soon learn is called Sophie, the foster sister and brother Fable and Eros, and the wet nurse Ginnistan, whose name apparently has no connection with the Greek ones given the others. After the initial sword-throwing, this group provokes most of the action of the tale. After drinking from Sophie's liquid, Eros grows mightily in size and erotic power. Taking on the form of Eros's mother (in order to avoid temptation!), Ginnistan travels with him to the castle of the moon. Along the way we learn that she is the daughter of the moon; after witnessing phantasmagoric spectacles, she and Eros make love. Previously the father had been having an affair with Ginnistan, and the opportunities for confusing her and the mother are maximized, with the incest theme inescapable.

Meanwhile, back home things have changed for the worse: the Scribe has fomented a revolt and imprisoned the parents. But Fable escapes to another realm, that of the evil spinning sisters, who are called *Parcae* only at the end (147). Fable gets there in a Blakean way, by descending a staircase behind an altar. Through her wit she outdoes the sisters as well as the Scribe, who turns up holding a mandrake root. Then she enters the initial realm, that of Arcturus, this time climbing *up*, using a ladder and a trapdoor. Thereafter she encounters Ginnistan, still in the form of the mother but transformed for the worse and enslaved to Eros, who is creating havoc everywhere. This is followed by the death of the real mother, which becomes a universal disaster as the sun burns itself out and falls into the sea.

The back-and-forth movement increases as Fable again visits the sisters. Each time she goes there she encounters a sphinx and she turns the tables either by asking the questions or by correctly answering them. She also visits Arcturus. Then she travels around the earth to the aged Atlas, who is refreshed not only by the magic liquid on his face but by a pot under his loins! Together with Atlas appears another piece of Greek myth, the Hesperides. Then in rapid sequence Ginnistan is united with the transformed father, Eros flies to awaken Freya, the latter couple become the new king and queen, war is banished, their throne becomes a marriage bed, and their nuptial embraces are imitated by the assembled, harmonious multitudes. Sophie recalls that the spirit of the dead mother is with them, and Fable concludes by singing this song:

> Gegründet ist das Reich der Ewigkeit,
> In Lieb und Frieden endigt sich der Streit,
> Vorüber ging der lange Traum der Schmerzen,
> Sophie ist ewig Priesterin der Herzen.

This summary is by no means exhaustive, since many zany details are omitted, but it may serve to convey the experience of reading this bizarre sequence, which, however, moves inexorably toward its millennial conclusion,[13] expressed finally in nuptial and royal terms. Still, although it is impossible to explicate in detail such an extended piece of writing, some selective close attention is in order. Let us observe the interspersed poems as well as the fantastic visions in the treasure room of the moon.

The last of the four poems, quoted above, is typical in that through its simple vocabulary and in its rhymes it expresses the central millennial themes: the foundation of the realm of eternity, strife ending in love and peace, suffering a dream long over, Sophie the princess of all hearts. The first poem had used some of the same words ("Ewigkeit," "Träume"), as well as motifs addressing the frozen state of Arcturus's kingdom (the end of night, the arrival of warmth) and the promise of Freya's fruitful womb. That poem also mentions Fable, who does not appear until the following segment, hence unifying the two. The second poem advances the action, or at least our understanding of it, even more clearly, in that through it we learn that Ginnistan is journeying to her father. Strikingly, but by now not surprisingly, sexual vocabulary ("Vorgefühl," "die wilde Glut") expresses her longing; it is not until the last line of the penultimate stanza that we realize that we are dealing not with a lover but with a "Tochter."

In the third poem Fable thwarts the evil sisters by weaving unified existences in anticipation of the millennium evoked at the end. In its artful simplicity the next-to-last stanza again encapsulates the central themes:

> Ein jeder lebt in Allen,
> Und All' in jedem auch.
> *Ein* Herz wird in euch wallen,
> Von Einem Lebenshauch.

Every word of the first line is subsequently repeated (appropriately, "ein" is repeated twice), and in the first two lines the words for "one" and "every" change place with that for "all." The rhymes contribute, in that the second word of each rhyme contains the previous rhyming word in its entirety. A key word, "Herz," recurs not here but, as we have seen, in the final poem. One, each, all, united in heart through the benign influence of Sophie: this again is the message of universal harmony and peace that the tale repeatedly expresses. But at this point the time is not yet ripe. In a concluding stanza of the third poem for some reason omitted from the translation, Fable sends the creatures she has been weaving as flamelets to annoy the evil sisters. The strange detail is never lacking.

The scenes at the court of the moon are a dense and complex piece of prose writing, accurately translated on pages 129–31 with the exception of the introduction of paragraph breaks that do not appear in the original. The breaks are justified by subtle shifts in the German text, which however sweep the reader even more powerfully along. The scenes, beginning in midparagraph right after the reunion of king and daughter, are intended as a spectacle ("Schauspiel," a theatrical word) for Eros, until "das Zeichen des Aufbruchs" is given. What this "disbanding" may be is unclear: Ginnistan's departure, the hoped-for golden age? In any event, the immediate outcome of the experience is the love-making between Eros and Ginnistan in the form of his mother.

The spectacle occurs in the treasure chamber, which is said to be a "great garden." This conflates architecture with human-modified nature and sets up a convention, exploited later in texts such as Rimbaud's *Illuminations*, according to which we seem to perceive what cannot be perceived. In this case there are not only air castles, familiar from fairy tales, but "weather trees," linked by the vocabulary of concrete description: "between," "were" (literally "there lay," "lagen"). Words like "colossal," "countless," and "surpassing" add an impossibly hyperbolic dimension to the objects that we are supposed to perceive. More familiar creatures (sheep, though in unfamiliar colors) then mingle with extraordinary scenes ("merkwürdige Bilder"), processions, strange vehicles, flowers, buildings. The latter contain what we might expect to find in a treasure room, but in infinite profusion: weapons, rugs, tapestries, curtains, drinking vessels, all kinds of utensils and tools in endless array, presented in virtually infinite enumeration, another tactic of this phantasmagoric writing.

To this point these objects have been impersonally proposed to the attention ("beschäftigten die Aufmerksamkeit"). With a shift of perspective, from an eminence "they [Eros and Ginnistan] saw" a romantic country containing signs of human habitation but also scenes of the desolate extremes of nature, all in the most luminous color. With another impersonal shift ("Hier sah man") there follows a succession of tableaux contrasting disaster with happiness, from peasants eating a picnic against the background of a shipwreck to the burial of a youth before a madonna accompanied by angels. Without transition the scenes are said to be transformed into a mysterious and horrendously violent spectacle ("Vorstellung") in which death, as an army of corpses, seems to conquer life, then is routed. Motifs of music and rainbow accompany the apparition of Sophie and a splendid man who in place of a scepter holds a "palm of peace." Fable sings; Eros leans over a beautiful sleeping maiden, and both are enclosed in a flower. Peace and wisdom reign, but not without the potential for sexual ecstasy that will be realized at the end of the tale. Despite its disconcerting quality, this sequence too ends with the recurrent millennial theme.

We have thus far seen, then, that not only the succession of dreams and encounters but also the strikingly original tale at the end of the first part serve tantalizingly the golden age myth that Novalis shares with Blake and Nerval, though in highly original ways. As indicated at the outset, and as we have seen with regularity, those experiences and that myth are closely linked to sexuality, which, together with equally important historical notes, we need now to explore.

It is apparent by now that the idealized familial-sexual theme of the work gradually is shown to have its somber aspects. The innocent young man Heinrich (in our terms, perhaps, a sheltered twenty-year-old experiencing a late adolescence — what a target for Maldoror!) fatefully encounters the beautiful Mathilde, a conjuncture favored throughout by the adult figures. With only a hint of sadness about leaving his father, Heinrich is led by his protective mother to Augsburg, where he is fairly propelled into his relationship with Mathilde through the approving comments and actions of his grandfather and Klingsohr. Along the way he has heard of other instances of benign support by parents for young love. There is Atlantis, in which a commoner's love for the princess is clandestinely fostered by his father, an adventure that, through the power of poetry and the presence of an illegitimate child, results in the king's acceptance of the young man as his son-in-law. And there is the experience of the miner, whose foreman adopts him and offers him his daughter's hand and who is married on the day when he strikes a rich vein, thus earning promotion and the gratitude of his lord.

Both of these examples look like wish fulfillments, the perfect coincidence of true love and societal-economic success, and hence are small embodiments of the millennial myth expressed later. But the potential threat of the all-powerful king in Atlantis, the mistreatment of the captive Eastern girl Zulima in the Crusades chapter, and the fatality that shadows Heinrich's love for Mathilde point in an opposite, negative, direction.

Indeed, this negative theme is pervasive, as the happy family relations throughout the work inscribe a curious and systematic *separation* of husband and wife. Once Heinrich has left his father's house in the company of his mother, he learns of or meets a series of older men, all alone and most of whom speak of the death of their wives: the father and the king in the Atlantis tale; the foreman, the miner, and the hermit; his grandfather, Klingsohr, and Sylvester at the end of the first and the opening of the second parts, not to speak of Arcturus and the moon in Klingsohr's tale. Hence the intensity of reunions between daughter and solitary father (Schwaning, the moon); hence the young hero's penchant for calling Klingsohr, and later Sylvester, father; hence Mathilde's references to her dead mother and to the Virgin Mary (117, 119). Hence also Heinrich's question to Sylvester: "Did the mother have to die that the children might thrive, and does the father sit alone at her grave, doomed to everlasting tears?" (161). Indeed, an essential feature of the structure of Novalis's book is that its hero is aided in his search for a love partner by a series of father figures who no longer have a wife. And Mathilde will die, of course.

This death of the wife, which represents something like the law of the work, is also a flagrant ingredient in the conclusion of Klingsohr's tale.[14] Whereas the unfaithful husband is transfigured and united with Ginnistan, the ashes of the mother are turned into a divine liquid and drunk by all her family, who, as Sophie announces at the end, feel her continual presence. It would be difficult to imagine a more troubling expression of the sacrificial effacement of the maternal as an apparently necessary contribution to the positive outcome of Klingsohr's, and his creator's, millennial myth.

Another provocative feature of the tale and of the whole work concerns the figure of Eros and the importance of sexuality in general. The contrast of north and south, and Schwaning's insistence in initiating Heinrich to love, have been noted and constitute a reiterated thematic. In particular, Schwaning's poem (100–101) recalls Blake in theme and image. In it young girls rebel against guilt and the sickness of sexual repression imposed by the old, particularly "die strenge Mutter." Characteristically too, a poem placed between the two parts of the work is filled with sexual imagery, but, equally characteristically, with death imagery too. In Klingsohr's tale the sacrifice of the mother, multiple incest suggestions, the sexual power of Freya and Eros, and the degradation of Ginnistan have been mentioned. When Fable comes upon her (136–37), Ginnistan is in a terrible state, physically wasted, her features expressive of "a hopeless sorrow and touching loyalty." Indeed, although she describes Eros's cruel triumph over her and her humiliation, she blames herself and rejoices in her experience: "Like a heavenly robber he appeared to want to destroy me cruelly and to triumph proudly over me, his quivering sacrifice."

Clearly the sexual havoc that Eros wreaks throughout the world at this point indicates that Novalis is exploiting the traditional meanings of the Greek myth. Presumably too, the transfiguration of the father and Ginnistan and the union of Eros and Freya at the end are meant to represent some transcendence of that destructive sexuality. On this score, the link with Sophie is curious. At the conclusion she is said to reign in the hearts of all, but only at the end of the process initiated by Eros, for it was in drinking her liquid that he first magically grew. This implies a partnership between the two, yet she at points tries to exercise control over him, preventing the first lovemaking attempt by him and Ginnistan (126). But it is Sophie who thinks of transforming Ginnistan into the image of the mother (127)! And Ginnistan does not make use of the magic liquid Sophie furnishes to ward off temptation; instead, recalling Heinrich's dream, bathing is the prelude to sex (131).

From all of this it is safe to conclude that Novalis's visionary project is closely linked with, and dependent upon, liberated sexuality.[15] But there is a puzzling relation between sex and wisdom, a relation far more ambiguous than what we saw in Blake — who of course is *vastly* disturbing in his own way ("Sooner murder . . ."). Most troubling in Novalis though is the death of the mother, which echoes throughout the work. If *Heinrich* is a *Marriage*, it is one purchased at a high cost.

Finally, the sexual motif cannot be separated from historical and political considerations, even in a work set early in the thirteenth century and seeming to have little to do with the modern world. The nuptial pleasures of monarchs bring universal harmony and the abolition of war, which fits with Novalis's presentation elsewhere of royal marriage as emblematic of the good society.[16] Written after a decade of revolution and warfare, *Heinrich*, with its reiterated millennial theme, represents at the very least a deep desire for reconciliation and peace. Its apparent lack of specific political content reminds us that some forty years later Marx lamented the still-persistent political and economic backwardness of the Germans, visible most of all, he argued, in the preeminence of idealist philosophy. Hegel was his particular bête noire, whereas Novalis had immersed himself earlier in the work of Fichte; perhaps there is some link between these philosophers and the vaguely optimistic view of the course of history expressed by the hermit at the end of the mining chapter and Sylvester at the opening of the second part.

But *Heinrich* in fact is far from vague, has indeed a good deal of historical point, although, one may say, ideologically idealized. Here we may recall that the hermit thinks that the best history is written by poets (85). The call for a new crusade in chapter 4, and projected references to warfare and travel in Italy as well as the Middle East in the second part, situate the action in the realm of the emperor Friedrich II, who began the Sixth Crusade in 1229. Heinrich was to have delivered a magical talisman to him in the later portions. This historical period is relevant for ennobled, but ideologically mixed, versions in the book of socioeconomic activities and sites — merchants, mines, cities, and war.

The significance of the trip to the Augsburg is great. Although by 1800 Rousseau's Emile had long since discovered the corruption of modern Paris and Blake had written "London," no echo of which we hear in Novalis's book, the medieval city plays an important role in his poet's development, since as Klingsohr explains it contains artists, experienced statesmen, cultured merchants, all classes and crafts (110). Augsburg was later made an imperial city (1276) and was subsequently associated with the Fuggers, bankers who also developed mining and trade with the Levant, both of which play a role in *Heinrich*.

The merchants in whose company Heinrich and his mother travel to Augsburg are presented in both a realistic and an idealized manner. They know how to get there, how to avoid danger, and how to find hospitality; they make good company, but always have a sharp eye for profit. For example, amid the wonders of the mining chapter they consider the possibility of starting trade with Bohemia (76). They are the source of the exalted views of poetry and the myths of Arion and Atlantis in the early chapters, but they admit that the press of business gets in the way of poetic enjoyment (32). The problem of specialization and the deadening effect of the economic are already on this medieval horizon. Indeed, before the journey begins, the *narrator* reflects nostalgically on the romantic period in which Heinrich lived as one of a lovely *poverty* in which one's few possessions were more precious than the larger number of uniform items available in the world of 1800 (24–25).

Similarly, chapter 5 describes miners as a class of workers who contribute essentially to the dominant political-economic-social order but who purport to be idealistically uninvolved in it. This chapter marvelously conveys how in occult, alchemical, and scientific studies mining becomes a privileged site for the experience of the primeval. In keeping with this, the old miner is from Bohemia, just as according to Mathilde her father is often in Hungary (99), in an eastward-moving symbolism. Hence, according to the miner: "Our occupation is very ancient and widespread. It may well have migrated out of the east with the sun, as our race did, toward the west, and from the center towards the ends" (86). But we should keep in mind more down-to-earth implications of such localities. The foreman Werner was also a foreigner, from Lusatia, a region that was for centuries the object of dispute between Bohemia, Hungary, and German states. Where is it located now? In what until recently, in this long-term historical conflict, we called East Germany.[17]

The miner now presents a highly idealized version of the members of his trade. Without much reference to the rigors of their work, he presents them as satisfied with their low wages, as moved by religious faith (in references to the Lord's Supper and to contemplating crucifixes underground), as opposed to private property, and as losing all interest in precious metals once they are turned into commercial articles ("Waren," 69–71). Marx too is on this medieval horizon. Yet this is the man who struck a rich vein the day of his marriage and was rewarded by the duke of Bohemia with a gold chain and a coin bearing the duke's likeness, as well as the promise of replacing his father-in-law as foreman. And, later, Heinrich recalls that even more magnificent success story, the poet who became the king's son in Atlantis (77–78).

The discrepancy between the miner's disinterested idealism and his contribution to the sociopolitical order is apparent earlier, in the description of Werner's impact: "Through him mining flourished and provided the Duke of Bohemia with immense treasures. Thereby the whole region has become inhabited and prosperous and a flourishing country" (68). Similarly, the miner's first view of gold is that of a king, rescued by the miner so that the metal "might attain to honor in royal crowns and vessels and holy relics, and might rule and direct the world in the form of respected and well-preserved coins adorned with portraits" (67). Here the miner enriches the sovereign, but also thereby the entire region and population; he also directly provides the materials not only for the wealth of but also for the emblems of the power of monarchy and church. This support for the feudal political and religious order is hardly surprising in the author of *Die Christenheit oder Europa*. What insinuates contradiction, however, is the co-presence of visionary exaltations of mining, straightforward presentation of its socioeconomic role, and somewhat ambiguous claims of virtuous noninvolvement by those who fulfill that role.[18]

The poems interspersed in the passages under consideration here lend some support to this attention to socioeconomic notes. One of the songs in the Atlantis chapter makes the contrast between palace and hut plain — "Was du umsonst gesucht in Hutten, / Das wirst du finden in Palast" — and concludes on a rhyme between the words for "throne" and "son":

Ein Herz voll Einklang ist berufen
Zur Glorie um einen Thron;
Der Dichter steigt auf rauhen Stufen
Hinan und wird des Königs Sohn.

(50)

"Heart" and "harmony," the millennial vocabulary, are slanted more in the direction of what Fredric Jameson might call the "political unconscious," the glory of a throne, transformation of a poet into the king's son.[19] Similarly, in chapter 5 familiar motifs, pride and womb, the primal world ("Vorwelt"), do not obscure the miner's essential economic function: "Er führt des Goldes Ströme / In seines Königs Haus" ("He leads the golden streams into his king's house," my translation, 72–73).

Finally, at Heinrich's request the miner sings a poem of unknown origin so obscure as to resemble music and to have the fascination of a dream seen in a waking state. This describes the text well, which is fascinating also because, in an almost Blakean way, it mixes political and sexual motifs and seems unusually revolutionary (73–75).

Although mysterious, the poem is also strangely personal, opening with an individual expression of knowledge: "Ich kenne" ("I know"). Moreover, an "us" will appear in the last line. What the speaker knows is an example of abuse of feudal power, a rich king who lives underground surrounded by water and protected by invisible guards and who prevents his subjects from having access to the heavens and higher regions. Phrases like "des Reiches Untertanen" and statements such as "Ein jeder spielt den treuen Knecht / Und ruft den Herrn mit süßen Worten" use the political vocabulary of realm, subject, knight, and lord to stress this abuse of traditional authority.

But whereas most are submissive, others await their chance to overthrow the king, bringing closer the dawn of freedom: "So bricht der Tag der Freiheit an." These are given the characteristics of persistence, courage, and power of heart and hand; they are able to link spirits together; and they are masters of the floods. In the last stanza a figure rages through the world; this recalls Blake except that the text here claims that the more he rages the more his power is reduced. Does he represent monarchy or an early form of revolution that must be surpassed? At the same time the number of the free grows: "Je mehr die Zahl der Freien werden." The last lines of the poem propose an apocalyptic destruction quite different from what we have seen thus far in Novalis:

Am Ende wird von Banden los
Das Meer die leere Burg durchdringen
Und tragt auf weichen grünen Schwingen
Zurück uns in der Heimat Schoß.

We must translate this way: "At the end free of fetters the sea will pour through the empty town, and (the sea) draws us on soft green wings back to the homeland's womb."

The switch of tenses and use of the first person, now collective, are notable. Political rebellion, leading to annihilation of traditional power, also takes on mythic overtones (one thinks of the end of Rimbaud's "Après le déluge") from the key word "zurück," the metamorphosis of water into flight, and the heavily charged "homeland" and "womb."

But these motifs, familiar from much else that we have discussed, also serve to illuminate the most obscure portion of the poem, the description of the king's solitary pleasures at the beginning. His old and marvelous castle is said to have sunk downward from deep seas, in accordance with the biblical myth of upper as well as lower waters. The streams that rush down from the roof of the castle serve both as mirror for the stars (is this a myth of fall and exile?) and as water for the king's bathing. The limbs that the king bathes are called "zarten," perhaps an overused word but certainly a sexually charged one. The description of the bath ends with the king brightly looking from within his mother's white blood ("Aus seiner Mutter weißem Blut")! Presumably it is the water that is called white blood, and this sentence may suggest that another mother has died, that the king has his own return-to-the-womb need. Significantly, there is no paternal figure, and the story of political abuse coincides with suggestions of solitary sexuality. The familial-libidinal theme merges again with the political, in a text difficult to situate because it seems more potentially revolutionary than recurrent expressions elsewhere in the novel.

But the history to which *Heinrich* most overtly alludes is the conflict between the West and the Middle East that still convulses the world. How write of the thirteenth century without considering the Crusades? How read such a book in ignorance of the continuing conflict? We have seen some hints already — reference to central European countries and to the theory that mining originated in the East, Novalis's version of Blake's position: "The philosophy of the east taught the first principles of human perception." We have not stressed that the hermit in chapter 5 is identified as Count Friedrich von Hohenzollern, who died in 1201, nor that he speaks of the Crusades and his experience in the Middle East, with which he associates India, Africa, and Spain for their treasures, known since antiquity (88–89). Anachronistically, the king of Atlantis claims to come from an ancient Oriental line; his wife was the last descendant of the famous hero Rustum (38). We should not forget that behind this small "Orientalist" appropriation of the history of another region[20] lies the association between Rustum and the violent clash of religious and military warfare in the eighth and ninth centuries A.D. involving Algeria, Persia, and Shiite Moslems. Saïs, another privileged mystical site for Novalis, and Nerval, also has its own painful real history.

But it is in chapter 4 that Heinrich is frontally exposed to the Crusades and what they represent. The structure is simple: he hears first from the victors, then from the victim. The victors recount heroic exploits, work themselves and him up for another crusade, and express themselves in truly bloodthirsty fashion. Not for the Moors and Saracens the desire to wash the Holy Grave with the adversary's blood or to be carried in triumph to heaven — it is the crusaders who voice such fanaticism. Although Heinrich is at first uplifted emotionally, he might have been given pause by the old crusader's statement that Eastern girls are very attractive "to us in the West," to the suggestion that prowess with the sword can bring sexual rewards. Almost casually he notes, "You can also see an oriental girl in my house" (55).

Zulima is this victim, and her presumed sexual submission fits into the erotic thematic of the work as a whole and of course changes Heinrich's attitude. She is allowed to make a thoroughgoing critique of the Crusades, lamenting the killing of her family and her imprisonment, condemning the crusaders as men of barbarous character, defending her own people from the negative images perpetrated by the Europeans, and arguing that the violence was wholly avoidable: "How tranquilly the Christians could have visited the Holy Sepulcher without the need of starting a terrible, useless war which has embittered everything, spread endless wretchedness, and separated the East from Europe forever" (61). Whether this is a fully accurate version may be debated, but it is very significant that Novalis has such a sympathetic and vulnerable personage articulate it. Although at another point Klingsohr speaks of war, especially the perfect example of the most destructive kind, religious war, in exalted terms (113–14), and although in the magic book Heinrich sees himself engaged in warfare, it is *not* with Saracens and Moors, with whom he on the contrary engages in friendly conversation (91). Here again we see that *Heinrich* is hardly ahistorical. Although it seems initially to glorify holy war, it instead condemns it as a disaster, a major Western error; this certainly adds historical content to the symbolism of millennial peace at the end.

At the same time, chapter 4 also constitutes a *large* instance of Orientalist appropriation. In the second part, Heinrich, like many nineteenth-century writers, was to go on an extended *voyage en Orient*, to Jerusalem and elsewhere (the voyage is foreseen in the hermit's manuscript, naturally). But he has already imaginatively traveled East, and so have we, through Zulima's description of her homeland (59–61). This description justifies Klingsohr's reference to the Middle East as the country of poetry, as the privileged site of visionary glimpses of the primeval, almost of the numinous.

Themes of recollection and recognition are strong as Zulima is reminded by Heinrich of her brother, now studying with a famous poet in Persia. Although her memory is weakening, she says that Heinrich has called up "strange recollections of happy times" ("eine sonderbare Erinnerung aus frohen Zeiten"). The inhabitants and the landscape of Arab regions, presented in glowing terms, are also characterized by this preternatural quality of recollection. The people are noble, especially sensitive to the extraordinary beauty of the land, and there are remnants of the ancient past ("mannigfaltige Überbleibsel ehemaliger denkwürdiger Zeiten"). Two decades before the exploits of Champollion (1822), but contemporaneous with the discovery of the Rosetta stone (1799), mysterious symbols, incomprehensible constituents of a primeval language ("uralten Schrift"), abound, and they provoke a deeply meditative response to the surroundings:

Life has special charm on land inhabited for ages and glorified by former diligence, activity, and affection. Nature appears to have become more human and intelligible there. An obscure recollection amid the transparent present reflects the images of the world in sharp outlines, and thus one enjoys a double world which in that very way sloughs off its crude and violent nature and turns into the magical poesy and fables [Dichtung und Fabel] of our senses. Who knows whether an incomprehensible influence of former, now invisible inhabitants does not also play a part . . . [?] (61)

This is the archetypal expression of the Middle East as the preeminent visionary locus. More than the mines, where there is no primitive human presence; more than the content of dreams, myths, tales, even such a strange one as Klingsohr's; more than the wisdom of the sages, which derives from it, this scene obscurely puts Heinrich and the reader in the presence of the primeval. The earliest of human inhabitants (are they still near?), nature irradiated, *doubled* by poetry and fable, even the visible symbols of the lost original language: here we are closest to the other world, on the edge of the noumenal.

Nonetheless, an idealistic male Western poet, steeped in the lore of the visionary, has put this passage in the mouth of an Arab female character of his invention. This may be thought of as one of the final complexities of Novalis's fascinating novel, which repeatedly expresses mystical apprehensions of a primal human experience and millennial visions of future harmony. The latter are not devoid of historical, even contemporary, content, as we have seen. As we might criticize Blake for being "utopian," we might think of Novalis as "regressive" in nearly leaving the modern period for the medieval. Yet *Heinrich* treats history, the city, commerce (and poetry) in

Heinrich's move from Eisenach to Augsburg, riches, and the feudal order, not to speak of warfare, and in highly mixed and therefore unsettling ways. The Middle Eastern theme is equally mixed, for whereas Novalis criticizes Europe, the Arab regions are imaginatively put to use and indeed furnish him his most compelling visionary landscape. Finally, we must not forget that, as implied in Blake's title, sexual union in marriage is the central metaphor for eternity or millennium and that *Heinrich* functions throughout on the basis of fearful cost, the death of the mother. It is not incidental that Zulima is a mother and that only her child keeps her from suicide (59). The beauties of *Heinrich* are inseparable from its revelation of discrepancies in economic, military, political, and familial, but also poetic/visionary, spheres. It is a book that both illuminates and disturbs.

Visionary Insanity ✍
Nerval's *Aurélia*

Gérard de Nerval's *Aurélia* is beautiful and frightening, indeed harrowing. Although Nerval variously recalls Blake and Novalis in presenting visionary transpositions as part of a myth of universal history replete with orientalism and extreme religious syncretism, *Aurélia* is unique. For it presents its exalted and anguished persona, hardly distinguishable from its author, as *insane*; its content is the story of his illness and apparent cure, entirely in the first person and largely in the form of a recital of his dreams and visions. Ross Chambers has brilliantly shown how this narrative tactic is a form of "oppositional writing."[1] Whereas Blake's *Marriage* and Novalis's *Heinrich* were produced in the immediate and not-so-immediate aftermath of 1789, respectively, Nerval's last work (published in 1855) is situated after the failed revolution of 1848, under the repressive regime and society of the Second Empire. That repression is brutally signaled two years later in the government trials of Flaubert and Baudelaire on grounds of sexual immorality and sacrilege. But even in *Aurélia*, whose author is often considered apolitical, historical, religious, and sexual themes treated in Blake and Novalis take on an exacerbated intensity.

In earlier works, journalistic efforts and a play, *Léo Burckart* (1838), (the first version of which was written with Alexandre Dumas), Nerval had fenced with the censor of the preceding régime,[2] but he is better known for the intensely beautiful and hermetic (in both senses) sonnets entitled *Les Chimères* and for other exalted productions. These include what might be considered obsessively magnified portraits of women and goddesses, *Les filles du feu*, and the translation of the first part of *Faust*. Nerval traveled frequently in Germany and was a conduit for German romantic literature to France, although not for Novalis, whose work he did not know, and we shall see that there is a pale Faustian note in *Aurélia*.

Although some of his prose, notably *Sylvie*, has a novelistic strain, the nocturnal wanderings evoked in *Les nuits d'octobre* are protosurrealist and include a reflection on the inadequacies of the novel and realism in conveying "les combinaisons bizarres de la vie." Nerval's contrary devotion to "rêverie *super-naturaliste*" is stated in the prefatory letter to Alexandre Dumas for *Les filles du feu*, a concept also used in relation to eighteenth-century illuminism.[3] The last allusion is to *Les Illuminés*, in which notable writers and practitioners of occult doctrines are celebrated, just as Nerval's preoccupations with the Middle East are reflected in his *Voyage en Orient*. From this list it will be seen that he was an adept, like Blake and Novalis, of esoteric doctrines and religions.

Despite the parallels with earlier writers, with Nerval there is the striking difference that in *Aurélia* the visionary is experienced as madness and is diagnosed as such in the case of the author as well as his narrator; the suicide by hanging of Nerval between the publication of the two parts of *Aurélia* apparently "justified" the diagnosis. (See fig. 3.) This judgment of mental illness gives rise to interpretation of portions of *Aurélia* as symptoms, say, of schizophrenia, but has also led "subversive" thinkers like Deleuze and Guattari to make Nerval a capital case of the repressiveness of modern society.[4] In provocative prose poems such as "Le Mauvais Vitrier" and "Assommons les pauvres" Baudelaire had *at the time* made a similar argument, although not directly concerning Nerval.[5] In the case of *Aurélia*, what is striking is that the narrator evidences symptoms of what *we* "recognize" as insanity, even accepts that judgment himself, yet as Chambers shows, insidiously subverts it.

Hence early on (118) the glimpse of a house number that is the same as his age convinces the narrator that either he or his beloved Aurélia is about to die; similarly, he later anticipates literally the Apocalypse and the Flood. On the occasion of his first internment, the appearances of the world change; he disrobes and believes himself possessed of supernatural power: "There was something comic in the care I took to spare the strength and lives of the soldiers who had picked me up" (121). In a similar situation later he drinks ether, escapes from his guards, and is captured while calmly picking flowers. Several times he falls into a state of dissociation from the

3 Gustave Doré, *La Rue de La Vieille Lanterne (mort de Gérard de Nerval)*, 1855.
© cliché Bibliothèque Nationale de France, Paris.

external world lasting several days, on one occasion adding: "The cataleptic state in which I had been for some days was explained . . . to me in
scientific terms" (129). Most astonishingly perhaps, in the third chapter of
the first part, illustrating what he calls "the overflowing of the dream into
real life" ("l'épanchement du songe dans la vie réelle," 120), he recounts
an extraordinary alienation from self and normal time-space events as he

witnesses the arrival of friends, an occurrence that "in reality" happens only later on. Here the well-known theme of the double is introduced for the first time.

What is sketched above is in itself quite fascinating for the reader, as "content" and as narrative tactic. The interest is increased by elements that subtly or blatantly challenge the psychoanalytic position. These include appeals to the reader's experience of suffering and dreams (115–16, 121, 130) as well as questionings of scientific reasoning. The narrator is irritated by the use of the vocabulary of cataleptic state to describe what for him was "a series of logical events" (129), just as at the outset the concept of his sickness causes him to wonder what he will lose if he accepts "what men call reason" (115), a version of a theme already encountered in Blake and Novalis. Once again interned, he accepts his visions as "illusions" but retains the promises of the goddess Isis, whom he had perceived in these visions (164). Elsewhere, moreover, his disregard for the constraints of "reason" is flagrant, recalling certain formulations in Blake: "However that may be, I do not think that human imagination has invented anything which is not true either in this world or in others, and I could not doubt what I had so clearly *seen* myself" (139). This visionary logic is by now familiar to us, and in fact it has been asserted from the opening page. There Nerval puts *Aurélia* under the patronage of authors also familiar to us, Swedenborg and Dante as well as Apuleius, a prelude to the massive invocation of literary and religious traditions in service to his "insane" quest.

Here then we have an unusual narrative tactic: exploiting our interest in mental illness, which as modern readers we fear but accept as real, to draw us toward visionary or supernatural experience, in which we are perhaps greatly interested but to which we may have trouble attributing reality. Further, the tactic is practiced with high intensity, particularly in the first part, where there is very little external event or story, aside from the unnamed fault that has caused the narrator to lose Aurélia, and where virtually everything involves the recounting of dreams. Although Nerval is thus more extreme than Novalis in emphasizing dream, from what we have already seen it is nonetheless clear that the concept includes as well unusual waking states, which could be dismissed as hallucinations, and extended periods of sleeplike experiences, "scientifically" called cataleptic trance. We shall have to delineate still other forms. The multitude of dreams and related visions constitutes as complex, powerful, and effective a tissue of visionary textuality as can be found anywhere, and Nerval's techniques as well as his obsessive themes will repay attention.

Concerning dreams proper, the opening sentence, in my translation, sets a grave and mysterious tone: "Dream is a second life," an echo of the subtitle, "Le rêve et la vie." This is followed by a classical epic allusion to the gates of ivory and horn and a reference to sleep as the image of death, a state in which the self continues its existence in another form. Shifting visual imagery (the dreams in *Aurélia* are overwhelmingly visual) leads to the concluding note of this liminary paragraph: "le mondes des Esprits s'ouvre pour nous" — "the world of Spirits opens for us." This is followed in the next paragraph by the citing of Swedenborg, Apuleius,[6] and Dante. The experience of falling asleep and beginning to dream, the elusiveness of the self and the closeness of death, but also the ancient traditions of dream as illumination, are thus all evoked.

The first dream the narrator recounts (118–19) seems to confirm his belief that he, or more likely Aurélia, will die, since he views an immense winged creature of undetermined sex in desperate and unsuccessful struggle. Typically, changing visual effects are noticeable, and Nerval gives a precise pictorial equivalent, Dürer's *Melancolia*. Moreover, before viewing that scene, the narrator had wandered in a vast edifice, part place of learning, part hotel, in whose corridors he got lost before being struck by the "spectacle étrange." Shortly afterward, during his first trance experience and after perceiving shifting colors and forms, he has the "celestial vision" (121) of a divinity, constantly changing yet finally Asian in setting.

The anguish, but also the wonder, associated with the Nervalian version of visionary voyages, and the emergence of a larger-than-life figure, thereafter always female, are then developed in a sequence of dreams (chapters 4–6 of the first part, 123–31). These involve a regression in familial and universal time reminiscent of Novalis, including Heinrich's opening dream. First transported to the Rhine and an earlier century where he is spoken to by a magical bird, the narrator then seems to fall into an abyss that, fusing geology with the physiology of the brain, traverses the globe ("I felt myself carried painlessly along on a current of molten metal, and a thousand similar streams, the colors of which indicated different chemicals, crisscrossed the breast of the world like those blood-vessels and veins that writhe in the lobes of the brain," 124). Thereafter he sees a new horizon and enters into contact with his long-dead relatives and, indeed, with the totality of the human race. This is followed by a Blake-like statement of enlarged and intensified consciousness:

The costumes of every nation, visions of every country, all appeared to me distinctly at the same time, as if my faculties of observation had been multiplied — and yet not muddled — by a phenomenon of space comparable to that of time, whereby a century of action is concentrated in a minute of dream. (125–26)

Here, as in Heinrich's dream and in Blake's visionary state, the Nervalian *rêve* produces a transcendence of normal space-time, a magnified form of consciousness and a universalization of the limited self.

Despite this confidence, the following dream is introduced by an expression of fear that the narrator is going too far in his quest. Nonetheless, after finding himself in an unknown city on a mountain and after much climbing and descending, he encounters the original inhabitants, the "primitive, heavenly family" (129), a paradisal experience causing liberating tears. This is followed by a dream in which he is once more with his ancestors, and in fact seems to have regressed to a childhood phase. This does not prevent him from following a woman into a garden, whereupon a kind of sexual allegory, sensuous and of mythic intensity, unfolds. Heavy clusters of grapes, a profusion of plants, the garden returned to "l'état sauvage," the plashing of a fountain with water lilies provide the setting. The now pointedly sexualized woman, rolling her hips and caressing the stem of a "rose trémière"[7] (hollyhock in English, for Nerval mystical), becomes identified with the garden, grows gigantically out of sight, and disappears. The narrator finds himself alone against a fragment of a wall and the sculpted bust of a woman. Later he learns that Aurélia has died.

Most of the motifs and themes noted above recur in the concluding dream of the first part, which follows upon the narrator's perception of his evil double, who is to marry Aurélia in his place (138–39). In chapter 10 he again traverses the interior of the globe, lands on a mountainous shore, and exhausts himself climbing and descending in a castle that is also an immense city and then a casino, arriving at the room where the marriage is to occur. Despite the atmosphere of anxiety, a dreamlike absurdity at first prevails as a sofa in the shape of a throne (painfully recalling the end of Klingsohr's tale) is tested for its springiness by several in attendance! But then the horror returns as the narrator is threatened by a worker holding a bar with a red-hot end ("dont l'extrémité se composait d'une boule rougie au feu," 142). Those around him seem to jeer at his impotence, and he wakes to the sound of what seems to him the scream of a real woman. Here indeed is the very opposite of the successful nuptial culmination of Novalis's tale. Quite understandably after such a dream, the narrator concludes the first part on a note of utter defeat, sorrow, and despair.

The dreams in the first part thus reveal recurrent movements and motifs, including voyage, globe, city, mountain, and garden as well as marriage. The sense of unbearable psychosexual trauma, though inescapable, is accompanied by the experience of wonderful transformations, immeasurable distancings from the here and now, which we as readers also undergo. Mental illness here indeed seems the vehicle for the visionary.

The dreams in the second part bring the divinity glimpsed earlier into focus, although not without a continuing threat, and thereby (ambiguously) accomplish the redemption of the narrator. I will discuss these dreams only briefly. Early on the dreams are painful. In the second chapter, amid familiar motifs (climbing, houses, rooms), the narrator is not sure he has received Aurélia's pardon, and in the next chapter another woman seen in a dream emphasizes his guilt. By chapter 4 his dreams have reduced him to virtual incoherence, but after the narration of many confused waking activities, including repeated internment, he later in his sleep has a vision of the divinity, who tells him that she is the same as Mary and his mother and that she will soon appear fully to him (162). And this later occurs (172) as the divinity of his dreams, now dressed in almost Indian fashion, explains that his ordeals are over, giving him the confidence to conclude the work in a positive fashion.

In this sketch of the dreams in the second part two aspects of the work that require further investigation are visible: syncretism, as in the divinity who is Mary and mother — and Venus and Isis, and spouse as well as mother (168); and the narrator's effort to impose coherence, which long ago led Charles Mauron to portray Nerval as emblematic of the victory of artists over mental turmoil rather than of submission to it.[8] Actually the two features are part of the same process, and in treating them we will also confront themes (family, sex, religion, history) that were salient in Blake and Novalis and already appear to be obsessive in *Aurélia*.

In terms of structure, we note the effort to surmount a persistent tendency to disunity, to dichotomy, even an alienating doubling within the self, as reflected in the division of the action into two phases (115), two parts, the second opening with a reiterated evocation of Eurydice and the exclamation "Lost a second time!" (my translation, 145, 147). Whereas at a certain point the narrator refers to the completion of one of his best stories (autobiographically, *Sylvie*, 161), in *Aurélia* he apparently eschews invention, modestly following the example of the visionary authors cited at the outset in "transcrib[ing]" the "impressions" and "notes" of his illness and his dreams (115). Early on the evolution of various phases is noted: "Here began"; "From that moment on" (120). Later, in the effort to overcome his guilt, his writing takes on the character of a systematic examination of conscience (155). In keeping with that goal, in the second part he gives us more external information, a firmer sense of history, family, setting. Throughout he insists on the moral usefulness of such sincere self-analysis, viewing it as the writer's mission (121). At the end (176) his description of the effort to dominate his dreams is couched in confident terms: pursuing a "bold undertaking," "I resolved to fix my dream-state and learn its secret." He stresses the will and the ability to force, dominate, tame, impose upon the "spirits of the night which play with our reason." Here he seems to accept the notion of psychological rationality, but he returns in the concluding sentence to the view that his ordeal has involved an initiatory descent to hell. At his most controlled he balances rational and mythic modes.

In keeping with the drive to coherence, despite conflicting tendencies, which we will note,[9] in both parts the narrator engages in a major effort of syncretism, attempting to reconstitute the past — first that of the world, then that of his own life, that is, both universal and personal history. Significantly, both efforts take place in asylums; both involve dreams but, just as important, conscious intellect and synthesizing energy.

Like the second, the first of these passages (chapters 7–8, 132–37) opens with the prospect visible from the narrator's asylum, which quickly leads him to want to draw his visions. He covers the walls with frescoes depicting Aurélia as the divinity of his dreams, but these are destroyed by the other inmates, called "the lunatics" ("les fous") by the narrator. Furnished with paper, he sets about writing and illustrating the primeval history of the world, "representing, by a thousand figures accompanied by stories, verses and inscriptions in every known language, a sort of history of the world mixed with memories of studies and fragments of dreams" (my translation, 133).

These passages could serve to epitomize Blake, Novalis, *and* Nerval in their syncretism and mixture of media, including the visual. Think of Blake's illustrations, the images in the hermit's book in *Heinrich*. As in the other two authors, the history here is ancient, drawing on "oriental traditions" involving talismans, genies, and divinities from Persian, Greek, and Scandinavian mythology and biblical Elohim interpreted in cabalistic fashion. Later, in the second synthesizing passage, Nerval again characterizes these materials as cabalistic: "My role seemed to me to be to re-establish universal harmony through cabalistic art and to seek a solution in evoking the occult forces of various religions" (my translation, 165). Nerval's cabalistic readings are detailed in notes to editions of his work,[10] and we recall similar materials in Blake and in Klingsohr's tale.

Although the narrator's work begins while he is awake, it continues in dream as he seems to be "transported" to another planet where the origination of life is occurring. This passage reads like an extended development of the opening phase of Heinrich's first dream, as the narrator participates in battles with monsters (he possesses a body as strange as theirs), witnesses wars and revolutions that last thousands of years, suffers in captivity with a part of humanity, and narrates the theft of the secret of the Cabala by evil genies. Although his memory begins to fade, he brings us up to biblical time with the story of the Flood and then into modern historical time. For after the evocation of the Eternal Mother suffering throughout the ages, the last scene of conflict is one well known to us, recalling Novalis once again:

The last one took place at Granada, where the sacred talisman fell before the hostile blows of Christians and Moors. How many more years yet has the world still to suffer, for the vengeance of those eternal enemies must inevitably be renewed under other skies! They are the severed sections of the serpent that encircles the Earth . . . separated by steel, they join together again in a hideous embrace [baiser!] cemented by human blood. (136–37)

The mythic history (suffering Eternal Mother) leads to a vision of *our* history, a hideous vision of bloodshed focusing on the conflict between European and Moor and ominously repetitive. Individual psychic disarray and occult investigations here do not exclude historical consciousness.

This is subtly the case also in the other syncretist reconstruction, that of the narrator's personal life in the asylum near the end of the second part. This very moving passage (168–70) describes the narrator's pleasure in the scene he views from his window as well as his separation from the life outside and his joy in rediscovering the objects and books that recall his whole past life. A reference to these as being like Faust's capharnaum reminds us that earlier the narrator had expressed the guilt inflicted on him by Christian religion because of his interest in Oriental religions and his occult studies and projects (148).

Precisely, the objects he rediscovers embody his French and European past but also his interest in the Middle East, his travels, like Nerval's own, to Constantinople and Cairo. At the opening of the chapter the setting reminds him of the shores of the Bosporus, and among his long-forgotten possessions are his Arab clothes and a map of Cairo (165, 169). Then too there are the books on the basis of which he produced the first synthesizing passage:

My books, an odd assortment of the knowledge of all ages, history, travels, religion [religions], the Cabala, astrology, enough to gladden the shades of Pico della Mirandola, the sage Meursius, and Nicholas de Cusa — the Tower of Babel in two hundred volumes — they had left me all that! (169)

Here the syncretic masters, students of Middle Eastern languages and proponents of the synthesis of religions, are named, and not without historical

point: Cusa published an irenic treatise on the occasion of the capture of
Constantinople by the Turks in 1453.

Surprisingly, at the end there turns out to be a link as well between the
personal and the historical in the intimate relation established in this passage between past and present, narrator and reader. Changes in tenses bring
us *presently* into the personal situation of the narrator: "My room lies at the
end of a corridor"; "Above the bookshelves stretches an enormous map of
Cairo"; the arrangement of his things "aptly summarizes my wandering
life"; the books are "enough to drive a wise man mad; let us try [now] to
ensure that there is enough to make a madman wise." Note the continuing
conflict between structure and incoherence: even as he organizes his possessions ("Avec quelles délices j'ai pu classer dans mes tiroirs l'amas de mes
notes et de mes correspondances," 169), madness and the Tower of Babel
are close. Nonetheless, even the correspondence with Aurélia is said to be
preserved: "I find Arabic letters, relics of Cairo and Stamboul [. . .] faded
drafts, half-crumpled letters, these are the treasures of my only love . . . Let
me read them again . . . Many of them are missing, others torn or scratched
out; here is what I find:" (170). But even this fragmentary evocation of the
discourse of the past is followed by a gap; the writing in this passage brings
us into the immediate presence of the narrator in the asylum, where we virtually identify with his experience, which yet is finally elusive.

Directly after this gap the narrator describes a kind of ecstasy, a waking
dream gradually impregnated with Eastern and finally Indian imagery,
namely the caves of Ellorah, but which is transformed into a vision of
human history written in blood, epitomized by the mutilated body of a gigantic woman accompanied by similarly dismembered bodies of women of
all races and classes. The narrator's response: "There [. . .] is what has re-
sulted from power bestowed on men," who have destroyed the eternal type
of beauty and therefore reduced the races of humankind (171). The racial
reference is part and parcel of the cabalistic myth, but a different kind of
history soon intrudes as the narrator's doctor distracts him with the spectacle of another inmate, apparently blind, deaf, and mute, who refuses to
eat, thinking, we learn later, that he is already dead. The narrator after-
wards calls him Saturnin and turns him into a type of a good or fraternal
double, but at first we learn only that he is "an ancien soldat d'Afrique" —
of North Africa, that is. France's ongoing subjugation of Algeria is on the
horizon.

The syncretist passages in both parts, the one mythic-historical, the
other personal, both "orientalist" and to some degree perhaps open to that
criticism,[11] nonetheless end lucidly with references to historical warfare
between Europeans and Arabs. We recall that the first passage represents

that recurring conflict as a bloody kiss, having previously evoked the sufferings of the Eternal Mother. In the second the bloodshed takes the form of the mutilation of another larger-than-life woman and provokes a critique of power as exercised by men. The reference to the current form of that violence, France's colonization of Algeria, is discreet — inevitably so only a few years after Napoleon III's coup d'état.

Discreet or flagrant, what is striking in the conclusion of both of these passages is the link between military violence and sexuality, warfare and the female body either sublimated or horribly mutilated. We shall now discuss systematically themes of sexuality, inevitably linked to religion and history, the first two insistent from the outset, the last more explicit in the second part.

Blake's view of the destructive effect of religion, particularly in the creation of guilt and in the realm of sex, illuminates *Aurélia*. As the reference to Faust suggests, there is a timid, nearly repressed demonic theme in the work. Early on the narrator reflects that he is "displacing" the conditions of good and evil (116), and in the nearly biblical struggle with his companion before his first internment he cries out that he is from a prior ("antérieur") revelation (120). In the first chapter of the second part, he explains his confusion and skepticism regarding Christianity as a result of the upheaval of the Revolution, then attempts a reconciliation of reason and faith but quickly condemns this as satanic and heretical, a worse-than-Faustian attempt to make a pact with God (148). Hardly a Blakean or Nietzschean, let alone Goethean, success in "displacing the conditions of good and evil."

In fact, in accord with arguments by Blake and Nietzsche, religion in *Aurélia* is associated with overwhelming guilt and distress. The protagonist's unpardonable "faute" against his beloved (116), apparently so reprehensible as to be unnameable, his self-criticism for compensating through facile love affairs (138), the accusations of women in dreams in the second part, his frenetic effort to expiate all, even minor, faults ("The mass of reparations to be made crushed me because of my impotence," my translation, 158) — all of this is unbearable. But at the end he feels purified of his faults and engaged in the "luminous paths of religion" (my translation, 177).

Yet the link between religion and sexual trauma is insistent, and, as we shall see in discussing the first "Mémorable," undissolved at the end. There is a familial component here, apparent in the sequence of dreams discussed in the first part and rendered painful by the brief allusions in the second part to the narrator's actual parents. He never knew his mother, who died in Germany during revolutionary or imperial wars (155). His two attempts to see his aged father are unsuccessful: once he is absent, once so irascible as to cause the narrator to leave in consternation (158, 161). What a chasm between these absent parental figures and the heavily overdetermined dream presence of the Isis divinity throughout.

As for expression of sexual desire, we have seen it only in the garden-woman sequence, where it emerges from a regression to a state of childish innocence (130). In contrast, the naked female body is evoked only in the vision of universal mutilation, and the most provocative male imagery is the phallic threat to the protagonist in the concluding dream of the first part. We should not forget that when he afterward reflects on this dream, it is to condemn himself and to identify the figure of the double with Jesus! "This preferred spouse, this king of glory, it is he who judges and condemns me, and who has forever taken away into his heaven her whom he would have given me and of whom I am henceforward unworthy!" (my translation, 150). This makes Jesus the sexual rival of the protagonist (but it is *his* fault), the author of the earlier threat to his masculinity.

Whereas these themes are evident from early on, the historical dimension, with the exception of the Granada conflict, is not visible until the second part. In the first part, in keeping with the visionary theme, conventional space-time is eclipsed. After unspecific reference to Italian cities and a return to Paris the "urban configuration" melts away (my translation, 117), and it is not until well into the second part (155) that we realize that ten years have passed. By this time, the narrator is starting to give us a sketch both of his experience of French history and of the Parisian geography in which he circulates.

We have already mentioned allusions to the Revolution and to European wars. Then, in explaining his religious ideas, the narrator tells of being given a copy of the New Testament by an Englishman in 1815 (156), that is, after Napoleon's final defeat and the reestablishment of peace between the two countries. The next upheaval, the July Revolution of 1830, is at first evoked indirectly through the opinions of a friend called Georges, in reality Georges Bell (Joachim Hounau, politically active in the revolution of 1848[12] and Nerval's first biographer). Quite in character, he speaks eloquently against the skepticism and political and social discouragement following upon the failure of the 1830 uprising. Although the narrator soon moves on to his usual preoccupations, Aurélia and the need for forgiveness, his initial reaction is like Georges's: "I had been one of the young men of that period and I had tasted its ardors and bitternesses" (157). As for 1848 and its aftermath in the coup d'état of 1851, it too had better be evoked in vague terms: "Political events worked indirectly, not only by worrying me but also by removing the means for my putting my affairs in order" (158).

Vague but quite systematic — 1789, the period of continental wars, 1815, 1830, 1848–51. Then there immediately follows the reiterated narration of the protagonist's nightly insomniac wanderings through Paris, sketching a geography of personal suffering and historical resonance.

In regard to the latter one must recall that the February revolution of 1848 led eventually to tragic confrontation with large numbers of workers, many of whom were massacred in June of that year, as evoked in Flaubert's *L'Education sentimentale* when Rocques fires into the crowd of prisoners in the lower level of the Tuileries, provoking a slaughter (chapter 1 of the third part). One recalls also Baudelaire's poem "Le Cygne," which laments all forms of suffering and exile but which is specifically located in the place du Carrousel, between the Louvre and the Tuileries (a palace burned during the defeat of the *next* revolution, in May 1871). Critics have unearthed the many pro-Republic, anti-Empire motifs hidden in this poem, which Baudelaire was trying to publish as early as two years after his trial for immorality and blasphemy.[13]

But no special research is needed to see that Baudelaire's suffering over the changes in Paris refers to Haussmann's transformation of the city, beginning with the place du Carrousel. How interesting then that the relics of the narrator's past life at the end of *Aurélia* include wood paneling from the demolition of a house where he (and Nerval in fact) had lived — "on the site of the Louvre" (169 — actually l'impasse du Doyenné, close to the Carrousel).[14] That is, like Baudelaire, Nerval and his protagonist were very directly and personally uprooted by the Second Empire, as is expressed in masked ways by Baudelaire and by the scantiest of references in *Aurélia*.

The narrator's nightly wanderings in Paris are not unconnected with the above. They originate in Montmartre, near the cemetery where Aurélia is buried, in keeping with his overwhelmingly personal motivations. Starting from the Clichy gate, he speaks frequently with peasants and workers, then moves toward the center of the city, stopping at Les Halles and various churches, particularly those known for their Marian devotions, before reaching the Louvre and often the Palais Royal, which attracts crowds but which also has a revolutionary history beginning in 1789. The first of these nightly wanderings is especially charged with individual,[15] religious, and historical meanings. For the narrator believes that John's prediction of the Apocalypse is about to be realized, since he sees "a black sun in an empty sky and a red ball of blood above the Tuileries," as well as a dance of multiple moons over the Louvre (159–60). The Tuileries and the Louvre, where the workers were massacred in those "political events" vaguely evoked a page earlier: together with the exalted experiences and the tortured psychological themes of *Aurélia*, the devastating history of violent political turmoil is also shadowed forth.

The themes that we have been pursuing are not absent from the "Mém-orables," which the narrator includes just before the confident, yet precarious, closure of his text. This occurs after the dream in which the now-Indian divinity has told him that his ordeals are over and after a break in the text: "I inscribe here, under the title of *Mémorables*, the impressions of several dreams which followed the one I have just reported" (my translation, 173). The convention of direct transcription reappears, although the breaks and divisions among the "dreams" that follow are ambiguous (perhaps due to the fact that Nerval did not see the final proofs) and although not all of the passages in fact look like dreams. We might view them instead as a final sampling of several kinds of Nervalian visionary writing — hymnic, dreamlike, allegorical.[16]

The briefest of the passages is the most apparently dreamlike, but it also has subtle connections with the others:

I found myself *in spirit* in Saardam, which I visited last year. The ground was covered with snow. A very little girl was walking and sliding on the frozen ground toward, I think, the house of Peter the Great. Her majestic profile had something Bourbon about it. Her dazzlingly white neck emerged half-way from a *palatine* of swan's feathers. With her little pink hand she was sheltering a lighted lamp from the wind and was going to knock at the green door of the house when a skinny cat that was coming out got tangled in her legs and made her fall. "Why, it's only a cat!" said the little girl as she got up. "A cat is something!," answered a soft voice. I was present at this scene, and I was carrying on my arm a little grey cat which began to mew. "It's that old fairy's child!" said the little girl.

And she went into the house. (my translation, 175)

The northern setting, actually the Dutch city of Zaandam, the reference to Peter the Great, and the girl's Bourbon quality prepare the reader for the imperial allegory in the following text. So does what the girl is wearing, since a *palatine* is a fur collar such as that worn by the *princesse Palatine*, hence evoking like Novalis the history of empire in Germany. The erotic theme of the first "Mémorable" also appears, but in subtle and childlike form. This is a rare evocation of a female body in this work, and although that of a child, the body is sensuously evoked in terms of color, form, resemblance to animals associated with beauty and sensuality (in particular the way in which her strikingly white neck *half* emerges from the collar, which, normally of fur, here is of swan feathers). The cats, the fall, and the fact that the first cat is female ("une chatte maigre") and a mother could be seen as suggestive of sublimated or prospective sexuality. The involvement of the dreamer (if it is a dream; he says he is there *in spirit*) seems sublimated too: it is he who describes the details noted above, yet he admits only to being present. The voice that speaks is unlocated. Is it his? If not, whose? And, although supposedly only "present," he seems to participate, since he carries the cat whose mother has caused the girl to fall. Yet it is she who brings the "dream" to an end: "Et elle entra dans la maison." The dreamer may be present, project, participate, but he does not control.

As this *innocent* dream looks forward to the political allegory to follow, it echoes in childlike ways the strong eroticism of the first "Mémorable" (173–75). I consider the passage using Scandinavian mythology to be part of the opening paragraphs of that "Mémorable," which are heavily syncretist. These paragraphs may also be read as strophes in this hymnic, biblical, sacred prose poem. Note that the eroticism, although strong, is again deflected by religion, as we recognize in a dream that this passage contains: "I have come out of a very sweet dream. I saw the woman I [had] loved, radiant and transfigured. Heaven opened in all its glory and I read the word *forgiveness* written in Christ's blood."

The pluperfect seems significant, since in the following lines the erotic imagery is projected away from any individual and throughout the cosmos. To the accompaniment of hosannahs a dual note rings out, "the first octave of the divine hymn." The religious reference is clear: "From Sunday to Sunday [. . . .]" (my translation). So is the universal scope:

The hills sing [. . .] to the valleys, the springs to the streams, the streams
to the rivers, and the rivers to the sea; the air thrills, and light gently
bursts the budding flowers [brise harmonieusement les fleurs naissantes].
A sigh, a shiver of love comes from the swollen womb [sein] of the earth,
and the choir of stars unfolds itself in infinity; it parts and returns again,
contracts and expands, sowing in the remoteness of space the seeds of
new creations.

Different from Novalis's work in that it involves separation from the beloved and forgiveness by Jesus, this passage nonetheless enacts a universal creative ecstasy.

The passage closes as though it were a refrain, echoing references to stars, flowers, foreign languages, and the Greek word *Myosotis*, with which this initial "Mémorable" had opened. Without analyzing each of these in detail, we may say that the writing at the beginning — and throughout — is indeed hymnic and ecstatic. Exclamations, parallelisms of (again) a syncretist nature, and apostrophes abound. Auvergne and the mountains of

Himalaya are related. Shepherds invoking Mary ("*Pauvre Marie!*") cause corybants to leave the grottoes of Love, although somewhat chauvinistically the text asserts the superiority of "la Patrie" to Paphos. Or is this another sign of the threat that hangs over writing in France in this period? Even a shepherd's song that Nerval like the German romantics is said to have collected[17] is added: "Là-haut, sur les montagnes, — le monde y vit content; — le rossignol sauvage — fait mon contentement" ("Over there, on the mountaintops, the world dwells content. The wild nightingale creates contentment"). And all of this in the interest of provoking a universal *and holy* sexual experience: "Pure loves, divine sighs! Inflame the sacred mountain . . . for you have brothers in the valleys and in the bosom of the woods thy shy sisters are hiding." Again, the universal erotic awakening at the end of Klingsohr's tale comes to mind.

That tale is also recalled, though differently, in the concluding portion of this first "Mémorable," with its host of Scandinavian deities. The difference is that they are identified finally as the authors of the destructive tendencies in history, as those who tried to break the cabalistic unity of macrocosm and microcosm. However, "le pardon du Christ" has been pronounced for them too, and the "Mémorable" thus concludes, "Que Dieu préserve le divin Balder, le fils d'Odin, et Freya la belle!"

Christ and forgiveness are important in a segment of this "Mémorable" not yet discussed (173–74), another dream in which the troubling religious-sexual themes noted earlier reappear undiminished. This passage begins with a grateful celebration of the protagonist's "great friend" for pardoning him and the world. Then it describes a dream, a night in which he was to join her in her palace on his reddish-brown horse ("cheval alezan-brûlé," the first adjective having an Arab root). The horse, however, exhibits the symptoms of exhaustion and impotence: "the stallion slipped from beneath me. The broken reins streamed along its sweating flanks, and it required enormous efforts on my part to keep it from lying down on the ground." The translator is right to give "stallion," because the great friend now appears mounted on a white "cavale," a poetic word for "mare." As in an earlier dream (172), the narrator is helped by the apparition of Saturnin, and this moment of sexual weakness is overcome and he rides off with his beloved in a mixture of biblical, Arab, and Greek motifs. Her hair is full of the perfume of Yemen, and they are guided by the bird — "la huppe messagère" — considered prophetic among Arabs, under the protection of Apollo and Adonis, male divinities emblematic of sexual power and superior vision.[18]

At no point in this passage is Aurélia named. In fact at one point we read: "I recognized the divine features of ———" (my translation, 174).

Nerval's editors assure us that the manuscript contains the name not of Aurélia but of Sophie, at one level at least evoking the Sophia of Gnostic tradition, and again recalling Novalis. Once more there is the possibility of
self-censorship in fear of the accusation of heresy. Quickly, too, Saint Paul
and Jesus are invoked:

"Oh Death, where is thy victory," since the conquering Messiah was riding [chevauchait] between the two of us? His garment was of sulphur
yellow hyacinth, and his wrists, as well as his ankles and feet, sparkled
with diamonds and rubies. When his light wand touched the pearly door
of the new Jerusalem, we were all three inundated with light. It is then
that I descended among men to announce to them the good news. (my
translation, 174)

The concluding extravagance (why does this seem more demented than
anything in Blake?) perhaps fits with the sense of sexual unease that emerges
for this passage: Jesus' delicate and bejewelled extremities, his position
mounted "between the two of us." There is sexual anxiety, replacement by a
divine other, followed by a "dream" of childlike simplicity.

As already mentioned, that "simple" dream leads to another, the last
"Mémorable," also called a dream and universally read as a statement
in favor of the settlement of the Crimean War (1854–56), which was in
progress during the composition of *Aurélia* and which ended after Nerval's
death. Indeed, the dreamer goes east and north, first to Vienna, where there
are references to pardons and Solomon (behind the scenes in the Song of
Songs imagery of the first "Mémorable," we realize), then to the Baltic,
which seems about to engulf Saint Petersburg and surroundings. But suddenly the scene is illuminated and we see the rock that supports the statue
of Peter the Great and then a succession of regal and imperial females.
These include the two Catherines of Russia, the empress Saint Helen
(mother of Constantine, hence implying the Eastern theme — and the
conflict of religions — again), and the princesses of Muscovy and Poland.
In dreamlike fashion their gentle looks, directed toward France by long
crystal telescopes, seem to suggest that Nerval's country will arbitrate the
eastern problem ("la querelle orientale"). "My dream ended in the sweet
hope that peace would at last be granted us."

Not revolutionary like Blake (but we have seen the external and internal
mechanisms of censorship at work), here Nerval's protagonist, and certainly Nerval himself, wistfully appeal for peace. The appeal is couched in
imperial terms, evoking "great" Russian and Roman/Christian rulers of
the past, and implicitly and inevitably the emperor Napoléon III. Recall,

though, that the Crimean War primarily concerned the clash of English and Russian interests in the Middle East and that its outcome strengthened the emperor's hand in France. Furthermore, despite Catherine the Great's reputation as an enlightened monarch, her despotism and depravations are well known. They include the annexation of Crimea and Russia's participation in the repeated partitioning of Poland. Putting the Russian and Polish princesses cozily together in this passage would hardly have endeared Nerval to the generations of Polish and French who made the liberation of Poland a rallying cry for republicanism throughout the nineteenth century.

And this history too is still with us, as evident in an aptly titled article about the potential for conflict over the Crimea between the republics of Russia and the Ukraine: "Les Députés Russes Lorgnent Sur La Crimée."[19] In the context of continuing violent conflict in eastern Europe and the Middle East, this example again indicates the relevance of our apparently otherworldly texts to our this-worldly concerns. And if wistful, Nerval is still powerful. The Granada conflict was imaged as "a hideous kiss cemented by the blood of men," and the question asked: "How many years still will the world have to suffer?" (136). The mother dead in Germany, the traumatized North African veteran, the black sun and the blood over the Tuileries of 1848, the reference to conflict in eastern Europe then and now — add it all up. *Aurélia*, for all its harrowing psychic content, its unresolved religious and sexual trauma, and its visionary flights, is a compelling political message.

Antivisionary Subversions 🙋
Lautréamont's *Chants de Maldoror*

Les chants de Maldoror is considerably more disturbing than *Heinrich von Ofterdingen* and *Aurélia*, yet perhaps as exhilarating, though perversely so, as Blake's *Marriage*. In an arguably more oppressive social and ethical context, *Maldoror* constitutes a demonic response to all that is idealized in *Heinrich* — youth, family, love, visionary history — and to all that causes anguish in *Aurélia*: religion, dream, sexuality, recent as well as cosmic history. It is demonic but also "antivisionary." For amid the plethora of motifs utilized in this strange piece of writing, both infernal and visionary themes are prominent but also parodied. The effect is something like a massive extension of certain portions of *The Marriage of Heaven and Hell*, in that diabolical rebellion and biblical forms are burlesqued while nonetheless retaining a powerful impact. This is the sense of my chapter title, "Antivisionary Subversions."

The reader will want to decide for herself or himself the validity of this notion of the "antivisionary" on the basis of the passages that I will analyze. But for the sake of clarity let me state at the outset the conclusions to which I have come, implied already in my allusion to Blake. As in that English protoromantic, the original source of the visionary impulse, traditional religion, is attacked in *Maldoror*, often through outrageous parody of visionary motifs. Nonetheless the visionary transformations are as powerfully *re-*

alized as in any of our authors, are impossibly but explicitly *claimed to be real*. This curiously makes us think of Isaiah's "firm perswasion," Blake's insistence that "Truth can never be told so as to be understood, and not be believ'd," and similar glimpses in Novalis and Nerval, not to mention the truth claim we shall encounter in *Naked Lunch*. As we shall see in the next chapter, too, the concept of surrealism implies a reality that, recalling numerous mystical and occult traditions as well as Blake's contraries and Freud's arguments about dreams, surpasses the normal opposition between true and false, existing and not existing, real and unreal. That is, whereas absurdity and parody in *Maldoror*, as in Blake, might be thought to undermine the visionary, the opposite is true; instead parody *furthers* the visionary. Finally, again as in Blake, parodic visionary motifs in *Maldoror* are placed in the service of a violently subversive attack on society and all its structures and values — to the point this time of class warfare.

Maldoror is indeed subversive, an extreme instance of oppositional writing. Although many have seen "oppressive social and ethical" features *in* the work, we cannot forget the repressive environment in which it was produced: the last years of the Second Empire, before the defeat by the French at Sedan, at which the emperor Louis-Napoléon was captured. The Prussian siege of Paris, during which the book's author, Isidore Ducasse, died, led to the proclamation first of a republic then of the Commune. The latter, a workers' republican government, was crushed in May 1871 not by the Prussians but by reactionary French forces under the direction of Adolphe Thiers. Part of *Maldoror* appeared in 1868–69 anonymously; later it appeared in complete form under the pseudonym "le comte de Lautréamont." Additionally, Ducasse's letters to publishers subject to government harassment and the later ironic and parodic *Poésies*, which was published under his own name and which could only simple-mindedly be read as an unambiguous recanting of *Maldoror*, show the need in such a historical climate for defensive tactics. As we shall see, *Maldoror* is so outrageously corrosive of conventional values and institutions as to require such defense.

It is subversive and terroristic textually as well, augmenting Blake's imposition on the reader and parody of the sacred, the discrepancies in the narrative tissue of *Aurélia*, the bizarre personages and events and shifts of Klingsohr's tale. A proliferation of intrusive devices undercuts the story, threatens but also involves the reader, hyperbolically mobilizes an array of conflicting modes and codes. Although the conventions of "normal," especially novelistic, writing are thus pulverized, the cantos and prose strophes nonetheless obsessively reenact several themes and events. These include violent attacks on humanity, a gigantic struggle against God, and an attraction to and brutalization of male adolescents culminating in the murder of

Mervyn in the thirty-page "novel" of the last *chant* (173). And *Maldoror* is bulky; in dealing with it, it is as if we were to treat *Jerusalem* with *The Marriage of Heaven and Hell*, as if Klingsohr's tale were not twenty-five or thirty but two hundred and fifty pages long. Our discussion will necessarily employ selection and summary, and it will point toward that ironic closing "novel."[1] There, as with the concluding strophe of the fifth canto, close commentary will illustrate more directly some of the dimensions of textuality and reading in this antivisionary visionary work.

Readers of *Maldoror* are subjected to a moral attack on human beings that is all the more vehement for being contradictory. At the opening of the last chant (172–73) the speaker admits that he has been insulting himself along with man and the Creator, adding in a Marx-like manner (Groucho, that is), "I laugh . . . to think you reproach me with spreading bitter accusations against humanity, of which I am a member (this remark alone would prove me right!)." This is in fact a double contradiction, since earlier he had claimed to be incapable of laughter (IV, ii, 115–16). Contradiction and comedy notwithstanding, there are repeated assertions of humanity's hypocrisy and propensity for evildoing, including sexual sordidness and prostitution, rebellion against God, indifference to the vulnerability of abandoned children, and deception of one's parents (I, v and ix; II, i, iv; IV, i and iv).

That the narrator-Maldoror is guilty of all of the above, and worse, in no way lessens his bitterness. Hence in the face of our immorality he mutilates himself by cutting his lips in a fruitless attempt to laugh (I, v). His addresses to us progressively insist on our appetite for evil (I, ii; V, i). Indeed, although he initially warns us about the danger of our reading ("direct your heels backwards and not forwards," my translation, I, i, 1), at the end he triumphantly claims to have totally cretinized us (VI, viii, 200). He envisages pederasty as a sexual practice that could lead to the elimination of the race (V, v) and in mock-visionary style describes his mating with a louse in order to unleash a plague on humanity: "Three successive nights I was seen to lie with her [. . . .]" From his numberless insect offspring he quarries quantities as big as mountains that, hurled to earth, appear as meteorites. Again he imagines the annihilation of the race: "What a sight! And I, with angel's wings, motionless in the air to view it!" (II, ix, 58–59).

Here we glimpse the antivisionary mode. (See fig. 4.) The attack against humanity loses none of its force for being couched in a grotesque version of now-familiar visionary motifs, which in the end seem to transcend parody: "Moi, avec des ailes d'ange, immobile dans les airs, pour le contempler."[2]

Maldoror also embodies perhaps the single most concentrated and hysterical attack on the divinity in Western literature, again no less powerful for its satirical form. As made explicit in his correspondence and the *Poé-*

4 André Masson, *Maldoror*, 1937. © 1996 Artists Rights Society (ARS), New York/ADAGP, Paris.

sies and shown allusively in *Maldoror*, Ducasse/Lautréamont draws on "the noisy series of cardboard devils," the diabolical figures of *roman noir* and *Faust* and epic from Renaissance to romanticism. These include Milton and Byron, among many others, not to speak of their ancient antecedents in the European Middle Ages, in Greece, and in Egypt (*GF* 334). The absurdly hyperbolic writing of much of *Maldoror* corresponds with this parody of the visionary and demonic syncretism seen in earlier writers.

From early on the speaker represents himself and his "hero" as fighting the battle of evil versus good (I, iii, vi), as punished by God with hideous appearance and pestilential breath (I, viii). Although later the narrator claims to contribute positively to morality by unmasking human evil, he admits that Maldoror risks divine retribution, which may strike the reader as well (II, i). In the following strophe God does retaliate against this diabolical writing with a lightning bolt. Thereafter the speaker defies God, explains that the laws of mathematics, emanating from the highest power, have given him the logic to defeat the Creator, and recounts the oppression felt by him and all children in the face of the irrational power of the divinity and his religion of prayer and guilt (II, iii, x, xii).

Maldoror also encounters and battles God and his emissaries in passages that sometimes comically use biblical motifs. These scenes are Blakean in their satire and exuberance and sometimes worse than Blakean in their moral message. Maldoror is warned by a toad (I, xiii), struggles with a lamp that is also an angel (II, xi), and in the shape of an octopus fights God to a standstill (II, xv). In a parody of infernal and prophetic motifs (bloody light, chattering teeth, monstrous animals, incomprehensible inscriptions, metamorphoses, and cosmic flights), he defends prostitution, kills conscience, and dispatches hope (I, vii; II, xviii; III, iii).

In the first of these scenes he combats a glowworm as big as a house, crushing it with a stone that rebounds as high as six churches, and concludes, à la Blake, that prostitution is caused by God. But he goes further, not only renouncing sexual virtue but presenting prostitution as a universal force to be adored by humans. In the second he is seen descending valleys, mounting towers, and hurling himself into space. Conscience disposed of, he tops off the action by guillotining three young girls. In the third Maldoror takes the form of an eagle, and only at the end do we learn that the dragon he kills is really hope, signaling his even more definitive engagement in the career of evil.

In addition to the conflict of ethical values and fantastic metamorphoses, Ducasse-Lautréamont demeans the divinity in gross bodily terms. We see God lying drunk amid floods of vomited wine and with bloodied nose, insulted by animals, shat upon by man; a parting insult compares his arms, when he is finally on his feet, to a "consumptive's testicles" (III, iv, 99). The next strophe shows him in a brothel and relates unsavory details of his sexual union with a prostitute followed by his flaying of a male adolescent. Here God resembles Maldoror himself. This last is recounted by one of God's giant-sized hairs, left behind in the brothel — a grotesque magnification of the physical in an effort to degrade utterly the divine.

Elsewhere God is shown to be a pederast (V, v) and is described as sitting on a throne of excrement and gold, torturing and devouring human beings (II, viii). The details here are absurd but excruciating, as we see people swimming in blood, being fished out with the claws on God's foot,

God's sniffing of their bodies before devouring head, limbs, trunk. Blake showed us a similar vision of religion *inside* the Bible; Lautréamont, perhaps using or abusing Dante and Goya, ascribes it directly to God. The accompanying black humor is no fun. The men's heads emerge from the blood, "for after all these men weren't fish!" The involvement of the reader is hardly pleasant either: "O reader, does not the latter detail make your mouth water?" (52–53).

Finally, an impressive meditation in favor of lucidity seems to oppose the Nervalian cult of dream. Here the narrator refuses sleep, arguing that it is at night that the individual is overwhelmed by the divine. God is called the "Great Exterior Object" and the "Celestial Bandit," sleep the place where the incense of religion burns. In opposition, the narrator insists on his willpower and, again opposed to Nerval, on the unity of his person: "If I exist, I am not another [. . .] My subjectivity and the Creator — it is too much for one brain" (V, iii, 151).

So the demonic theme is incisive, outrageous, and deliberately disgusting in *Maldoror*. Familial and sexual motifs, variously disquieting in the earlier writers, are flagrantly repulsive too. The first page refers to filial respect for mothers, but by the opening of the fifth chant the narrator asserts that he has cured us of our illness. The best proof of this will be for us to rip off and eat an arm of our mother or (perhaps) virgin sister. Indeed the speaker has made a pact with prostitution against families in a strophe (I, vii) that in passing mentions fratricidal relations between children. Later we encounter abandoned and prostituted children (II, iv, v). We also witness outlandish examples of familial sexual violence: a man hung by his hair, tarred, and whipped by mother and wife for refusing incest (IV, iii); a man imprisoned and tortured by his brother but who later escapes to the sea, where he metamorphoses into an amphibian (IV, vii); brothers transformed by a woman, and their revenge: one of them, a beetle, eternally rolls what turns out to be her mangled body. The narrator/observer concludes: "And I believed it to be excrement! Really what an utter simpleton I am!" ("Grande bête que je suis, va," V, ii, 149). Again the fantastically horrible becomes comic. Amid all of this, early on (I, xi) there is only one instance of "good" family relations, a parody of respect, obedience, religion, work, economy — but this provides the occasion for Maldoror's first murder of an adolescent boy.

The reader has had a foretaste, if I may say so, of the truly horrendous ways in which the body and sexuality are treated in *Maldoror*. The narrator has a glorious dream of being transformed into a hog (IV, vi); elsewhere he lovingly details the hideous corruptions of each part of his body (IV, iv). A curative potion is made up of any number of unpalatable substances and body parts (V, i), and throughout there are demeaning offhand references to sexual organs, for example at the end of the second chant: "It is time to curb my inspiration and to pause a while along the way, as when one looks at a woman's vagina" (84).

The last may epitomize the hatred of the female body and of sexuality expressed throughout the work. There are numerous evocations of brutalization of girls and women and excruciatingly explicit scenes of rape, mutilation, and murder of women by men and animals (II, v; III, ii, v). The exclamation "La femme est à mes pieds!" in *Poésies II* (*GF* 356) corresponds.

The preferred form of sexual attraction in *Maldoror* is attraction to adolescent males, but this leads to danger, temptation, perhaps suicide, sadism, and finally murder (I, vi; II, iii, iv, vi, xiv; III, v; V, vii). A synthesizing strophe on this homosexual theme (III, i) expresses love but is not lacking in bathetic overstatement. An earlier version gives the logic for murder: to prevent the beloved from growing to be like adult men (II, iii, 39). Still another (IV, viii) has the structure of a deranged memory of a murder. It is very different from the strophe opposing sleep in that it exhibits compulsive repetition, fragmentariness and lack of control, splitting of the subject, the recurring motifs of hair, scalping, and slingshot, and a psychoanalytic vocabulary: "in a fit of insanity" ("dans un accès d'aliénation mentale," 139).

Such materials doubtless have contributed (1) to the opinion that Ducasse, more perhaps than Nerval, *was* insane, or (2) in mitigated form to biographical and psychoanalytic[3] interpretations. Regardless of where one stands on those issues, it is difficult not to recognize in this work a tragedy of sexuality enormously exacerbating such themes in Blake, Novalis, and Nerval. Thus a strophe not yet mentioned, that on the hermaphrodite (II, vii), is rare in expressing sympathy. It is also not lacking in comic notes — once thought insane, the hermaphrodite is now supported by a government pension. The lack of sexual adaptation expressed there has an absurd parallel in another strophe. Having rejected both male and female, the narrator mates in suitably viscous manner with a shark. Here too humor cannot be avoided, as he concludes, "I was facing my first love!" (II, xiii, 78).

We may think of the hermaphrodite and the shark strophes as part of a structure of confusion or disguise; this is confirmed by the fact that in the second canto two boys are spared and it is a girl who is in imagination murdered. But, just as more and more it is male adolescents who are harmed, finally a tortured homosexuality is affirmed in a complex strophe (V, v, 155–59) on what the narrator calls pederasty. This strophe mirrors the general movement from indecision or disguise to hyperbolic assertion.

Thus in addressing pederasts the speaker first calls them incomprehensible but immediately defends them against a narrow morality. He repeats the hostile view that they are adequately punished by their shameful and almost incurable diseases. (How upsetting, that "almost" — history has bested us again.) He asks understanding of them from the young, then goes on to express veneration and love for them. Regarding the body, the shift in attitude is as rapid: using medicolegal vocabulary he states that he will not scorn their "infundibuliform anus," but then imagines kissing various parts of their bodies. This produces a vision of the universe as a celestial anus and of a cosmic orgasm that is as explicit as other passages and that emphasizes not only sperm but also blood and rupturing. If Steinmetz is correct in finding homosexual tenderness in *Maldoror*, this is not it.[4] Thus the narrator's invitation to the adolescent male reader to join him in his bed, with the clarification now that he likes neither women nor hermaphrodites, is accompanied by a threat as well as by the claim to have earlier murdered an uncompliant partner. And when he then tries to reach us readers sexually through the opacity of the page, we perhaps, regardless of gender or orientation, have to control a shudder.

So the counterimage of sexuality that emerges most clearly in this strophe is hardly free of destructive features. This is all the more apparent in the closing insult to God. How much more negative can one be than to show him opening his door to a pederast? The universal, sacred projection of sexuality in the texts treated in earlier chapters also finds a parodic echo here. The narrator imagines hordes of people from the exotic extremes of the world attracted by his seminal odor. It is for this reason, he informs us, and not out of a desire for cleanliness, that he changes clothes twice a week! In what seems a homosexual satire of the kind of writing encountered in the first "Mémorable," he calls himself the one whose "sacred sperm perfumes mountain, lake, heath, forest, promontory, and the vastness of the seas!"[5] This is a cosmic sexuality, no longer holy but sordid, a brief version of what we will encounter in Burroughs's *Naked Lunch*.

Hence in treating the issues that are more or less insistently disturbing in the *Marriage*, *Heinrich*, and *Aurélia*, *Maldoror* is horrendous — and the more so for being outlandishly funny. Recall the claim made in *Poésies* that the exaggerations of *Maldoror* are intended to cause an opposite, positively moral, reaction in the reader. At the least *Maldoror* and *Poésies* might be thought of functioning as a Blakean pair of contraries, profoundly challenging our moral sense.

We have also seen some of the myriad tactics by which *Maldoror* subverts the conventions of writing,[6] including visionary writing. I will discuss these systematically before examining the last chant, which contrary to its announced function (173) effects a synthesis of what precedes.

In keeping with the strictures against the novel in *Poésies* (GF 330–31, 351) and the parody in the last chant, *Maldoror* is from the outset anti-

novelistic, a kind of prose poetry in the form of cantos, strophes, and re-
frains. Are novels often biographical in form? Early on that's dealt with: "I
shall set down in a few lines how upright Maldoror was during his early
years, when he lived happy. There: done" ("C'est fait," I, iii, 2). Or do you
genuinely want realism about childhood? "Hear, mankind, the thoughts of
my childhood, when I used to wake with red prick" (II, xii, 67).

In addition to not presenting the main story, that of the hero, sequen-
tially, Ducasse/Lautréamont starts any number of plot lines in apparently
representational contexts that lead nowhere. I will cite not the most well
known, extensive, and extremely complicated examples, particularly the
strophe (IV, ii) included by André Breton in his *Anthologie de l'humour noir*,
but rather the briefer passage about a temple much debated by Egyptologists
early in the century and that Novalis or Nerval might have put to exotic use.
"The ancient temple of Denderah lies an hour and a half away from the left
bank of the Nile. Today [. . . .]" (IV, i, 111). "Today" the temple is infested
with wasps, the noise of whose wings the narrator compares to that of arctic
ice, provoking a reflection on his own unhappiness and numerous other
analogies. In the process the Egyptian temple disappears from view.

By this point in the text the reader is accustomed to such features as the
very un-Flaubertian intrusion of the narrator and the frequent confusion of
him with his protagonist, and even with the author, born in South America
and anxious for glory in Europe (I, vii, 8; xiv, 33). Whereas at times the separation between narrator and character is stressed ("the hero I bring on
stage," II, i, 34), they are frequently elsewhere confused, as in the very next
strophe. There the narrator takes up pen but after God's lightning strike it
is Maldoror's blood that flows (37). Elsewhere the confusion is not that
between persons but the surreal one between persons and the nonhuman:
"It is a man or a stone or a tree that is going to begin the second canto" (my
translation, 110).

Whether identified with his protagonist or with something wholly inhu-
man, the narrator is insistent in drawing our attention to the act of writing,
to the performance of reading, to the present not of the story but of the text.
As for us, even the cases already cited do not adequately convey the constant solicitation of the reader. Quite horribly, we receive instruction in
how to torture a child (I, vi). If we continue reading after this, isn't there
indeed something wrong with us? At the end of the first chant our indul-
gence is asked for the writer's fledgling efforts; by the opening of the fifth,
we are addressed as friends and it is insinuated that by now we must have
become sympathetic to what we have been reading. In the second canto (vi,
45) the narrator relies on us to guess the identity of the threatening individual who addresses a child, but later (II, xii, 75) he tricks us by telling us one

thing and then denying it. We even begin to play an active role: we seem to ask a question (IV, iv, 124) and to advise the narrator to conclude the first chapter of the last chant (179).

We have seen that he, or it, is ever-intrusive as well. He interrupts his discourse because it's making his hair stand on end (I, iv) and howls in anguish that he is being beaten on the head with an iron bar (I, viii, 11). He also stresses the activity of composition, announcing that he will declaim the strophe on the ocean (I, ix), explicitly noting the beginning and ending of various cantos, drinking not one but two glasses of water before returning to an interrupted narration (IV, iii, 121), and preparing pen and ink and even blowing his nose before beginning the story of Mervyn's murder (176).

As for the text, the texture of the writing rather than the story it supposedly tells, it is foregrounded by the techniques just discussed and by all manner of other zany devices, including the undigested mixture of styles, codes, and parodies; to this we can add scientific and technical vocabulary and whole passages cribbed from books of natural history. There are frequent absurdities of expression: "Direct your heels backwards" for "retrace your steps" (I, i, 1); "planches somnifères," literally "somniferous boards" (V, iii, 150), which produces the Scribe-like annotation "autant dire un lit (par métonymie)" (*GF* 414).

Famously, too, analogies proliferate from the opening page to the last canto. Among many examples we may mention the evocation of the ocean as a huge bruise on the body of the earth, a comparison that the narrator likes (I, ix, 12); others he judges less appropriate (I, x, 18; xii, 27), disquisitions on resemblance and difference (V, 6). There is extended discussion of the "criminal use" of this rhetorical figure in incomprehensibly long sentences, notably in the second strophe of the fourth canto. The narrator even apologizes for the length of the sentences (114), a prelude to his forgetting the beginning of one of them (VI, ii, 176).

But the most flagrant of the features that deconstruct narrative conventions is the antivisionary. As suggested at the outset, this element exacerbates questions of belief and doubt in the earlier writers, from the skepticism of Heinrich's father to the menace of insanity in Nerval, not forgetting the role of contraries in the self-confident Blake or Isaiah's comment about the rarity these days of "firm perswasion." As seen throughout, contradiction and parody rule in *Maldoror*, notably in the text's playing with the "reality" of visionary modes. Here we may delineate passages treating supernatural combats and the "male sadistic" theme; urban settings for the fantastic; strophes in which the limits of belief are pushed to the extreme; and, despite the rejection of dream discussed earlier, the power of hallucination or trance.

In the first strophe of the third canto the merging of speaker and protagonist reappears as the narrator describes the "imaginary beings" (85) he had created earlier and then produces another. Thereupon a new narration abruptly begins: "Mario and I were riding [. . . .]" No sadism is ascribed to the couple, who are put through the standard demonic and visionary moves. In conflict with God, they are viewed with awe by ordinary people, flee the earth, sprout wings, and undertake cosmic flights and subterranean, volcanic voyages. The forbidden homosexual theme here takes its recurrent although not destructive form, and for all its imaginary quality, and perhaps a degree of comedy, is compelling as emotion and as theme.

Two other versions of these motifs more explicitly and ironically raise the issues of reality and belief. The battle with conscience in the form of a dragon, in which Maldoror transforms himself into an eagle (III, iii), a passage filled with satirical echoes of the Apocalypse, is narrated by another youthful companion, Tremdall. Understandably, Tremdall is surprised by what he sees: "I have not been accustomed to such sights" (95). And, whereas the allegorical theme is apparently serious, since conscience is killed, the visionary is merely amusing. Since he is now an eagle, Maldoror can't speak but clucks his intention of eating the dragon's posterior. That done, he changes back to human form, which Tremdall finds entirely *reasonable*.

The battle with the lamp/angel (II, ii, 63–67) is more insistent with regard to the question of belief. Again the love theme, this time sadistic, is present as Maldoror's bite hideously deforms the angel, who however exchanges a look of eternal love with him as he retreats to heaven. The surprise expressed by Tremdall is developed by Maldoror: the lamp glows in ways inconsistent with the laws of optics, and it is not "natural" for it to turn into an angel. Although Maldoror struggles against this unnatural perception, he cannot resist it; "in reality" the lamp and the form of an angel are *glued* together. Moreover, amid explanations by the naive and superstitious, we are told that, since Maldoror threw the lamp into the Seine, it reappears and progresses on the river each night, where *we* are sure to see it. But it doesn't show itself to everyone . . .

In addition to passages paradoxically and ironically insistent on our ability to see the impossible, others provide a realistic urban setting that "naturalizes," so to speak, the fantastic. Steinmetz is right to stress this in the strophe (II, ii) in which the narrator/Maldoror is struck with lightning by God, since suddenly a conventional setting emerges — a dog, a servant, a cleaning woman (who won't come because it's raining). This is an "effet de réel" not in the Barthian sense, but rather something more like the reverse of Todorov's description of the fantastic as momentarily troubling our sense of the real.[7] *Maldoror* regularly unfolds in various fantastic ways, occasionally touching base with what we take to be normal reality. Again, the absurd strophe concerning God's hair in the brothel is set in a realistic urban and class setting and is framed by references to the physical locations from which the narrator is supposedly able to perceive certain things. There is, then, a repeated contradiction between parodic visionary events and forms asserting their presence.

Lautréamont exacerbates this contradiction in two infuriatingly complex strophes (IV, vii; V, ii) in which we see impossible things and are subjected to tortuous reasoning to justify them. The first describes the amphibian, a man with webbed feet and dorsal fin who swims a kilometer with every stroke. The second describes a beetle as big as a cow, then puts us through a page or so of digression and technical vocabulary before we realize that we are in the presence of a man who is part bird. There is also the decomposed body of the evil woman, together with other men transformed by her into birds.

The second of these strophes begins by stressing a "realistic" framing position: "I saw before me an object standing on a hillock. I could not clearly discern [. . . .]" (144). It claims to be able to furnish reliable witnesses and proofs, which are not produced, and ends with the amusing "Grande bête que je suis, va." The first introduces some subtle philosophical-scientific reasoning about the possibility of abnormalities in the laws of nature and the deceptiveness of the limits imposed by good sense on imagination. The illustrations of these arguments, rains of frogs and states of rage and pride, are in the first case absurd and the second insufficient. No more satisfying is the pseudoscientific explanation that the amphibian became so by long-term adaptation. Additionally, some peasants who are on hand do not see the amphibian, but their gullibility is demonstrated by the statement that their mouths are open wide enough to swallow three cachelots (corrected to three baby elephants). As the strange creature swims away, though, the narrator introduces a further "epistemological" feature, the role of instruments. He observes the amphibian with a telescope and insists at the end, "However, everything was real in what had happened, during this summer evening" (my translation, 137).

Despite the absurdities, in part because of them, much in *Maldoror* affects us with oneiric power.[8] The general resemblance to Klingsohr's tale, the revealing viciousness of the attack on Nerval (no one wants to wear *his* tie, *GF* 352), Breton's recognition of Ducasse's writing as a locus of the surreal — all converge, and all remind us that, despite Freud's insistence on the need to accept the reality principle, he recognized it as a construction of the conscious mind. In the unconscious, on the contrary, absurdity and contradiction reign, according to him, and the distinction between what exists and what does not exist is null. Again this corresponds with descriptions of the surreal by Aragon and Breton.

A number of passages in *Maldoror* apply closely. In particular, the claim not to have slept in thirty years (V, iii) and the resistance to the catalepsy of dream ("he who sleeps is less than an animal castrated the day before," 150) are contradicted: earlier the narrator presented himself as castrated and described the cataleptic dream of becoming a hog (IV, iv, vi). Even within the strophe rejecting sleep, although he claims that when dreaming he retains free will and the ability to move, he recounts the opposite, a dream of being led enraged and powerless to the guillotine. And in the last strophe of the fifth canto, when Maldoror is nightly tortured by a spider, he precisely lacks the ability to resist or move: "Remarkable thing! I who make sleep and nightmare recoil, feel the whole of my body paralyzed" (164). Maldoror later claims to have produced a similar hallucination in Mervyn (VI, ii, 182), and the narrator's goal in cretinizing us is also to put us to sleep, to hypnotize and paralyze us, making it "somnambulistically impossible" for us to move (VI, viii, 200).

Dream and trance, in spite of the anti-Nervalian notes, ultimately figure the status of the visions in *Maldoror*. And remark that the note of reality is repeatedly, and confusingly, introduced. Of the impossibility of movement in the guillotine dream, the narrator says: "The weight of an obelisk stifles the spread of madness" ("l'expansion de la rage"), adding: "Reality has destroyed slumber's dreams!" ("Le réel a détruit les rêves de la somnolence!," 152). But at the end, he says that if ever he does fall asleep, his suicide will prove that sleep was indeed the more real: his razor "will prove that as a matter of fact nothing was more real." There are similar confusing suggestions concerning reality in the strophe on the torturing spider, which is worth examining in some detail (V, vii, 164–71).

As in a couple of other instances, this opens with a speech within quotation marks, and only later do we learn that it is Maldoror who has been speaking. He describes how each evening an old spider "of the large species" (what is that?) emerges from "a hole set in the ground at one of the corner intersections of the room." Again a representational convention prepares a nonrealistic narration, accompanied by an inanely "metaliterary" note. For the spider has to rub its mandibles if it is to "increase the treasures of literature by brilliant personifications." Indeed, the spider *contains* two youths formerly attacked by Maldoror, thus literalizing the figure of personification.

The narrator chimes in, telling us to look at the spider. Then, in perhaps his most flagrant violation of distinctions between text and reality, he adds: "We are no longer in the narrative [. . . .] Alas! we have now reached the real as regards the tarantula, and although an exclamation mark might be put at the end of every sentence, that is perhaps no reason for dispensing with them!" (165). Characteristically, the closing focus on punctuation reminds us that whatever "real" is involved here is within the language of the text. At the same time, the trancelike vision that unfolds is said to leave the frame of narration. In what sense, though anchored in language, can it be real?

Now the spider opens its stomach, "whence sprang two youths in blue robes, each with a flaming sword in his hand, who had taken up their places by the bedside as if thereafter to stand guard over the sanctuary of sleep." The narration of the attempted murder of the two, Réginald and Elsseneur, repeats familiar motifs: the murder of a swimming youth (II, 13) and Maldoror's avoidance of cities and preference for savage nature (much of the first canto). Absurdities of language recur: "one of your hands seized the binarity of my arms in its vice." The confusion as to the source of narration persists: the spider keeps talking, but refers to itself by the name of the second of the youths. This is resolved when we learn that an archangel has told the two to become a single spider with a mission to avenge their suffering. God's victory is announced, Maldoror is downcast, and the two youths are seen ascending entwined to heaven.

The murderousness of the adolescent love theme is here overcome, reversing the lamp strophe, only to be itself reversed at the end of the work. Moreover, despite the clash of the realistic and fantastic modes, the absurd language and even more absurd metalinguistic notes, and the scrambling of the source of narration, the vision of the youths stationed with flaming swords at Maldoror's bed comes through with a hallucinatory intensity. "Nous ne sommes plus dans la narration": having by his absurd tactics exacerbated the problem of belief, Lautréamont/Ducasse's narrator never stops insisting on the reality of the visions he shows us.

As indicated at the beginning of this chapter, the confusing reality of the antivisionary takes on a new meaning in the last canto. For that canto is inevitably understood as a disguised but transparent allegory of murderous class conflict, eerily if inversely prophetic of closely following historical events.

At the beginning of the canto (172–74) the narrator again addresses us, taxing us with the error of thinking that what we have already encountered — his "explicable hyperboles" (have we not been engaged in explaining his exaggerations?) — is complete. In this "hybrid preface" he explains that the first five cantos constitute the "frontispiece" to a more important task, the analysis of a preceding synthesis. I have already stated that I think this is backwards. He also announces the irresistible unfolding of a fundamental thesis, or theorem. In part this essential theorem concerns the recurrent "sadistic male" scenario, which we are said to recognize: "You have recognized the imaginary hero who for a long time has been shattering my unhappy intelligence by the pressure of his individuality! Now Maldoror approaches Mervyn [. . . .]" (i, 178).

Our involvement, and the slippage between narrator and character, persist. So does that other recurrent note, the antivisionary demonic element, since the murder of Mervyn involves an increasingly absurd battle with an archangel and with God himself that the narrator claims to be both unbelievable and real. But—somewhat resembling *Aurélia*—the inevitable theorem of the last chant of this most extreme oppositional work also foregrounds historical and political themes only barely hinted at earlier. *Maldoror* ends as a work of sociopolitical hatred and violence.

The hybrid preface also humorously claims that the last chant will be different in that it will be a novel: "Today I'm going to fabricate a little thirty page novel [. . . .] It's the best, since it's the novel!" (my translation). Hence the narrator asserts that the unnatural events that we have encountered earlier will no longer be involved (172–73; VIII, 200). But of course this proves not to be true. Ridiculing fiction's pretensions to representing physical reality and psychological energy, the speaker claims that the characters will be "placed only a few paces away from [us] so that the solar rays, striking the roof-tiles and chimney-pots first, will then shine visibly upon their earthly and material hair." We will even get *inside* them, glimpsing their "spiritual principle" and touching their aortas — "and then the sentiments!" Thus, after a strophe (ii) devoted to preparations for writing (174–76), the text is divided into chapters (given capital roman numerals) that mix realistic conventions with the wildest of antivisionary events.

In this parodic novel the coexistence of fictionality and of the present of writing with the claim to referentiality is stressed: "in this spot my pen [. . .] has just made mysterious, you will see — if you look in the direction of where the Rue Colbert meets the Rue Vivienne [. . .]" (I, 177). We will not neglect the historical allusions connected with this mystery and with the precise evocation of Paris streets, but for the moment let us examine the devices that one might expect to subvert such reference. Only a few lines later, for example, after asking a series of questions that could reasonably supply a clue to Mervyn's behavior, the narrator is self-referential and self-deflating: "(It would show very little command of one's profession as sensational writer [écrivain à sensation] not to advance at least the qualifying questions after which immediately comes the sentence I am on the point of completing)" (I, 178).

Then there is the granddaddy of surreal analogies, describing Mervyn's beauty, on which one might (but I will not) comment interminably:

He is fair as [beau comme] the retractility of claws of birds of prey; or again, as the uncertainty of the muscular movements in wounds in the soft parts of the lower cervical region; or rather, as that perpetual rat-trap always reset by the trapped animal, which by itself can catch rodents indefinitely and work even when hidden under straw; and above all, as the chance meeting on a dissecting-table of a sewing-machine and an umbrella! (I, 177)

Another "beau comme" series, equally grotesque, occurs in the fourth "chapter," where the struggle with God is ascribed not to Maldoror but to the narrator. That chapter begins: "I became aware that I had only one eye in the middle of my forehead!" (188).

Additionally Lautréamont plays with the convention of narrative suspense, telling us at one point that God will have to battle Maldoror himself but that it is not yet time to narrate this conflict, and later that the end is fast approaching (VI, 194; VII, 200). In the first of these he says that each "truc à effet," or trick designed to produce an effect, will come in its proper place, when the plot will be ready for it, thus exposing the false sense of inevitability generated by fiction that Breton and Sartre, as we shall see, were also to criticize.

These trucs à effet occur at the end of chapters, sometimes involve questions or directions to the reader, and become more and more zany. How could the pont du Carrousel bear the awful cries emerging from a sack (ii, 176)? Do we know why the narrator shudders at the thought of a maniac and an iron ring (I, 179)? Next we are directed (II, 182–83) to proceed to a lake with swans; we are promised that later we will be told why one, which is black, carries an anvil and the putrefying corpse of a giant crab. The end of the next chapter (187–88) announces future events involving flying fish tails, burning beams, the shooting of a rhinoceros, a beggar, a crowned madman, a "snow daughter," and "the truth about the fidelity of the fourteen daggers," and the following chapter (189) gives us a cock's prophecy, a caravan of pilgrims, and a narrative by a Clignancourt ragman.

Needless to say, all of these elements unfold rigorously in the narration of the culminating "supernatural" battles, as Maldoror dispatches first an archangel disguised as a huge crab and then God in the form of a rhinoceros after having attacked Mervyn on the Carrousel bridge. In this sequence the appearance of God as a rhinoceros covered with sweat at the corner of the rue Castiglione (VIII, 203) is an amusing convergence of antivisionary and realistic registers. After the wounded divinity withdraws, Maldoror proceeds to accomplish the final truc à effet, "the incredible incident in the Place Vendôme" (VI, 198). Indeed, Maldoror kills Mervyn by whirling him on a cable around the top of the column in the Place Vendôme, then hurling him across right- and left-bank Paris to crash to his death on the dome of the Panthéon.

The final scene (my translation, 203–05) is hauntingly *realized*:

On the entablature of the massive column, leaning against the squared balustrade more than fifty metres above ground level, a man has thrown and unrolled a rope [. . . .] the escaped convict [. . .] imparts to the youth an accelerated motion of uniform rotation [. . . .] The sling hisses in space; Mervyn's body follows it everywhere, ever distanced from the centre by centrifugal force [. . .] in an aerial circumference independent of matter.

Maldoror begins to run around the balustrade so that gradually Mervyn rises, finally turning "majestically on a horizontal plane." In accordance with the "theorems of mathematics," when the murderer then releases the cable the backlash causes the balustrade's joints to crack and Mervyn to fly through the air, striking the vast dome of the Panthéon, the rope coiling around its superstructure.

This scene concretizes several earlier phantasies or memories involving slingshots, hair, scalping, and hurling adolescents to their deaths (II, v, vi; IV, iii, v, viii). Although horrible, it has an eery beauty as an illustration of the laws of mechanics, for in his flight Mervyn has become "independent of matter." The element of resemblance or appearance is reintroduced critically, for it is an "illusion" that as he flies through the air Mervyn is a comet, and the immense cupola of the Panthéon resembles an orange only "pour la forme." Yet, in an extreme version of his earlier insistence on the reality of the antivisionary, although the event is indeed "incroyable" the narrator claims that the youth's shrunken skeleton is visible up there. He complicates the claim by suggesting that the flowers the corpse is holding are a sculpted garland desperately grabbed by Mervyn from the base of the Vendôme column. He admits that the distance involved makes it impossible to assert that this is "really" the case. But, in convoluted fashion, he says that they are indeed missing from the base of the tower. Hence his last words to us, recapitulating the antivisionary, the supposed visibility of the impossible: "go there and see for yourself, if you don't want to believe me" (my translation, 205).

Readers familiar with the period may be persuaded that the murder of Mervyn has another kind of reality as an allegory of political violence in a work that displays a remarkable prescience.[9] This is especially visible in the foregrounding of Paris monuments and of street and neighborhood geography, with historical resonances and clear notes of socioeconomic class, features only hinted at earlier. Indeed Maldoror's preferred habitat at the outset is the solitary and fantastic countryside, where he is associated with wild dogs, Norwegian grave diggers, leaches, and toads (I, viii, xii, xiii). In his travels with Elsseneur he avoids the Middle Eastern cities that would have attracted Nerval (V, vii, 168). Early in the last chant the narrator, again indistinguishable from his protagonist, even recalls having existed at a time prior to modern urban history, a sadistic version of such prehistoric glimpses in our earlier writers. But now Maldoror approaches the "human agglomerations" of Madrid, St. Petersburg, Peking, and finally Paris in search of victims (ii, 174–75).

In fact a number of earlier passages point in this direction. Specific historical-political allusion is rare, deft, but if grasped unmistakable. If the name for an exotic bird, the russet sea-eagle (II, ii, 35), can be traced to an anti-imperial poem by Victor Hugo that provoked suppression in 1867 of two plays by the exiled bard, this work is not innocent of political dimension. In addition, the supposed progress of the lamp on the Seine (II, xi) from the pont Napoléon (constructed early in the Second Empire, 1852, and of course renamed in 1870) to that of Austerlitz (commemorating a victory of Napoléon I) and finally to the pont de l'Alma (named after the first victory of the Crimean War in 1854) traces a historical pattern. Slyly, *Maldoror* here seems to begin where *Aurélia* left off.

Moreover, two references to the guillotine appear to be incidental but by the last chant will no longer seem so. Maldoror, we recall, kills three innocent girls on the spot where the guillotine stands, himself miraculously resisting execution (II, xv, 83–84). This at the time was the place du Trône, a site with monarchical and revolutionary resonances (Louis XIV's triumphal entry in 1660; as the place du Trône-Renversé, the site of the guillotine in 1794; presently the place des Nations, dating from July 14, 1880, the first *fête nationale* intended to unify the country after the upheaval of the Commune). The other allusion (V, iii), referring to an obelisk and to a reality that dissolves dream, evokes the guillotining of Louis XVI on a different spot, now place de la Concorde with its obelisk, originally Place Louis XV but called the place de la Révolution at the time of his successor's execution. Both passages relate to the sadistic theme of the work — the narrator/Maldoror is guilty of murder, seems doomed to or immune from execution. Both also evoke the horrors of revolutionary history and the process of renaming for reconciliation.

Some earlier urban (including class) notes also anticipate the last canto, as always in connection with the sexual-sadistic theme. Maldoror's first victim is from a hard-working, poor, apparently rural family (I, xi). In the strophe on pederasty the narrator admits to being attracted to poor adoles-

cents, school children and factory workers, and claims to have been genitally wounded by an ungrateful bootblack (V, v). Here the word "décrotteur" vividly conveys the working conditions of this individual. In two
strophes whose Parisian setting is highlighted (II, v, vi), Maldoror first encounters a girl, apparently a child prostitute, in an extremely poor area. He
fantasizes her death by the preferred slingshot method. Next he tempts a
boy, seemingly of the middle classes, in the Jardin des Tuileries, then as
now the site of homosexual encounters.

The brothel that God visits is situated on the outskirts of Paris, the dangerous zone that separates the city from the "suburban slum alleys" (III, v,
101), and its filth and squalor are stressed. When a client leaves, he returns
to breathe the "pure air" of the center of the city. This reminds us in a more
grotesque way both of the speaker's nightly wanderings from the Clichy
barrier through working-class areas to the center in *Aurélia* and of the expulsion of poorer segments of the population to the outskirts in the Hauss-
mannization of the Second Empire.

There are related implications in the eery Parisian night scene (II, 4) in
which the egoistic riders of an omnibus ignore the appeals of an abandoned
child. He is rescued by a *chiffonnier*, a ragpicker, or rather more realistically,
a "refuse-picker." This figure is traditionally representative of the lowest of
Parisian livelihoods and of revolutionary anger.[10] The narrator calls our attention to his posture as he stoops over his pale lamp, to the care that he will
take of the child, and to the piercing look filled with animosity and obsti-
nacy with which he follows the departing bus. Then the narrator breaks out
in another condemnation of humanity and God. Significantly, the area of
the city mentioned at the outset of this strophe is that stretching from the
Bastille to the Madeleine, that is, right-bank geography, from the original
site of revolution to the privileged area where Ducasse lived for a time and
where he situates Mervyn and his family.

The anti-imperial and revolutionary hints, and the awareness of class
relative to urban geography, prepare the way for the murder of Mervyn,
which has as much to do with class antagonism as with sexual perversion.
The parodic but sociopolitically acute novelistic convention accomplishes
much of this as we follow Mervyn through the city and see him captured
and killed and as we observe the recruitment of Maldoror's accomplice in
the crime.

Maldoror first stalks his future victim through a precisely noted series of
right-bank streets in the rich area of the Madeleine, highlighting the display
of costly items in the stores on the rue Vivienne (I, 176, 179) and later the
many signs of affluence in the "hôtel moderne" ("modern mansion") where
Mervyn and his family live.[11] Here (II, 179) as in the next chapter there is

an absurdist piling on of detail to evoke wealth in terms of furniture, decor, clothing, and food, including exotic items. Although most of Maldoror's victims have foreign-sounding names, curiously Mervyn is English, his father a retired commodore. But is there a suggestion of English maritime power in his remembrance of combat, a rare echo (together with references to South America) of international economic dominance and conflict? More clearly to the point, this is an established and wealthy family, with servants and family portraits. Ducasse makes them a parody of the paternalistic family unit as well, with an authoritarian father, hysterically sensitive mother, and submissive children. We have seen that by no means are all of Maldoror's victims wealthy, that he often murders or brutalizes the poor, but the reference here to Mervyn's siblings as "this brood of adorable brats" (III, 185) aptly summarizes the class hatred that saturates the last canto.

Something similar is involved in the recruiting of the accomplice to the murder among the dropouts of society. The strangely named Aghone, a madman crowned with a chamber pot who in his insanity cannot distinguish good from evil (V, 194), is discovered in the garden of the Palais-Royal. His story seems socially realistic though bizarrely narrated. His father, an artisan in the working area of the Halles, alcoholic and violent, caused the death of his sisters and the departure of his mother. The realistic component is matched by the elaborate use of representational conventions: "On a bench in the Palais-Royal, on the near side, and not far from the ornamental lake, a fellow emerging from the Rue de Rivoli has come and sat down" (189). To win him over, Maldoror treats him like a prince, giving him food, clothing, lodging. Hence one of the participants in the culminating crime is emblematic not of sexual but of socioeconomic as well as familial depravation. The point is reinforced by the fact that part of the crime is to be recounted by another ragman (IV, 189, 202), this one from Clignancourt, another working-class area on the edge of the city.

Nor is he the last chiffonnier, just as the Palais-Royal is not the last Paris monument to be mentioned. Its revolutionary history had already been remarked in *Aurélia*, and when in chapter VIII we follow Mervyn's early-morning walk through the streets to meet Maldoror we are again in familiar territory: Mervyn is attacked on the pont du Carrousel, in sight of the Louvre. From the outset of the "novel," too, Maldoror's pursuit of the youth has been presented in terms of the violent history of Parisian geography. In the passage mentioned earlier where the scene is said to become mysterious, the *quartier* of the stock market and the Bank of France trembles. An owl flies over the Madeleine toward "la barrière du Trône" (I, 177), that is, from the center of finance and social power across the working-class areas and the Bastille, reversing the movement of the omnibus in the second canto. The owl shrieks, "Un malheur se prépare," "misfortune" being an understatement for the murder that is predicted as well as for the implied violence against the societal-familial-financial order.

Significantly, too, Mervyn's failure immediately afterward to turn to see who is following him is described both in urban and historical terms. It is contrasted with the combat between "un rôdeur de barrières," a dangerous person on the outskirts of the city (178), and a cat old enough to have witnessed past revolutions. The cat's skin will bring profit to yet another ragman. Again, difference in social class represented through city geography evokes an image of violent, mortal struggle, this time with an explicit reference to revolutionary history.

The path of Mervyn's flight to his death is of course also full of significance. A cock has already foreseen it: "It is not as far as one thinks from the Rue de la Paix to the Place du Panthéon" (VIII, 202). Like the pont du Carrousel and the Palais-Royal and the Tuileries wing of the Louvre, the latter two burned in May 1871, the last beyond repair, *Vendôme* and *Panthéon* resonate historically.

The place Vendôme to this day embodies memories of *grandeur* as well as present wealth and social ascendance. Since in the past the figure atop the column changed with the government, it was also a political barometer. As I have noted elsewhere, writers as different or as alike as Karl Marx and Herman Melville commented on this on the eve of the Second Empire.[12] Within months of Ducasse's death the Commune toppled the column, an act of political defiance corresponding to the symbolic implications in *Maldoror*.[13] To reinforce this symbolism the column is even called an obelisk (204). And the Panthéon has similar importance: conceived as a church in accordance with a vow by Louis XV but not substantially completed until the eve of the revolution, thereafter its function was secular or religious depending on the regime in power. In 1869 it was of course a church, but whether a church or a repository of France's intellectual and political patrimony (I use the word advisedly) it was a suitable target for the vehemently oppositional writer who earlier claimed to want to be the poet of the waning nineteenth century (I, xiv, 33).

A further irony appears on the last page: the reminder that when Mervyn grasped the garland from the "grandiose pedestal" of the Vendôme column it was within sight of the "new Opéra" (205), that is, the one still under construction to the glory of Napoléon III at the time of his defeat and capture by the Prussians. Mervyn's murder, like everything else in *Maldoror*, affronts us on the grounds of family, sexuality, and virtually every fundamental issue of morality and religion, not to mention the myriad subversions of sense and discourse that we have encountered. But, as in this ultimate reference to Napoleonic architectural grandeur, through the repeated symbolism of Paris geography and monuments *Maldoror* is also a most virulent expression of sociopolitical protest.

This does not necessarily make its author a "socialist" or a left-wing rebel à la Blake. As we have seen, there is as much murderousness as protectiveness of the poor in this work. But it does indicate that Maldoror's final act is one not only of literary terrorism but also of political rage. Perhaps most revealingly, in regard to the contradictions noted here, its prophecy of class destruction turns out to be backward. The revolutionary but peaceful government of the Commune did not exterminate members of the wealthier classes. But Thiers's troops did execute thousands of workers when they defeated the Commune in May 1871.[14] Repeatedly, history crushes opposition.

chapter five

Surrealism and Its Discontents ✍

Breton's *Nadja* and Aragon's *Paysan de Paris*

My title is unoriginal but serves to recall the impact of Freud and several kinds of discontent: that in the face of the constraints of defined mental and social reality which the name *surrealism* foregrounds; that represented by the fact of coming *after* writers like Lautréamont and Rimbaud; that experienced by me and others at what may fairly be considered the contradictions of surrealism, notably in its leading figures, André Breton and Louis Aragon.

Rimbaud indeed sketched a visionary poetics and wrote the poems that expressed it before, according to Breton, having the cowardice to give up (*M* 175–76).[1] And *Maldoror*, as we have just seen, subverts fundamental values and the conventions of depicting a supposedly stable reality. Lautréamont, who appears in virtually every enumeration of Breton's predecessors, is praised for these subversions. Breton took him to be as infallible in the mental realm as (in 1929–30) he viewed Marx to be in the "external" world of society (*M* 156). The dichotomy here is one of the contradictions suggested above. It ignores the destructive sociopolitical allegory at the end of *Maldoror* and hints at the ambiguities in Breton's political stance during his career.

Like Blake dynamiting the "real," and, even more than Blake, traditional religious vision, Lautréamont leaves writing utterly free. Aragon, influenced by Lautréamont early on and still writing about him in 1967,[2] flirts with self-focused modes in *Le paysan de Paris*, but both he and Breton are more characteristically in the position of being atheist and opposed to the mystical and supernatural, yet glimpsing some "reality" other than the one proposed to us, and of using writing to evoke it. Both approach this position in part through a reading of idealist philosophy. In his early work Breton more than Aragon relies heavily on Freud, whose writing on dreams seem to him to provide evidence of that other reality, yet later Breton insistently cites alchemical, magical, occult, and Gnostic traditions. Such eclecticism, although characteristic of the tradition, is not wholly convincing on intellectual grounds. But another assemblage of predecessors, the "harrowing" philosophy and poetry of Hegel, Feuerbach, Marx, Lautréamont, Rimbaud, Jarry, Freud, Chaplin, and Trotsky (*M* 155), is more attractive in its interdisciplinary scope, in its refusal to separate history and politics from philosophy and poetry.[3]

The historical context is again, as in the case of earlier writers, of extraordinary importance and is even more apocalyptically threatening. Aragon and Breton served as medical personnel in World War I, and Aragon was a decorated combatant in World War II. Both were influenced by artistic movements that in the period of the first war imagined universal transformations (for example, various futurisms) and by the writing of another precursor, Guillaume Apollinaire. There was also the tendency to subvert all societal and aesthetic values, most notably in the Dada movement. In the years between the wars and, as we shall see, during the second war and second *après-guerre*, they responded in radically different ways to the challenge of Marxism and Soviet Communism.

Two important recent books, Pierre Daix's revised biography of Aragon and Margaret Cohen's very positive revaluation of Breton's effort to combine Freud and Marx against the repressive "materialism" of Soviet and French Communist parties, are valuable in these connections. The first provides detailed historical information, including materials newly released from Soviet archives, the second subtle argumentation not only on *Nadja* but on what Cohen presents as the other two works in Breton's Parisian trilogy, *Les vases communicants* and *L'Amour fou*.[4]

Although they broke permanently over the issues of the party and Stalinism, Aragon and Breton both thought of their literary enterprises as contributing to the success of revolution, not only in France but throughout the world — hence the title of one of their reviews, first published on the eve of their rupture in 1930–31, *Le surréalisme au service de la révolution*. Thus in their writings we again encounter visionary tendencies in a period of unimaginable violence and revolutionary expectation.

This setting, and the range of sources evoked above, correspond to the achievement of the surrealist movement in a wide variety of fields, including nonverbal media. Despite the evident danger of using the avant-garde tactic to achieve recognition and success, surrealism involved a major effort of the arts, inspired by visionary aspirations, not to be separated from the historical field. Aragon and Breton, whom I will treat selectively yet with an eye to range, propose to us in the modern period an extensive meditation on surrealist goals and tactics, with a high degree of political awareness.

Most of these themes are visible in two relatively early and widely appreciated surrealist texts, Aragon's *Le paysan de Paris* (1926) and Breton's *Nadja* (1928). The latter, insistently autobiographical, recounts Breton's encounter with an unusual woman, the woman and the encounter closely associated with surrealist experience. The former, whose less obvious autobiographical dimension has been uncovered by Pierre Daix,[5] is more flagrantly antinovelistic. Yet, like *Nadja*, it is abundantly attentive to the Parisian setting while including philosophical reflection and passages of surreal expression. Both must be linked to Breton's manifestos of 1924 and 1930 and related documents for a sense of scope and evolution that nonetheless will not obscure the immediacy of two fascinating works.

In keeping with Breton's critique of realism and the novel form in the first manifesto (*M* 6–9), and his prescient sketch of what would later be called *le nouveau roman* in the second (*M* 162–63 n.), *Nadja* claims not to be a novel. It is a first-person narrative, supposedly true, based on the author's experience. Like Barthes's later *nyn-egocentrism*,[6] but unlike Barthes's work retaining the autobiographical referent, *Nadja* renounces the novelist's claim to create fictional characters (17–18). The book in a deeper sense is therefore also intended to be nonliterary or nonaesthetic, like surrealism in Breton's famous definition (*M* 26). But other features point in the opposite direction. These include the author's reiterated care for publication (147, as well as the preface to the 1962 revision);[7] various ponderous rhetorical effects; and Breton's belated realization that there is such a thing as *le poncif surréaliste*. Such clichés were indeed visible in that supposedly spontaneous production, automatic writing (*M* 40, 157–58), and had already been criticized in Aragon's *Traité du style* (192–96). Nadja herself predicts that on the basis of their experience Breton will write a novel (100).

This is to suggest a discordance between the claim to surreality in this apparent antinovel and the quite traditional aspects of its structure having to do with person, description, event, form. The preference for subjectivity and biography announced at the outset, but which Lautréamont contradicts (11–18), is at least in tension with Breton's argument that the true mission of psychoanalysis is to expel man from himself (24). Later I shall argue that, as many a reader has felt, the surrealist goal of risking person and all for the marvelous is in no way realized by the narrator's self-protective behavior.

One could say something comparable about the photographs that in the 1962 preface Breton says he used to replace description. He himself was dissatisfied with them (152); although some have a certain mystery, they on the whole assert the banality of the quotidian as effectively as any standard novelistic description.[8] The same is true for action, or plot, in that the events that lead up to the meeting with Nadja, said to illustrate mysterious coincidence and convergence,[9] also deftly sketch the early activities of Breton and his surrealist companions. Aragon manages something similar, but with a pinch of irony, in *Le paysan de Paris*. No more than *La Nausée* does *Nadja* violate the novelistic enchainment of events, at the outset apparently patternless, for the purposes of plot and conclusion. As Breton himself writes, everything prepares, "sans plus tarder ici, l'entrée en scène de Nadja" (60).

"Without further delay" — the sign, repeated throughout, of utterly *truthful* form, that of a journal scrupulously aware of the conditions of its composition. Although time and place are clear, from the place du Panthéon in 1918 to the manoir d'Ango in August 1927, the narrator is conscious of choosing them to frame his story (23). We are not to expect an exhaustive report, since the composition will proceed effortlessly without any preestablished order (23). I have already expressed doubt on this. Any forgetfulness will be sincere; what he recounts will not be "sujet à caution" (24). Sometimes memory serves: "Je revois Desnos" (31). Occasionally, though, the present not of the event but of the writing is foregrounded, as when, "a few days ago," Aragon points something curious out to Breton (56). In ways untouched by Lautréamont's subversive practice, the act of writing is stressed: "J'en arrive à ma propre expérience" (24). Once Breton even recounts part of a fearful dream deriving from his reflections on the preceding portion of the narration ("En finissant hier soir de conter ce qui précède," 49–51).

Despite the analogy with *Aurélia*, that is, the convention of faithful notation, though not fully of dream, the fundamental difference is what stands out: in *Nadja* the insane visionary, this time a woman, is not the narrator. Indeed, after a series of dated journal entries in the present tense, the concluding movements of the structure formalize the progressive distancing of the two (114, 116, 130). An especially painful instance: "On est venu, il y a quelques mois, m'apprendre que Nadja était folle": "They came, several months ago, to inform me that Nadja was insane" (my translation, 136). Then, after a final reflection on the present of writing (148), it is revealed that the author has fallen in love with another woman, whom he celebrates but may lose. We learn in *L'Amour fou* that he does lose her. The risk of a new love thus exposes Breton painfully to what at the end he calls convulsive beauty, for once undermining his mastery, through behavior and narration, of his situation.

Although later Breton stresses that surrealism concerns language and the *torpedoing* of ideas through their expression in language (*M* 151, 159), in *Nadja* language and form on the whole display an almost classical control. In contrast, by a variety of formal features *Le paysan de Paris* troubles the reader's perceptions and sense of reality.

First of all, resembling in various ways the works of Blake and Lautréamont, *Le paysan* mixes forms and submits us to radical shifts. The book displays an energy, a diversity, and an unevenness that are almost impossible to convey.[10] Although the two long central parts, "Le passage de l'Opéra" and "Le sentiment de la nature aux Buttes-Chaumont," involve the detailed description of a soon-to-be-demolished gallery of shops and other establishments and a nocturnal visit to a park, they are also filled with interruptions, metamorphoses, disquisitions. And they are framed by two short pieces, "Préface à une mythologie moderne" and "Le songe du paysan" ("The Peasant's Dream"), which have their own tricks but are on the whole theoretical in nature. The tendency of visionary texts to combine discussion of the possibilities and conditions of vision with the description of experiences, manifestos with revelations, reappears.

On the one hand there is a strongly realistic tendency. We are invited to observe (22–23) as the narrator takes us through each and every establishment in the *passage de l'Opéra*: "Now I reach the threshold of the celebrated Certa café" (my translation, 92). Descriptive formulas abound. Indeed, the representation of the gallery is so apparently complete that the narrator refers to it as a guide (109), and that of the park assumes appropriate conventions: "Note, to the right" (219). So "documentary" is the book as a whole that it reproduces a variety of advertisements, notices, menus, newspaper articles, and even the text, or lack of same, of every plaque to be found in the Buttes-Chaumont park.

Note the potential for parody in the hyperrealism of the empty plaques. Usually it is not emptiness but fullness that is excessive, as in the café Certa (93–94), where we are several times told what is to be found to the left and to the right, encounter eleven barrels and twenty-four stools, and follow a Jakobsonian array of prepositions[11] before contributing to the furnishings ("Throw in with this some plants next to the bar") and meeting the cashier. Later the taxi ride to the park enumerates every street followed, with a parody of geometric accuracy (167). And when we get there, the overall shape of the park is described, first curiously as a sleeping bonnet, then with an unvisualizable exactitude (69–70).

The narrator explicitly examines the convention of description, noting criticisms of his own "gift of observation." Like Breton he claims instead to be guided by chance, arguing that objects and persons that he notes, and that he threatens to describe "if you don't behave yourselves," represent his own inner limits, constraints he needs to transcend in order to reach a hitherto forbidden realm (108–9). Typical surrealist themes, inner and outer, chance and choice, limits and transgression, are enunciated here. Visible as well is an exuberant superiority to the reader close to that claimed by Blake in the *Marriage*.

A later passage (221–22), with an aggressiveness that recalls Lautréamont, attacks our submission to the realistic convention. At first there is criticism of the narrator's attempt to describe: he is "loin de compte," far from all-inclusive, not having enumerated the park's gravel, blades of grass, sperm on the grass . . . But quickly he switches to us: "They followed me" — "les imbéciles"; "Up this little hill, now clamber down again." This involves a Ducassian sense of superiority, as the "moi" stresses his pride, his openness to poetry, his "torrential" nature: he belongs to "la grande race des torrents." There is a rare burst of sadism too, as we are ordered to lick his shoes, give up our watches and wives, and lie down to be trampled, he wishing he had worn hobnailed boots!

We have in fact been solicited from the beginning, invited — to have a drink (99), to step right in (115). Once inside, depending on the establishment, we might become aroused. Such seems to befall one of our number, whose hands are seen to flutter: "Have the courage of your inclination, stranger"; "Oh, he didn't take very long, that one" (110). The scorn accords with attacks launched elsewhere against sexual hypocrisy. Again (150) the narrator sounds like Lautréamont as his cheeks "bleed with shame" at the thought that we are his fellows. A particular group of readers, journalists and critics, draws an even more hateful response (95n, 246). I claim not to be part of this group.[12]

But all of us are caught by our need for logic, as the narrator shows after a confusing paragraph about a dog and an employee of a hat store. Slyly he adds "Thus . . . ," then assails us for our need for logic, which he exposed by this whole long paragraph. He furnishes four different concluding paragraphs beginning with "Thus" (184–86), adding the possibility that the whole work may proceed from "le goût insensé de la mystification et du désespoir," a senseless taste for mystification and despair (186). Later he returns to this vein, denying our ability to understand: "What are you awaiting from me, you people? There they stand, agape" (210); "you cannot understand me. Park, park, and park" (220). But near the end of the chapter on the park he includes a letter to Philippe Soupault that serves to explain and rationalize much that has preceded (223–25).

The act of writing is highlighted as the narrator wonders if he will continue the lying description of the park (209). A page later we learn that the answer to the question is affirmative. But as is clear, there is no single narrative view. The section on the park switches between first and third person and singular and plural. Throughout, various persons, mental faculties, and objects are given speeches, including the faculty of imagination, but there is also a man conversing with his faculties, the surrealist Marcel Noll, a statue in the park. At other times, Louis Aragon is the sole enunciator, as when we encounter a large boldface "**LOUIS!**" because the author feels like seeing his first name in print (72–73).

But, like Breton in *Nadja*, Aragon claims to transcend subjectivity. True, he is inscribed in his work as an individual having a certain name and exercising activities in history, exposing unfair real estate transactions, forming part of literary movements: "have you . . . heard of the Dada movement?" (73). He can distance himself from the action in the park: "Here the three friends realize that they are not armed" (my translation, 166). But he also can personally experience exaltation: "Here I stand in the preeminence of destiny" (175). At the end (246–47) he claims that he has not been dramatizing himself. Now he sounds like Montaigne in arguing that the first person singular expresses concrete humanity and that all metaphysics, as well as poetry, is in the first person. Metaphysics is for him not abstract but concrete (237, 245). In keeping with these notions, the work, reminding us of Blake's proverbs, ends with a series of affirmations, or maxims, which I cite selectively as an introduction to discussion of surrealist themes.

Hence: "The marvelous is the contradiction which appears in the real" (my translation); "There is no love except of the concrete"; "God is rarely to be found in my mouth"; "Those who distinguish faculties in the mind"; "Your time is up, gentlemen, for individuals have finished their stint on earth"; "Push the idea of the destruction of individuals as far as it will go; then, go beyond it" (248–49, the last concluding the work). Surrealist positions on reality, religion, reason, love, and person, are articulated, including ambiguities. Among these is the fact that love and women are celebrated but those who are addressed, even as adversaries, are men, and the trace of subjective voice in the enunciation of transcendence of person.

The materials on the visionary and surreal, including love, in these works are voluminous. In a passage echoed by Breton and Aragon, Lautréamont had written about "de nouveaux frissons," or new shivers, in the "atmosphère intellectuelle."[13] Breton refers to the passage in a 1922 lecture, and the use of *frisson* marks two comparable pronouncements in *Le paysan* (135–36, 142–43).

In the first the modern world is said to be undergoing a crisis in which the abstract words for fundamental values, the beautiful, the good, the just, the true, the real, have lost their meaning. Challenging of basic principles is familiar at least as far back as Blake, with the word *surrealism* disputing as here the ultimate opposition, that between real and unreal. In apparent contradiction to claims for impersonality elsewhere, into this void steps Aragon, who like Hugo in the poem "Ce siècle avait deux ans" becomes the vision, passage, limit, and voice of meaning. The last word of this section, which concludes "Le passage de l'Opéra," is "frisson." A few pages into the next chapter, on the Buttes-Chaumont, having left behind a rationalist phase Aragon is aware of certain "frissons" evocative of the infinite. Again in Blakean fashion, he recognizes that "man is full of gods" (my translation) and describes himself confidently: "I began, effortlessly, to discern the face of the infinite beneath the concrete forms escorting me as I walked down the tree-lined lanes of this earth."

This is the first time we have encountered such apparent ease of access to the infinite, such uncomplicated recognition of the human as the source of the divine, since leaving Blake. Earlier, "Discours de l'imagination" (80–84), defining surrealism through a pitchman's come-on and concluding with a humorous prophecy of the movement's triumph then defeat by the forces of practicality, uses another formula reminiscent of Blake — "pouvoir visionnaire." In a Rimbaldian echo, too, the visionary is linked to "the deranged and passionate use of the narcotic *image*, or rather the uncontrolled provocation of it for its own sake and for whatever unforeseen upheavals and metamorphoses it introduces into the realm of representation: for each image each time forces you to revise the whole Universe" (my translation).[14]

This is more interesting than the derivative theory of the image and pale illustrations in Breton's first manifesto. If the emphasis on profusion recalls Blake and Rimbaud, the reference to troubling the system of representation leads from certain texts of the latter and of Lautréamont to the infinitely ambiguous play of representation in modern *écriture*. But writing is not the exclusive issue; rather, revising our whole sense of the universe is. And in a mystical-sounding note Aragon adds: "there is for each man an image to find which annihilates the whole Universe" (my translation).

But this is not traditionally mystical. Aragon too rejects both religion and morality (144, 153–54, 231–34, 247).[15] Nonetheless, he wants to invent a modern mythology (14–15). We need to ask whether it is new, like the monuments to strange divinities that turn out to be gas pumps (145), or old, like the siren whom he drunkenly imagines in a dimly lit umbrella shop in the passage and who is probably a prostitute (31–32, 53–54).

As this last indicates in a comic vein, Aragon makes good on the claim that the places he describes are propitious for unusual perceptions.[16] The raised seats at the shoeshine establishment in the passage "are highly propitious to reverie" (87), and the stamp seller returns him to the imaginative voyages of his childhood (89–90). The enumeration of items in a medical supply store produces a delirium of words and things: "stockings for varicose veins; slips; douches, some of which are decorated with little flowers; belts for women in pink, red, and white, of rubber, silk, and twill; irrigators; enemas; clysters; fumigators; nozzles; syringes" and much more (123). And when night descends in the absurd spaces of the parc des Buttes-Chaumont, desire and vertigo and madness are experienced: "I know against reason that my madness has in itself an irrepressible power, which is above the human" (173–75).

Above the human, and opening toward death, as is articulated in impressive passages in both long sections of the work. In the first (42–44) Aragon steps back from the detail of the economic struggle over the passage de l'Opéra: "I am putting aside my microscope for a while. Needless to say, writing with one eye screwed to a lens [. . .] decidedly impairs one's vision." The optical switch first makes quotidian objects seem enormous: an inkwell looks the size of Notre-Dame. But reversing the process makes the financial conflicts under discussion seem minute, "magnificent bacterial dramas" of phagocytes gobbling one another up, expressive not of justice but of death. Everything, even the productions of surrealism, reveals death, Aragon continues, recalling that the passage de l'Opéra is "a large glass coffin" where love and death, the *Libido* now followed by the little dog Freud, are visible in the place's prostitutes: "On stage . . . ladies, on stage, and strip a little." In *Traité du style* Aragon claimed to be attacking less Freud than the misuse of him by others (79, 143 ff.). But his visionary switching of optics returns us to an ancient certainty, a somber one that Freud also rediscovered and that perhaps balances somewhat Aragon's unsavory fondness for prostitution.

The other passage forms the conclusion of "Le sentiment de la nature aux Buttes-Chaumont" (227–30). Beginning in the first person present, the text presents Aragon dreaming while his detached head makes a survey of other human beings that is hardly favorable to them. Then, the head back in place, there is a switch to the third person, who rips the head off again and hurls it through nature, where in its rolling it discovers the experience of feet. The last paragraph describes the death and transfiguration of "he who had separated himself from his thought" (my translation).

The surrealist effort to transcend reason is physically actualized here as decapitation. With the use first of the imperfect, then the simple past, suggesting an extended process reaching culmination, the arteries of the decapitated body, risen into the pureness of the diamond sky, hurl its blood, which forms monstrous ferns in space. A brilliant play of light leads to this beautiful conclusion:

The man-fountain, dragged off by celestial capillary attraction, ascended to the planets in the wake of his blood. The whole useless body was invaded by transparency. Little by little it became light. A bloodbeam [Le sang rayon]. Its limbs froze in some incomprehensible gesture. And man was now but a sign among the constellations. (230)

In this transcendence of the human, this elimination of both mind and body, Aragon again finds a modern reenactment of ancient themes. In the terms of *Le paysan de Paris* he is a visionary who perceives the universe in wholly nonreligious ways but as infinite, as infinitely various, and as harboring annihilation.[17]

This may sound like a balancing act, but it is in the positions of Breton that one finds up and downs. He is constant, to be sure, in expressing vehement dissatisfaction with every aspect of mental and external existence. Hence the first manifesto opens with an attack on practicality, logic, rationalism, *le bon sens* (*M* 4, 9–10) and concludes that existence is *elsewhere*, even that the difference between living and not living is imaginary (*M* 47). But later Breton discovers that he holds fast to life (1962 preface), just as, at the end of *Nadja*, where the insubstantiality of existence is initially conveyed by a vocabulary of phantoms and haunting (11–13), he draws back from some of his extreme formulations. We note a less flagrant but still significant incongruity between the second manifesto's goal of restoring thought to its "pureté originelle" (*M* 124) and a related theme in *Nadja*. There (12) Breton hesitates to adapt the notion of having *forgotten* some essential aspect of his being, precisely because of its suggestion of anteriority — and of loss, punishment, and fall. Like some of the Aragon passages discussed, this suggests a glimpse of another reality, one unapproachable in conventional religious terms.

Another formula, used at the opening of the second manifesto (*M* 124), is similar, like Aragon talking of annihilation, but including also mystical motifs. As opposed to art or anti-art, the only activities to be pursued there are those whose goal is "the annihilation of the being into a diamond, all blind and interior, which is no more the soul of ice than that of fire." The religious connotation of *soul*, the emphasis on innerness, the vocabulary of jewels, ice, and fire, have a long mystical-poetic history, in modern times for example in the so-called *Derniers Vers* of Rimbaud, the poet attacked by Breton in this second manifesto for permitting the possibility of religious interpretations of his work. Recall that later Breton listed Theresa of Avila among his predecessors, in 1942 rejecting the charge of mysticism but concluding a 1953 essay with a reference to the Gnostic "supra-sensible Reality, 'invisibly visible in an eternal mystery' " (*M* 291, 304).

Nonetheless, Breton's early authority, particularly in the first manifesto (*M* 10–26), is Freud. With an important exception, namely the absence of anxiety or guilt in the description of dreams (*M* 13), he gives a balanced account of Freud's views on dream, the unconscious, "accidental" acts, and verbal slips. This leads him to celebrate the products of automatic writing, culminating in the definition of *surrealism* as direct expression of the supposedly real function of thinking, free of the influence of reason, morality, or aesthetic considerations (*M* 26). Regardless of the questions the definition begs, the assertions it dubiously makes,[18] Breton's project, a systematic attempt to reconcile dream and reality, is in the tradition of Novalis and Nerval, two writers whom he cites frequently. "I believe in the future resolution of these two states [. . .] into a kind of absolute reality, a *surreality*" (*M* 14), he exclaims, adding that in pursuit of this goal he is "unmindful" of life or death.

In the second manifesto (*M* 136–37), too, Freud is at the base of another formulation of surrealist activity and goals: "the total recovery of our psychic force." This will mean a "dizzying descent," illumination of the hidden and obscuring of the known, a "perpetual excursion into the midst of forbidden territory" so that we will no longer be able to "distinguish an animal from a flame or a stone." As seen with regard to Lautréamont, the effort to obscure the conscious, to render the unconscious visible, becomes an attack on principles of reality and identity whereby the learned distinctions between categories no longer hold. Note that this important argument occurs just before Breton's labored attempt to establish surrealism's "attitude politique," replete with personal attacks against communists and surrealists alike.

Thus Breton's thinking on the surreal uses Freud, and Lautréamont *and* Rimbaud, for the liberation of a reality hitherto denied us, another version of the visionary project that we have been studying. To Breton's credit he pursued the problematics of his ideas throughout his career, but the contradictions are nonetheless striking: overblown claims, the difficulty of balancing Freudian unconscious and mystical symbolism, the problem of political involvement. Striking most of all in *Nadja*, where, as in the *Paysan de Paris*, love is presented as an integral component of surrealism (see fig. 5).

5 Man Ray, *Noire et blanche*, 1926. © Artists Rights Society (ARS), New York/ADAGP/Man Ray Trust, Paris.

Nadja at first appears as the culminating encounter in a series of supposedly extraordinary coincidences and meetings narrated in this book. She is surreal in her behavior and in her provoking a state at least akin to that exceptional circumstance, love (*M* 4).

Breton, as has been shown,[19] celebrated heterosexual love throughout his long career, although in notably sexist ways. In the first manifesto the paucity of any man's existence is reckoned in part by the women he has had, and one of Breton's fantasies of happiness involves a castle where he and his friends would be masters not only of themselves but of women (*M* 3, 17).

Later works are less crudely sexist in their praise of women. But *L'Amour fou* (1937) evokes an ecstatic, hysterical form of female sexual experience under the patronage of Sade and Lautréamont, among others (12). The wartime *Arcane 17* (1945) understandably valorizes the ideas of women as against those of men yet follows Nerval and Nadja in representing women by the mythical figure of Mélusine, whose sexual attraction derives from the animal form that she takes as punishment.

Still later, in *Du surréalisme en ses oeuvres vives* (1953), Breton cites Abelard and Heloise, Goethe and German and French romanticism as a vast tradition glorifying women, finally evoking the "reconstruction [reconsti-

tution] of the *primordial Androgyne* that all traditions tell us of, and its supremely desirable, and *tangible*, incarnation within ourselves" (*M* 302).
This is an exalted conception of love indeed, in which we seem personally
to enact the most ancient myth, transcending sexual difference. We must
contrast it with the sexual suffering in *Maldoror*, including the strophe on
the hermaphrodite. In this late work of Breton, destructive and sadistic features of sexuality are accordingly reduced to a preliminary infernal phase
(300–301), and in this Breton perhaps resembles the Blake of *Milton*.

Significantly, Lautréamont is not named here, a rare omission. Steinmetz
correctly diagnoses the blindness of the surrealists to homosexuality in
Maldoror (*GF* 14, 57 n. 20), and Gauthier stresses the unrecognized homosocial or homosexual element in their own work.[20] Concerning Breton
specifically, whereas my overview of his ideas on love shows an increasing
celebration of women, it also reveals that, even amid many pages of beautiful writing, the sadistic dimension, sufferings inflicted and horrible transformations, is rather little scrutinized. From Sade to Goethe to Breton those
features coexist but hardly square with the salvific function ascribed to
women in the words of *Arcane 17*: "l'idée du *salut terrestre par la femme*, de
la vocation transcendante de la femme" (48–49).

Although she appears initially as the term of a surreal series, Nadja thus
turns out to be one in a sequence of women, as the book ends in Breton's
unexpected falling in love with another woman. With her, he feels, the *sub-
stitutions* stop (158), although in *L'Amour fou* he again has to wrestle with
the problem of absolute love that can yet change its object. The unexpected
and transforming impact of love in *Nadja* reminds us that at the end of
Le paysan de Paris Aragon's life also undergoes the upheaval of love (238–
42). More disconcertingly, in Breton's book there seems something self-
justifying in his explanations of why he drifted away from Nadja as her state
worsened. He doubts he has been "à la hauteur," but answers that only
love, "mais alors le mystérieux, l'improbable, l'unique, le confondant et
l'indubitable amour," could have produced the miracle (136).

Yet earlier Breton wondered if he loved Nadja (90), and she is hardly
uninterested in a relation with him, expressing surprise upon learning that
he is married (70) and offering her lips to him on several occasions. He is
fascinated by her eyes, by her appearance (sometimes splendid, sometimes
expressive of utter poverty). They spend a night together, although — in
the revised text — with no mention of love-making.[21] At one point he
kisses her teeth, which makes her think of holy communion; this is followed
by the coincidence of his receiving a postcard from Aragon depicting a
painting called *La Profanation de l'Hostie* (107–8). A good deal might be
said of the possibly sexual iconography of the detail of the painting that the

French text, but not the translation, reproduces, and certainly desire, sublimation, transgression are suggested in this sequence.

This is the place to recall that throughout his work, while celebrating women and his daughter Aube, Breton in a principled way rejects the institution of the family and also argues that passionate love transcends all moral interdictions, all sense of wrong or sin. The likely inhumanity of such principles is visible in the figure of the wife, unnamed, who functions only to receive calls from Nadja and take cabs with Breton in search of her, and who is not even mentioned at the end. As if in passing, too, we learn that Nadja has a child (89), to whom there is no further reference as her mother sinks into insanity.

A good deal of what is troubling in Breton's conception of love and in the treatment of Nadja can be related to the earlier passage on his admiration for the play *Les Détraquées* (39 ff.), which Susan Suleiman correctly shows to be preparatory to the arrival of Nadja and which she deflates on feminist and class grounds. Breton takes delight in describing the degraded theater where he sees the play and where, despite his criticism of bordellos in *Les vases communicants*, he savors the flagrant presence of lower-class prostitution.

For his part Aragon exalts prostitution, candidly describes a *fille* washing his penis, and rejects our predictable reaction as hypocrisy, concluding that his masturbations are worth anybody's. The only social awareness he shows in that passage (125–31) is his rejection of the designation *maison de tolérance*, presumably for what it implies of political and moral condemnation. No thought about the selling of a woman's body intrudes, and he enjoys her submission to his will: "la femme épouse docilement mes volontés" — literally, "the woman docilely marries my wishes."

Another aspect of his defense is that he fears neither skepticism nor vulgarity in the search for the fantastic (144), just as Breton strives for the worst of the bad taste of his period (*M* 16).[22] Taken seriously, this amounts to an age-old pursuit of the absolute in the midst of the sordid; in the case of Aragon too it is accompanied by numerous amusing, lyric, and mythic celebrations of women and love (12–13, 51, 147, 157, 204–18). More critically, as Suleiman argues, it allies an exploitative male sexuality with an almost exotic appeal of the lower classes, a feature already suggested in Nadja. Indeed, the lesbian murderers of girls in *Les Détraquées*, associated like Nadja with drugs and prostitution, also have "ce rien de 'déclassé' que nous aimons tant" (48). The degraded social note, the collusion among "us" men, are apparent. Elsewhere indeed Breton proclaims sexual cynicism to be one of surrealism's subversive arms (*M* 129).

Suleiman has shown that Breton's depiction of the murderers, which seems a melodramatic version of the Blakean proverb that has troubled us from the outset, is based on a strange repression. According to his text, even as reprinted in 1962, Breton could not find in the play any explanation of what moved the women to become "ces superbes bêtes de proie" ("magnificent predatory beasts," 50). On the contrary, in the play, which in the meantime Breton had published, the women are condemned as monsters. There is a second omission, in that it is Breton's reflection on the play that produces the horrible dream that he first refuses then proceeds in part to recount, although in explicitly incomplete form (50–51). Although the passage closes with references to the impressions provoked by the play and to dreams in general as beyond good and evil, the dream itself, in which a hideous insect drives its "huge hairy legs" into his throat, causing "an inexpressible disgust," hardly fills the bill. Anguish, punishment, guilt might all be interpreted.

Ecstatic passion, celebration of women, moral rebellion are thus, as in several earlier writers, integral components of the visionary in both Breton and Aragon. Disappointing aspects — sexism, the sordid (sometimes for its own sake) — nonetheless persist. Nowhere is this more the case than in the interaction of Nadja, an unimpressive visionary, and Breton, an unpersuasive surrealist.

Nadja recalls Nerval in having apparitions, in sensing that she has lived earlier lives, in wandering at night through Paris and experiencing anguish at the horrors that have occurred and will recur at certain spots. As mentioned, she identifies with a favorite Nervalian mythical figure, Mélusine, who is associated with French history and the Crusades but who also embodies the animal punishment of female sexuality. Some of the reactions she produces and coincidences she predicts astonish Breton more than they do me; but then this is also true of similar material from his prior experience in the first part of the book.

Despite arguments that she is a frustrated and manipulated female visionary,[23] Nadja's sayings are not particularly powerful or poetic, and most express her sad dependence on Breton. Neither are the drawings very good. The ones that show her as Mélusine emphasize her hair and her siren tail, whereas in *Arcane 17* Breton stresses the traditional snakes. In the Mélusine drawings her face is averted. Another one, which Breton calls "La Fleur des amants" and which carries the words "L'Enchantement de Nadja," is a banal composition of eyes, hearts, arrow, and serpent. On it is also written "Vous devez être très occupé en ce moment? Trouvez le temps d'écrire quelques mots à votre Nadja": "You must be busy these days? Find the time to write a few words to your Nadja" (my translation, 116).

Rather, Nadja is surreal in her indifference to what Breton normally dismisses as the vile practicalities of existence. She calls herself "l'âme errante," the wandering soul, perhaps the soul in limbo that the translation gives (71). When she claims to pass her entire life in recounting stories to herself, Breton adds a note: "Ne touche-t-on pas là au terme extrême de l'aspiration surréaliste, à sa plus forte *idée limite*?": "Does this not approach the extreme limit of the surrealist aspiration, its *furthest determinant?*" (74). At the very moment of his separation from her, Breton launches into an extended development of these themes (108–13), claiming that reality is supine at Nadja's feet, that together they had been far from earth, in a wonderful "stupeur" beyond the wreckage of old systems of thought. He took her for a "génie libre," and for her he "*was* a god or the sun." Her scorn for the "compensations de la vie" was absolute, but his own drawing back from such a stance is preluded by a rare, and pale, introduction of familiar visionary motifs:

Perhaps life needs to be deciphered like a cryptogram. Secret staircases, frames from which the paintings quickly slip aside and vanish (giving way to an archangel bearing a sword or to those who must forever advance), buttons which must be indirectly pressed to make an entire room move sideways or vertically, or immediately change all its furnishings; we may imagine the mind's greatest adventure as a journey of this sort to the paradise of pitfalls. Who is the real Nadja [. . .]? (112)

The hesitancy, together with the bloated expression (the sentence on Nadja runs for another page), the literally mechanical nature of the transformations, the questions and traps, bring us close to the increasingly impossible situation described in the following pages, Breton's attempts to aid, Nadja's insanity. Here again, despite the sympathy we may feel for Breton's sense of helplessness in the face of Nadja's behavior, it is impossible not to be struck by the discrepancies between his surrealist claims and his actual way of living.

On the one hand, there is the ringing declaration on freedom as something to be pursued "without pragmatic considerations of any sort," on human emancipation as "the only cause worth serving" (142–43) — echoed by numerous statements of "*non-conformisme* absolu," "de la révolte absolue, de l'insoumission totale, du sabotage en règle," of disinterestedness, contempt for risk, refusal to compromise (M 47, 125, 129). On the other hand there is Breton's surprise that Nadja doesn't attend to the simple arrangements of life, doesn't know how to resolve difficulties "normalement" (115, 130). Were she not poor, were she able to afford proper treatment, she could return to "un sens acceptable de la réalité" (142). What happened to the surreal? Most of all Breton didn't believe that she had lost "cet instinct de conservation" that he evokes early on (20) and that he illustrates here by the prudence exercised by him and his friends when the flag passes, as they refrain from acting "sacrilegiously" (142)![24]

There is contradiction too in Breton's attack on Nadja's internment and on psychiatry in general. In the first manifesto he claims not to fear the risk of insanity (*M* 5–6, 45–46). And Nadja's insanity provokes a tirade against those who have imprisoned not only her but figures from Sade to Nietzsche. This passage (136 ff.) includes the shocking assumption by Breton that for Nadja there is little difference between the inside and the outside of an asylum. It also expresses the threat of revenge by murder that caused fear among psychiatrists and, generalized as the ultimate surrealist act in the second manifesto (*M* 119–26), drew Sartre's ire.[25] They need not have worried. Breton doesn't know what happened to Nadja, because, although he makes an effort at rhetorical camouflage, he admits that he didn't dare inquire: "Le mépris qu'en général je porte à la psychiatrie, à ses pompes et à ses oeuvres, est tel que je n'ai pas encore osé m'enquérir de ce qu'il était advenu de Nadja": "The scorn that I have for psychiatry, for its pomps and works, is such that I have not yet dared inquire about what had become of Nadja" (my translation, 141).

The impersonality of the expression is perhaps what is most painful here: Nadja has been reduced to a nonentity not only by the psychiatrists but by Breton's writing. Suleiman makes the point well by citing the 1962 preface's claim to medical, even neuropsychiatric observation, an idea already expressed, in apparently inoffensive form, in the first manifesto: "Les confidences des fous, je passerais ma vie à les provoquer": "I could spend my whole life prying loose the secrets of the insane" (15). These last notes reformulate with utter clarity the point made earlier concerning the contrast between *Nadja* and *Aurélia*. Nadja is a pale figure compared to Nerval or his protagonist. And Breton, at least in *Nadja*, is at a far remove from the visionary, even if at the end, under the influence of his new love and the violence in Paris following the Sacco-Vanzetti executions in 1927, he again aspires to situations that involve "the most absolute sense of love or revolution," to the negation of everything else (152–53).

Overstatement is in evidence again, but this assertion reminds us that the surrealists, among them Breton and Aragon, were passionate about both love and revolution. The reader may feel that something of an excavation job was involved in discerning historical-political meanings in Novalis, Nerval, and Lautréamont. But Aragon and Breton, not to speak of figures like Eluard and Char, are more like Blake in having lived a long time and written a great deal in response to history — the world wars, the Russian revolution, fascism, communism, Stalinism, the struggle to liberate the colonies.

The story of their confrontation with such events is an object lesson in contradiction, even dissembling, certainly courage, one too complex to recount in detail here.[26] Nonetheless it will be useful to sketch their conflictual and emblematic itineraries in the wake of the texts that principally concern us.

Aragon's *Traité du style*, written in 1926–27 and published in 1928 over the objections of Gide and Valéry, seriously criticized therein, is an astonishingly vehement attack on all things French, all things sacred, and is overtly oppositional on political and religious themes. Aragon's participation in 1930 in the Soviet-manipulated congress of Kharkov, concerning which he prevaricated, was followed by tergiversations as to where his commitments lay, censorship, and indictment for the poem "Front rouge." The public defense by Breton was formulated in terms that Aragon felt obliged publicly to reject. The charges against him were eventually dropped, but all of this led to the bitter break between the two writers that divided the surrealist group from the early thirties on.

Thereafter Aragon had a long career as a communist journalist and organizer and wrote quantities of political and love poetry, including Resistance poetry that had an enormous resonance, a series of large and impressive novels in a realistic mode with attention to historical and political themes, a justification of socialist realism, books on the literatures of Russia, *Les Communistes*, and much else. Before and after the war, during which he fought for the French then became an important member of the Resistance, he was a committed Stalinist, never denouncing the Soviet-German pact even after its secret provisions became known, persisting in his illusions into the 1960s, when for the first time he protested against trials of writers and the invasion of Czechoslovakia.[27]

Claiming to be prorevolution, and certainly consistently antifascist, anti-Stalinist, and anticolonialist, Breton throughout his career struggled against the suppression of thought in the communist movement. He attacked the "cretinizing" impact of *L'Humanité* in 1925, tried to ally surrealism with marxism in the second manifesto (1930), and produced lectures and publications on art, surrealism, and politics during the thirties, including one coauthored with Trotsky. In 1942 he warned communists to reflect on the likelihood that, if in a quarter century their system had not produced the results predicted, it must be basically flawed. In *L'Amour fou*, written in 1936, he told us that the birth of his daughter kept him from going to support the revolution in Spain. In 1944, away (understandably) from the scene, he composed *Arcane 17* in Canada as the allied armies neared Paris. From these works one may retain especially a movingly idealistic quote from Trotsky (*M* 106) on the socialist society that is still to be created and Breton's own reflections, in 1944's "sombre veille de deux fois l'an mil" (we are even closer), on the total transformation necessary for war to be eliminated (*Arcane 17*, 33, 127–38). Back in France, in 1947 Breton organized an international surrealist exhibit in which Antoinin Artaud refused to participate on the grounds that Breton had wholly given himself over not only to initiatory versions of religion but also to capitalism.[28]

Nadja and *Le paysan de Paris* are themselves historically precise. The former is set in the years immediately following World War I, with references to the war and to the Commune (14–15), which in *Arcane 17* Breton says was still very much alive in spirit during his youth (14–15). Evoking the war briefly (31–32), Aragon's book concerns in part the prolongation of the Boulevard Haussmann and the impending destruction of the passage de l'Opéra, "now destroyed" by the time of the writing of *Nadja* (37–38). Breton does not here mention *Le paysan*, but both works elsewhere refer to the other author, as I have suggested in sketching the early evolution of surrealism in its historical setting.

Nadja unfolds in a Parisian geography reminiscent of *Aurélia* and *Maldoror*. Not to speak of its point of departure, place du Panthéon (23), the story of Breton's encounters with Nadja begins to unfold in the right bank area, indeed on many of the same streets in which we saw Mervyn pursued by Maldoror.

The narration of the third meeting with Nadja corresponds to differences between the two persons noted earlier, although the translation obscures this dimension. "De manière à n'avoir pas trop à flâner," Breton leaves about 4 P.M. for a bar "où je dois rejoindre Nadja" at five-thirty. He plans to take the boulevards to the Opéra, "où m'appelle une course brève," and contrary to his ordinary custom he takes the right-hand sidewalk of the rue de la Chaussée-d'Antin. Here he runs across Nadja, who is again in a dilapidated state, and who later admits that she had planned to miss the rendezvous with him (74–77). Nadja's decision-making and changes in appearance remain rather mysterious, but Breton's navigation in the urban scene is explicitly not that of the Baudelairean *flâneur*, nor obviously that of the obsessive narrator in *Aurélia*. He has practical errands, a fixed time schedule, a habitual plan for expeditious movement.

Later lengthy nocturnal walks as well as a trip to Saint-Germain reproduce something of the strange intensity of *Aurélia* and other works by Nerval. The place Dauphine, Palais de Justice, Conciergerie, Louvre, Tuileries, and Palais Royal provoke in Nadja the historical anguish mentioned above. She wonders who she was in the entourage of Marie-Antoinette and repeatedly sees a burning hand over the Seine. The train trip to Saint-Germain is a modern version of Nerval's movement between the capital and the then supposedly still-romantic space of myth and poetry. The chateau and the evocation of Mme. de Chevreuse constitute a memory of distant, romantic French history, since she is famous both for her affairs and for her political intrigues, including those carried out during the Fronde.

Breton, and the reader, I suspect, are less attracted to this version of the past than is Nadja. Current politics and history are, however, of strong interest to the author. The day of his first meeting with her, an empty day on which he finds himself wandering aimlessly on the rue de La Fayette, the site of Mervyn's house, he nonetheless inspects the window of *L'Humanité*'s bookstore, buys Trotsky's latest, and snidely thinks of the crowds of workers: "No, it was not yet these whom one would find ready to create the Revolution" (63–64). He expands this judgment in response to Nadja's characterization of the workers she observes in the subway as "braves gens." So long as they submit to work, do not revolt, accept even military service and war, these people can never be free, he explains. The logic is doubtless correct, but the scorn for the workers is unbearably smug, and the tirade again gives the effect of a set piece (68–69). Nor is Breton personally at risk during the "magnificent" Sacco-Vanzetti pillage, which, during his absence from Paris, corresponded to his desires "en matière de désordre." In fact, explicitly contrasting himself with the Baudelaire of "Le Cygne," he prepares again to leave the capital in pursuit of his new love (152–54).

This striking of a revolutionary pose without accepting personal risk contrasts surprisingly with allusions to two figures, Etienne Dolet and Henri Becque, the latter of whom suffered lack of success and the former *death* because of their oppositional stances (24, 143–44). In each instance, Breton seems to miss the point. He disagrees with the advice Nadja thinks she has received from Becque, and he denies that the "insupportable malaise" that Dolet's statue causes in him has a psychological explanation.

Another historical allusion, to the Manoir d'Ango, where in August 1927 "on m'a offert" the possibility of hunting but also a place in which to compose *Nadja* (23), is also curious. No further explanation is given of the identity of this "on" (the manoir was a hotel at the time), but it is historically suggestive that Breton lodged at the house of the shipbuilder Jean Ango (1480–1551), who was associated with the earliest explorations of Canada, Brazil, the East Indies, and Africa. Nor is there an explanation of the description of the destruction of the manoir at the end of the first part, just before "l'entrée en scène de Nadja":

Enfin voici que la tour du Manoir d'Ango saute, et que toute une neige de plumes, qui tombe de ses colombes, fond en touchant le sol de la grande cour naguère empierrée de débris de tuiles et maintenant couverte de vrai sang! (60)

This is *Nadja*'s negative apocalypse, unsituatable in any normal chronological frame: how could this be happening "now"? — in the now of writing in 1927, in the reediting of 1962, in the destruction of World War II? Rather it might be interpreted as Breton's premonition in 1927 of the horrors that *were going to happen* in succeeding decades. The house named after one of those who "started it all," the period of worldwide exploration and commerce that characterized the origin of capitalism, is destroyed. Human structures, towers and tiles, are reduced to debris. Nature, in the form of the doves that also symbolize peace, is destroyed as well. Some other fundamental oppositions, flight and the ground, snow and fire, past and present, are collapsed. And the blood at the end is real. Transcending perhaps the self-contradictions we have traced, Breton's surrealistic tactics here produce a terrorizing historical vision.[29]

Le paysan de Paris is also full of historical reference. The opening sentence of "Le sentiment de la nature aux Buttes-Chaumont" speaks of "ces temps magnifiques et sordides" (139), a formula that aptly characterizes Aragon's book. The park visited there is one of Haussmann's great achievements, a monumental triumph of engineering and landscape architecture that constitutes the "lung," the source of greenery and air, for the working-class areas in the northeastern part of Paris. As already mentioned, the preceding long portion of the book concerns the destruction of the passage de l'Opéra due to the prolongation of the boulevard Haussmann in the mid-1920s. Both places are the source for a sense of mystery in the line of Baudelaire and Nerval, the "métaphysique des lieux," "lumière moderne de l'insolite" mentioned early on (19–20). A corresponding passage on the park sounds more like Breton in celebrating in exaggerated fashion the surrealists' daring experiments with freedom, situated in the shadowy "banlieue" around Paris, scene of the most troubling French serial novels and films (166).

Surreal, perhaps, the intimate and strange glimpses of the shops, cafés, and massage parlors in the passage de l'Opéra and of the lovers, statues, and nocturnal scenery of the park. But not lacking historical and sociopolitical point. Aragon compares the opening created by the extension of the boulevard Haussmann to a kiss having unexpected results in "the gigantic body of Paris":

There is some prospect that a large volume of the human river which regularly ferries vast freightloads of reverie and languor from the Bastille to the Madeleine may spill through this new sluice, thus altering the whole mental course of a neighborhood, perhaps of a world. We are surely about to witness an upheaval in the modes of loitering and prostitution; it is not unlikely that this widened channel between boulevards and the Saint-Lazare quarter will open the way to strollers of a new, unfamiliar sort, their lives hovering between these magnetic poles, who stand to become the chief couriers of tomorrow's mysteries. (22)

The trajectory of the dreamy, languid population is the same as that in the omnibus strophe in *Maldoror*, which is also mirrored in the two long portions of *Le paysan*. But there is no trace of the threat that animates Lautréamont's passage, nor any of the indignation and argument in *Nadja* or that Aragon later displayed, or that would be needed to confront conditions in today's cities. Nonetheless, "Le passage de l'Opéra" is impressive and courageous in denouncing in matter-of-fact terms the complicity of elected officials and business interests in transforming the city to the detriment of various small establishments and individuals. Names are named, statements and articles cited, and an apparently quaint but actually very sensible urbanity is espoused, as in the case of the proprietor of the café Certa, who merits a better fate than that reserved to him by "une municipalité inconsciente," more concerned with widening streets than with preserving and encouraging "une urbanité si rare" (100). But all of this is to no avail. Nor did Blake have a noticeable effect on the direction of history.

"Le sentiment de la nature aux Buttes-Chaumont" is largely given over to explorations of a nocturnal form of the surreal, but it has its social awareness too, as in the mention of the metro line that derisively links the extremes of Nation and Dauphine (167), an extension of the Bastille-Madeleine axis. The park has its positive function, mainly as a degraded environment for the expression of all that is repressed in modern society (174). Despite contrasting passages of exaltation, the wistfulness of this view predominates, even producing an ironic vestige of the exoticizing tendency of earlier texts. Deciphering the messages on the plaques in the park, Aragon and his companions are called modern Champollions (201). It is a testimony to the power of his imagination that in such an environment he can achieve the experience of a superior state: "I attain myself beyond my own means [forces]" (175).

Although earlier the description of the park was mentioned as a parody of realistic conventions, the streets named are also inescapably suggestive of historical meaning. Most of the ones around the park refer to the Crimean War as well as to earlier events in the history of France and to those in other countries. This working-class area is called the "quartier du Combat" (173), and a couple of the streets are named for liberators of nations, including Bolívar. This reminds us that in the passage about the transporting power of stamp collecting in childhood Aragon evokes a confused sense of worldwide revolution. There he speaks, as we do now, of the "recent and unintelligible partition of the globe. Here are the stamps commemorating defeats and revolutions," which he claims not to understand, nonetheless evoking images of massacres, destruction of palaces, the song of a crowd marching toward a throne with its placards and demands (90).

Uncomprehending as he *may* be,[30] Aragon here evokes the scenario of global revolution that he was later to espouse. Nor is it insignificant that in the passage constituting the most violent attack on the reader he tells us that he will not complete the book, that not only will we understand none of his poetry but that we will get no description either of what the quartier du Combat is really like: "You will have to rely on yourselves to imagine this Siberia, . . . this Ural bordering the rue de Crimée" (222). The suffering of the extremely poor, which this book in no way conveys (although it does suggest what life is like for many who are not wealthy), is imaged by three regions of the former Soviet Union, a tactic repeated in some of Aragon's Resistance poetry.[31] Hence the link between Aragon's visionary mentality and his later revolutionary and communist politics is prophetically there. But so also are the continuing irony and massive destruction of twentieth-century history.

The Sordid Sublime ⚜
Burroughs's *Naked Lunch*

Aragon and Breton reveal much about the visionary impulse in the twentieth-century setting. The notion(s) of the surreal itself, passionate and con-
troversial stances on love, insanity, and history, premonitions of decentered
écriture, have a relevance beyond the subsequent manifestations of French
literature. This is the case for the work that might be considered the most
disturbing realization of the visionary later in the twentieth century, William Burroughs's *Naked Lunch*, completed in 1959.[1] Despite important
differences, this book is linked in many ways not only to the surrealists but
to a number of the writers treated earlier, from Blake to Lautréamont.

For one thing, like *Naked Lunch*, *Nadja* and *Le paysan de Paris* can be
situated in a tradition of "sordid" writing having its roots as much in
Baudelaire and Nerval as in Zola, writing that puts the reader in uncomfort-
able contact with all that is squalid in life: people, the body, the world
around us, language.[2] Lautréamont, Céline, Bataille, Genet, the Sartre of
Le Mur and *La Nausée*, Beckett come to mind here; on the American scene
some of those commonly associated with Burroughs are Henry Miller, Kerouac, Mailer, Southern, Ginsberg. But as I have shown elsewhere,[3] in *La
Nausée* Roquentin's unpleasant sexuality and his attraction to all that is
filthy and decaying leads to an overwhelming ecstatic experience as well as
to visions that, Sartre's attack on surrealism notwithstanding, remind us of

many a surrealist canvas and even of the dream in *Nadja*: a rag that turns into a hunk of rotten meat, spurting blood; a child who grows a third eye or a person whose tongue turns into an enormous insect; forests of penises and testicles, attacked by birds, oozing blood and sperm. Finally, in a book like Robbe-Grillet's *Projet pour une révolution à New York*, the sordid, the tortured female body, and the liberated language of écriture[4] propose a horrific worldwide vision of late-twentieth-century society and history.

Another strand mentioned at the outset but not significant in any of the works studied thus far, the experience of drugs, is important for *Naked Lunch*. In earlier works, exalted experience is conveyed with supposed immediacy as the account of prophetic inspiration, dream, hallucination, myth, love, generally within some "framing" narrative. Think of the various tactics in Blake Novalis, Nerval, Breton, even Lautréamont. But in Coleridge, De Quincey, Baudelaire, Rimbaud, and Huxley (whose title *The Doors of Perception* comes from Blake, who didn't need the stimulation of drugs), there is a tradition of drug experimentation, "direct" accounts of visions, and explanatory, even scientific and moralizing, analysis.

In spite of the allusion in my title and the recurrent references in *Naked Lunch* to "The Ancient Mariner," the master text here is not by Wordsworth but is instead another poem by Coleridge, "Kubla Khan."[5] In brief summary: this poem purports to be the spontaneous but inevitably fragmentary expression of drug-induced vision; this is expressed in a prose preface that claims not poetic but psychological interest and indirectly suggests Byron as the source of the impetus for publication; there are allusions to various ecstatic traditions; the exalted and trance states involve orgasmic imagery and the stimulation of an exotic Eastern "damsel"; its reference to Kubla Khan and his power, as well as to war, give the poem a faint political dimension.

That these features are of fundamental import may be suggested by their relevance to the range of works treated here, including those not concerned with drugs, and even some only glanced at, for example again *La Nausée*: unbearably intense experience conveyed in journal form; hallucination and the surreal; squalid sexuality yet exaltation of Roquentin's beloved Anny, who at the end is lost (to an Egyptian!); not a faint but rather a high degree of subversive sociopolitical commentary. In *Qu'est-ce-que la littérature?*, first published in 1948, Sartre analyzed *La Nausée* as intended to produce shame in its pre—World War II reader, which is close to the moral justification of *Naked Lunch* given by Norman Mailer at the book's celebrated trial for obscenity. Yes, drugs and the transformations of experience they provoke, together with provocative depictions of the body and a corresponding mixture of forms of writing, serve in *Naked Lunch* to generate a salacious and visionary, sometimes hilarious, universally frightening depiction of reality in America and the world.

In excerpts from the trial that preface *Naked Lunch* in the Grove Press edition, Norman Mailer finds it imperfect in form. Allen Ginsberg disagrees (xiv, xxxiii). In fact, the work reveals typical features of visionary form,[6] not the least of which is the surrounding of the central narrative, itself bizarre, by several other kinds of writing. True, Burroughs did not "write" the trial, but in it he is quoted on the scientific and medical validity of his treatment of drugs (xxxv). The book itself includes an introductory "Deposition" ("Testimony Concerning a Sickness") and, *after* the narration, an "Atrophied Preface," followed by an appendix on Burroughs's experiences with various drugs reportedly drawn from *The British Journal of Addiction* (vol. 53, no. 2). On a number of occasions the major narrative refers us to the appendix, and in other ways the various portions of the work tend to overlap and fuse. For example, the bad experience of a friend with marijuana, "I got the fear!," becomes that of the first-person narrator (20, 250), and the character Dr. Benway often uses language like that in the appendix. But in the main the surrounding discourses seemingly provide legal, medical, and scientific explanations of the strange events and visions of the narrative.

This reminds us of elements in Nerval and Breton, but the closest analogy is with "Kubla Khan," since in the introduction Burroughs claims that the main portion of *Naked Lunch* is based on detailed notes that he does not remember having taken during the "sickness and delirium" of drug addiction, from which he is now cured (xxxvii). The chapter entitled "Hospital" (55 ff.) corresponds most directly to the convention of direct note-taking, presenting "Disintoxication Notes," "Habit Notes," and "Habit Note continued." Similarly, the passage on the city of Interzone and the Meet Café is supposed to have been written "in state of Yage intoxication," and a later description of Yage as "space-time travel" recalls Burroughs's writing on that drug in the appendix as well as reproducing some of the language of the preceding description of the City and Café (106, 109–10, 253–54).

So removed is Burroughs in his cured state from the intoxication that is said to inform the narrative of *Naked Lunch* that the very title comes not from him but from Kerouac (xxxvii). As if to prove the point he proceeds to recount his cure with concision and clarity. And the introduction is severe in its moral condemnation of drug use, the appendix scientific in its vocabulary of "hallucination" and "psychosis," even if the effect of Yage, "a profound derangement of the senses," echoes Rimbaud (251, 253, 254).

So the "unmediated" experience/expression deriving from drug use, in a recognizable visionary convention, is framed by other kinds of discourse.

In the "Atrophied Preface" Burroughs generalizes from drugs to all sensuous experience in the well-known claim "There is only one thing a writer can write about: *what is in front of his senses at the moment of writing.* . . . I am a recording instrument. . . . I do not presume to impose 'story' 'plot' 'continuity' " (221). The advantage for the reader is that "You can cut into *Naked Lunch* at any intersection point" (224). Here Burroughs continues the antinovelistic tradition, humorously formulated in his explanation of the absence of notations of travel in the book: "I am not American Express" (218). As opposed to novelistic linearity, *Naked Lunch*, as the preface also claims, "spill[7] off the page in all directions, kaleidoscope of vistas, medley of tunes and street noises, farts and riot yipes and the slamming steel shutters of commerce [. . . .]" (229).

Nonetheless, even *Naked Lunch* cannot dispense with structuring elements. In addition to the frequent repetition that gives the book an almost musical texture as well as an uncanny familiarity, explanations and plots are furnished. The "Atrophied Preface" summarizes the story, but very late in the game: "Lee the Agent [. . .] is taking the junk cure . . . space time trip portentously familiar as junk meet corners to the addict . . . cures past and future shuttle pictures through his spectral substance vibrating in silent winds of accelerated Time" (218). Not only drugs but also the experience of withdrawal are described in the appendix as intensely hallucinatory (242), involving as in the above statement from the preface dislocations of space and time, dissolutions of body and person. In fact Lee is only intermittently noted, sometimes fusing with the narrative "I," in the preface and in other places (7, 68–73, 209, 219); elsewhere, another character, Carl, who also seems inseparable from the narrator, appears (47, 186 ff.). So the preface here attempts to stabilize an element, the human subject itself, that the experience of drugs radically questions.

In spite of, or in keeping with, his antinovelistic stance Burroughs also structures his narrative through two parodies of popular fictional forms, police stories and futuristic writing.[8] The book opens with a first-person narrative of a drug addict, called Lee on page 7, who is pursued by the police. The story is replete with details of New York City in the 1950s and reads like the B movie that it evokes (2).[9] The addict's escape is narrated in true non–American Express style, but we can nonetheless follow his trip, taken with various strangely named individuals and with a woman whose name, Jane, we learn only on page 19, to many localities in the American interior, Mexico, and finally Tangier. A year has passed by then, and Jane is dead (20).

More troubling than the names and discontinuities is the appearance already of the impossible bodily transformations characteristic of the futuristic portions of the book. We encounter Willy the Disk: "Willy has a round, disk mouth lined with sensitive, erectile black hairs" (7). Then there is the Vigilante, who loses ten pounds in ten minutes before disintegrating into a swarm of sex organs and defecating rectums: "I saw it happen" (8–9). Nonetheless, the major narration "concludes" by returning to New York (198 ff.). In another breathless first-person narrative, we see Lee kill two police officers, only to learn that no one remembers the two men: "I had been occluded from space-time" — "clawing at a not-yet of Telepathic Bureaucracies, Time Monopolies, Control Drugs, Heavy Fluid Addicts" (217).

In the intervening unfolding of the book, these futuristic experiences begin immediately after the notation of "normal" time and place: "A year later in Tangier I heard she was dead" (20). The "Benway" sequence is a nightmarish allegory of medical science gone mad in the control of human beings, a persistent theme from Nerval on. The names *Islam Inc.*, *Freeland Republic*, *Annexia* already suggest the geopolitical, economic, and religious propagandas and ideologies that will be displayed in succeeding chapters. The narrative is unhesitant and offhand: "So I am assigned to engage the services of Doctor Benway for Islam Inc."; "I reach Freeland, which is clean and dull my God"; "We are walking down a long white hall"; "We are eating lunch in Benway's office when he gets a call" (21, 28, 29, 36). Nonetheless, events are already impossibly wild; for example, there is a fight in an operating room in which Benway is aided by "Violet, that's my baboon assistant — only woman I ever cared a damn about" (30). And the call he receives alerts him and the narrator to the revolt of the patients in Benway's Reconditioning Center, "a scene of unparalleled horror" (37 ff.), a riotous enumeration and expansion typical of the impossible visions that Burroughs shows us.

The futuristic convention allows the reader, despite many difficulties, to make a good deal of sense of the major portion of what follows in *Naked Lunch*. A chapter like "Hospital," as already suggested, intrudes notes on disintoxication into the narrative, but then another crazy scene with Benway, this time with theatrical dialogue form, intrudes into *it*. An early chapter introducing Carl ("Joselito," 45 ff.) seems to be set in Mexico, whereas Lee's encounter with the junky Miguel might take place in France (65 ff.). The mistreatment of a vulnerable patient to which Carl is witness in the earlier chapter makes him its victim in "The Examination" (186 ff.) — since this occurs in Freeland it is out of temporal sequence. Who Carl and Joselito are is unclear, and this obscurity is magnified by the space-time confusion, but the underlying themes are apparent.

Elsewhere, despite the bizarre elements, including creatures like Mugwumps and food like the Black Meat, there is considerable progression and consistency. The Meet Café, the campus of Interzone University, the Market, and the City constitute *Naked Lunch*'s visionary geography. The first could be seen as Burroughs's version of the passage de l'Opéra: "The Meet Café occupies one side of the Plaza, a maze of kitchens, restaurants, sleeping cubicles, perilous iron balconies and basements opening into the underground baths" (54). And the "panorama of the City of Interzone" reenacts transhistorical experiences and terrestrial journeys reminiscent of but still different from those encountered in Novalis and Nerval: "The blood and substance of many races, Negro, Polynesian, Mountain Mongol, Desert Nomad, Polyglot Near East, Indian — races as yet unconceived and unborn, combinations not yet realized pass through your body." Vast migrations and voyages are evoked, then the "Composite City where all human potentials are spread out in a vast silent market" (106). Preceding and succeeding passages (53–54, 106–9) fill out the description of Interzone, at times recalling earlier texts (for example, some of the city poems in the *Illuminations*), but always with Burroughs's bizarre originality.

In the chapters emphasizing sexual materials we do not know the identity of Hassan and A. J., nor what Liquefactionists or Factualists are, and "Ordinary Men and Women" (121 ff.) is long and confusing. Still "Islam Incorporated and the Parties of Interzone" (144 ff.) lives up to its explanatory-sounding title. We get a lot of inane information on A. J. and Hassan, as well as two other zanies, Clem and Jody. But the narrator has to admit that the "exact objectives of Islam Inc. are obscure" (160). Nonetheless he clarifies the parties for us ("Now a word about the parties of Interzone," 162), only to conclude, "However the parties are not in practice separate but blend in all combinations" (167). With "The County Clerk" we think we are in the pre–civil rights American South but discover that the Old Court House is located just outside the Zone — a time and space warp that fits Burroughs's satirical aims regarding American and international realities. Finally we learn that Interzone is "a single, vast building" in proximity to the Island, a parody of a "British Military and Naval station" (178–82).

Nonetheless there are myriad features of *Naked Lunch* that are not "rationizable"; much in it, as in *Maldoror* and *Le paysan de Paris*, resists traditional analysis and understanding.[10] Note that there is absolutely no closure in the book, since the "preface" that *follows* the story itself ends with a brief, disjointed section called "Quick" (234–35). It begins in the first person: "I woke up with the taste of metal in my mouth back from the dead." At the end it returns to that "I," but not before introducing a brief exchange between Lee and an unnamed individual: "They are rebuilding the City"; "Yes . . . Always . . ." The last words, "No glot . . . C'lom Fliday," repeat-

6 Roberto Matta, Untitled drawing, D95/26, 1995. © 1996 Artists Rights Society (ARS), New York/ADAGP, Paris.

ing those of the Chinese dealer who refuses to service your habit (144), return us to the reality of addiction, as the book again spills off the page into the morosity of ordinary time and existence.

The analysis of the sprawling forms of *Naked Lunch* has already glimpsed the targets of Burroughs's satire, the obsessive themes of drugs and sex, and several outlandish sequences (see fig. 6). Amid all of this there is a serious visionary claim, evident early on in the contrast between terminal addiction, in the words of Benway, "virtual absence of cerebral event" (34), and the desire expressed in the introduction: "If man can *see*" (xlv). As in many of the works treated in earlier chapters, the visionary enterprise stresses the link between the writer and the reader.[11] The latter, "Gentle Reader," is on more than one occasion (40, 87) compared to the wedding guest in "The Ancient Mariner," compelled to listen to Burroughs's tales, even though conventional forms of fiction are later surmised to exist in order to keep the reader submissive, "Gentle" (218). Instead we are warned that the words of this text may tear us and imprison us (230).

At the outset the reader is inscribed in dual form, first as the "Ivy League advertising exec type fruit" to whom the narrator appears as "his idea of a character" (1), then as a more savvy type: "You know the old cop bullshit" (5). For the first various notes are provided, for example, what "junk" and the verb "to grass" mean (xxxvii, 2). These however rapidly become utterly unreal.

The second reader provides a takeoff point for the bodily metamorphoses that constitute an important portion of the strange things we see: "You know how old people lose all shame about eating, and it makes you puke to watch them? Old junkies are the same about junk [. . . .] their guts grind in peristalsis while they cook up, dissolving the body's decent skin, you expect any moment a great blob of protoplasm will flop right out and surround the junk" (5). We expect it, and pretty quick we start to see it, in the Vigilante already mentioned and then in Bradley the Buyer (15–18), who commits sex and murder by surrounding and assimilating people and who has to be destroyed with a flamethrower. In heroin overdose, Carl separates "clear and sharp from a great distance" from himself (49), and in more surreal fashion the Sailor's face dissolves, his mouth undulating forward "on a long tube" before coming back into focus (52–53). Thus among the notes and nightmares of disintoxication and withdrawal we are perhaps by now not surprised to encounter a hospital guard "in a uniform of human skin" (57) or, later, medical objects stranger than those in the shop in the passage de l'Opéra, "a jock-strap designed to protect some delicate organ of flat, fan-shape" (203).

We in some sense thus become accustomed to the hallucinatory metamorphoses induced by drugs, metamorphoses that elsewhere are presented in terms recalling experiences in earlier writers — Blake's sensuous Beulah, the timeless floating experiences in *Aurélia*, bathing and Oriental exoticism in Novalis and Aragon. "*Notes from Yage state*" (109) describe a serenity, a sense that "everything is free to enter or to go out": "A beautiful blue substance flows into me. . . . I see an archaic grinning face like South Pacific mask. . . . The face is blue purple splotched with gold. . . ." Burroughs quickly turns sardonic (110), as he is elsewhere (xxxix, 20), but the sense of peace, of total openness, of an experience of the archaic, is appealing.

Immediately, though, the room takes on the aspect of a Near East whorehouse and the narrator feels himself transformed into a Negress, followed by Polynesian, Near Eastern, South Pacific notes, "in some familiar place I cannot locate. . . . Yage is space-time travel. . . ." Again recalling Novalis and Aragon, exotic prostitution seems inescapable as a degraded emblem of the visionary realm, yet the expansion in time, race, and sex is again attractive.

This may indeed be the only nonhostile evocation of female sexuality in the book.

The "Atrophied Preface" treats the notion of the porousness of the body in tenser fashion. To those who think he is in possession of himself, mainly in control of the entity that occasionally "jumps in the body," Burroughs responds, "*Wrong! I am never here. . . . Never* that is *fully* in possession." He concludes: "I am always somewhere *Outside* giving orders and *Inside* this straight jacket of jelly that gives and stretches but always reforms ahead of every movement, thought, impulse, stamped with the seal of alien inspection. . . ." (221). Compared by one critic to the dualistic distrust of the body found in Gnosticism,[12] this is a literally alien experience of the flesh, of insideness and outsideness. In the following pages (222–23), it leads not only to the attack on "The Crime of Separate Action," that is, to the belief that everything is connected, explaining why all the elements in *Naked Lunch* are led "to occupy, at that intersection point, the same position in space-time"; it also leads to a sense that when the writer looks in the mirror his reflection may no longer obey, to a profound sense of the instability of the subject such as we earlier encountered.

Two other passages framing the description of *Naked Lunch* as spilling off the page echo prophetic and visionary themes more positively and in explicitly sexual ways (229). The first concerns the "Word": "The Word is divided into units which be all in one piece and should be so taken, but the pieces can be had in any order being tied up back and forth, in and out fore and aft like an innaresting sex arrangement." Slang expression and pronunciation, multiple and "perverse" experiences of sex, do not diminish the exalted vision of language as the Word, nor the sense that, despite the fragmented modalities of expression, some superior unity of revelation is imminent. The next paragraph does not hesitate to speak of revelation and prophecy, again as related to sexual activity:

This is Revelation and Prophecy of what I can pick up without FM on my 1920 crystal set with antennae of jissom. . . . Gentle Reader, we see God through our assholes in the flash bulb of orgasm. . . . Through these orifices transmute your body. . . . The way OUT is the way IN.

This is the only positive religious passage in the book, with "Revelation," "Prophecy," and "God" all the more striking because of the sexual allusions.[13] The out-in theme reappears not only in physical but in nearly mystical ways — "Through these orifices transmute your body." This recalls the Blake of the *Marriage*, in a homosexual version of his "improvement of sensual enjoyment." Nonetheless, in Burroughs's contradictory, degraded, and ecstatic presentation of the body, this positive passage in no way redeems other demeaning addresses to the reader, given in similar terms: "Gentle Reader, the ugliness of that spectacle buggers description"; "Why so pale and wan, fair bugger?" (39, 126).

Finally, another passage recalls Blake in its embattled expression of expansions from the physical to the visionary:

Black insect lusts open into vast, other planet landscapes. . . . Abstract concepts, bare as algebra, narrow down to a black turd or a pair of aging cajones. . . .

How-to extend levels of experience by opening the door at the end of a long hall. . . . (224)

Perhaps recalling Blake's angel's infernal vision, which narrows down to Aristotle's *Analytics*, abstract concepts here are reduced to the vilest of physical realities; but insect lust, which is often depicted in the book, can expand in extraterrestrial fashion. Extending levels of experience is the essential visionary project, one that, just above, the text claims to be combated by the "Press" of all political persuasions: "Above all the myth of other-level experience must be eradicated. . . ." Burroughs here is a latter-day Blake, the Blake of the *Marriage* and the preface to *Milton*, striving to open us to the possibility of the visionary, which according to both is opposed by the primary media of manipulation and control.

As frequently, then, the visionary involves other levels of experience, a provocative view of the body, and an oppositional sociopolitical stance, all inextricably linked. Recalling certain features in Breton, we know that Burroughs has adopted a position of utter opposition, a rejection both of politics and of political revolution, a hatred especially of family, nation, and prevailing (!) modes of procreation.[14] Sexuality, increasingly anguished in earlier works studied, in *Naked Lunch* (which in this respect apparently differs from the work of the surrealists) reaches a kind of destructive paroxysm. All of these themes are forcefully treated in Burroughs's book, in a combination of fierce moral seriousness, visions of the horrible and disgusting for their own sake, and bizarre forms of humor whose function is not always easy to define. Thus Burroughs on the body, morality, and history, in sordid enumerations, expansions, and apocalypses.[15]

Although Lautréamont certainly has his moments, no writer but Burroughs expands limitlessly on the infernal scene in *The Marriage of Heaven and Hell* where the simian-human body, mixing sex, eating, and excrement, drives us, along with Blake and the angel, away. Benway's baboon assistant Violet, "only woman I ever cared a damn about" (30), and any number of references to purple-assed baboons and the Upper Baboonasshole, correspond to repeated stress on male anal sexuality, animality, and murderousness.

As critics have by now come to note, misogyny is the rule.[16] Women are "cunts" or "gashes," and there are repeated outlandish denigrations of their sexuality: "nameless female substances, enough to pollute a continent"; "cunt saignant cooked in kotex papillon" (62, 130). This holds for futuristic fantasy, as the Divisionists are all homosexuals who tell boys, "If you go with a woman your replica won't grow" (166). Women's vaginal pressure is a threat, even to Steely Dan (91), and a related and recurrent element, the lynching of a black man, is fused with the ancient theme of vaginal teeth: "whimpering women catch his sperm in vaginal teeth" (85).

These themes are so extreme as to be farcical, and can be turned into farce at will, which in no way diminishes their maliciousness. At the end of Hassan's orgy a "horde of lust-mad American women rush in," screaming at the hanged boys, "You fairy! You bastard! Fuck me! Fuck me!" (82). Elsewhere there is anguish, and the threat of castration is not hidden: "Male and female castrated he them" (40). Burroughs knows his Freud or, others might think, his Lacan. Only once, in a scene from A. J.'s blue movies, typically after Johnny has removed Mary's vaginal teeth, does there seem to be a mutually satisfying male-female sexual experience (99–100). But there is much mutilation and murder in these passages as well, for example when Mary earlier lunches on Johnny's genitals (97). That this is supposed to occur in a film, and that Johnny is able to spring to life again (more precisely, Mark turns into Johnny), are perhaps mitigating features. Nonetheless this incomplete survey shows that, in *Naked Lunch* more even than in the other works examined, the visionary countertradition in no way opposes the antifemale dimension of mainstream literature; rather it exacerbates it and calls insistently for a feminist response.

Although Burroughs is quoted at the trial as striving through his work to help us control, and not be controlled by, sex (xxxv), and although one passage in *Naked Lunch* seems to correspond (43–44), the book creates the opposite impression: one of pervasive, uncontrollable, and destructive homosexuality.

From the vocabulary of the opening pages — "fruit," "fag," "queer," "A real asshole" (1–3) — to the activities or tendencies of numerous characters — Lee (7, 68–73), Benway (28), Carl (in "The Examination"), Clem (158) — homosexuality is virtually everywhere. In the opening chapter, only Jane's pimp lover, for whom the narrator reserves special scorn, in part, be it said, because "he degrades the female sex," is heterosexual (20). In Interzone Keif's vicious chauffeur is the only nongay (177–78). The narrative "I" is not different. He projects "disembodied lust" toward the schoolboys outside his hospital (58), and his explicit description of sexual sensations, although it involves girls as well as boys, focuses only on the male organ (101–2). As novelist, too, homosexuality and pedophilia are taken for granted: "If one of my people is seen in New York [. . .] and next sentence Timbuktu putting down lad talk on a gazelle-eyed youth [. . . .]" (218). Finally, it has been remarked[17] that the sole alternative to drugs in the introduction is precisely this kind of homosexual submission: "Only way to protect yourself against this horrid peril is come over HERE and shack up with Charybdis. . . . Treat you right kid. . . . Candy and cigarettes" (xlvii) — pervasive, obsessive, domineering, not at all liberating.

The anal theme is one source of grotesque humor, or lack thereof, in the actions of Sollubis (118), the fate of the Professor in the hands of the sultan's army (84), stories of talking asses (132), and Doc Scranton's ability to pass you his "on three feet of in-tes-tine" (126). The anal as erogenous finds its contrary in the constipation of the sexless drug addict (xlvi). But it also can be the means of domination, as in Benway's story of a boy he conditioned to defecate at sight, followed by sex — "And he was a lovely fellah too" (28). Excretion inevitably implies eating, "the long lunch thread from mouth to ass all the days of our years" (230), which accounts for the repeated mentions of repulsive foods and meals — the Black Meat, Mugwumps and Reptiles (53–55), the kidney worm (58–59), and A. J.'s practical joke menu (149).

Concerning organs of ingestion and excretion, in another scene Schafer argues that the body is inefficient: "why not have one all-purpose hole to eat *and* eliminate?" — to which, reminding us of the Vigilante and Bradley, Benway responds, "Why not one all-purpose blob?" (131). The extreme of this is the Liquefactionist program involving "the eventual merging of everyone into One Man" (146), which seems a parody of Blake's myth of the regeneration of the universal human being. But that casts an ambiguous light on the claim for an orgasmic vision of God discussed earlier.

The most extensive accumulation of sexual materials occurs in the chapters "Hassan's Rumpus Room" (74 ff.) and "A. J.'s Annual Party" (88 ff.), which Burroughs unpersuasively presents as a Swiftian tract against capital punishment. This does not diminish the importance, as executions increase in the United States, of the need indeed to see the death penalty "on the end of that long newspaper spoon" (xliv). Although both these chapters are not about capital punishment but about a murderous form of sex, they nonetheless involve expansions and apocalypses that are not exclusively parodic.

Both do contain outrageously wild elements: the invasion of the American women, the pornographic films produced by the Great Slashtubitch.

These features do not prevent homosexual activity from being extensively and explicitly evoked — to cite only one example, the Mugwump's rape and hanging of the boy. The earlier chapter also contains an anthology of pedophilic scenes (77–78): two Arab boys, a satyr, and a "naked Greek lad," a Negro and an "exquisite Chinese boy," a Javanese dancer and an American boy. This is a version of myth and Orientalism — the legendary satyr, the mixture of races. But the last scene in the series, that of Arab women bestially raping a struggling and crying "little blond French boy," leaps into history. The year of the American publication of *Naked Lunch*, 1962, was the year Algeria regained its independence from France, more than 130 years after the first French troops arrived and after years of guerilla warfare, terrorism, repression, and torture. Destructive sexuality and destructive history converge.

History and sexuality play roles in what I have been calling sordid enumerations, expansions, apocalypses. The first starts as a parody of apocalypse as last judgment — "the last Erection" (75 ff.). The blast is blown by a garbage collector, waking pimps and whores amid a landscape of fetuses, condoms, Kotex, and "shit wrapped in bright color comics." Then like Icarus a naked Mr. America, "burning frantic with self bone love," hurtles through space, insulting the Louvre, icon of traditional culture, through a nightmarish scenery that echoes early passages (4, 14): polluted harbors, flaring gas-well fires, and finally "black mud with tin cans and beer bottles, gangsters in concrete, pistols pounded flat and meaningless to avoid short-arm inspection of prurient ballistic experts." This is a wild but haunting scene, evocative of much in the book and in American life — the sordid body, the conflict of popular and high art, nationalistic expressions of self-love, crime, the ravaged environment.

After the youth is hanged and the "anthology" of pedophilia appears, the "expansion" begins anew, as Hassan dances the Liquefactionist Jig and unleashes an enumeration of orgasms, by couples outfitted with artificial wings, aerialists, equilibrists, boys by the hundreds, the strange creatures Latahs and Sollubis, Aztec priests sacrificing boys, junkies in trains, and many others, leading finally to "pictures of men and women, boys and girls, animals, fish, birds, the copulating rhythm of the universe," which flows through the room, "a great blue tide of life." As in the Yage state discussed earlier, but here through the sexual, a sense of universal energy is generated, a sordid ecstasy not without analogues in earlier writers. But again we are faced immediately with Burroughs's absurd comedy, as Hassan and A. J. argue: "This is your doing, A. J.! You poopa my party!"

The sexual "perversions" in the A. J. chapter also eventuate in apocalyptic and mythic expressions (93 ff.). Following the acrobatics of Mark and

Johnny, an extensive enumeration unfolds, once more including elements previously seen (harbors and skyrockets and penny arcades and dirty pictures, 76), then more and more a "non-Western" landscape in which repeated transformations between boys and old men alternate with scenes of youthful sex and aged destruction, a literally phallic death: "He stand up screaming and black blood spurt solid from his last erection [. . . .]" Near the end the effect of heroin on an old junky is to recreate the "immaculate" boy he once was, reversing an earlier process: "Time jump like a broken typewriter, the boys are old men, young hips quivering and twitching in boy-spasms [. . . .]" The impact is hardly agreeable, but in this sequence sex and drugs, normally at war, combine in a universal montage of space and a disconcerting jump in time.

Mythic expansions also crown the final Mary-Johnny encounter. They fall through space and to earth. From their decaying bodies "great rank buds" and tubers sprout and they explode into the natural scene, leaving behind only the statue of a boy smiling the "half-smile of a junky on the nod" (100). This seems a sordid version of the passage in *Aurélia* where the giant woman fades into nature, leaving behind a bust and a sense of desolation. As always the drug experience is there, and the chapter ends with a fade-out, reminding us of the particularly base medium, pornographic movies, in which the expansions and proliferations we have witnessed are achieved.

Sex in *Naked Lunch* is *very* much degraded, yet it has a squalid visionary potential. This is partly explainable, according to Catherine Stimpson,[18] in terms of the history of awareness and repression, as the writer's hideously parodic depiction of his own sexual orientation. Concerning homosexuality, one of the curiosities of the obscenity trial is the discussion between the judge and Allen Ginsberg about the possibility of a future political party representing homosexuals (xxviii–xxix). At the time Ginsberg thought it likely, and history has certainly moved in that direction. The sexual is indeed political, as is much else in Burroughs's book: not only government, nation, and law but also religion, medicine, and the media of communication. It is political — and prophetically historical, with simultaneous emphasis on America and the world.

Burroughs despises the United States as intensely as a century of French writers, from Baudelaire to Breton, hated the hypocrisies of their nation. The American interior is "a vast subdivision, antennae of television to the meaningless sky," but the evil is not recent: "America is not a young land: it is old and dirty and evil before the settlers, before the Indians" (11). No amount of censorship can prevent "popular songs and Grade B movies" from "giving away the basic American rottenness" (133). Racial violence and ethnic prejudice, including anti-Semitism,[19] appear repeatedly (14, 166,

174–75); they are localized however, in a delusion common in the early sixties, in the South.

Sex, satirized in the rout of crazed American women and the supremely narcissistic Mr. America, is shown to be a national obsession. In a ludicrous scenario inserted in "Hospital" (62–64), the likelihood that the singer of "The Star-Spangled Banner" is homosexual produces chaos. In the same chapter the narrator reveals that the president is a junky whom he services through what appear to be homosexual practices. Lately this has become more difficult, so that "I sometimes have to slip my penis under his left eyelid" (67). Lautréamont demeaned the divinity by calling him a drunk and a pederast. God in effect having died in the consciousness of many, it is now for the leader of the most powerful country on earth that such treatment is reserved.[20]

But Burroughs takes his shots at religion as well. Christ gets rejected with Mohammed, Confucius, and Buddha, a "notorious metabolic junky" (113–15). Ditto for Paul, "a really evil old shit," and the belief in "hypostatic union with the Lamb" — to be sure involving sodomy and bestiality (27, 150). In a typical fusion, American evangelical style is used to describe the manipulative effect of Islam: "And now The Prophet's Hour"; "Now friends of the radio audience, this is Ahmed your friendly prophet" (112, 161). The satire is broad, but one would have difficulty denying its aptness in America and the Middle East since *Naked Lunch* was published.

Burroughs is most compelling in his claim that the *"junk virus is public health problem number one of the world today"* (xliv). Think of what it has become during the intervening years! Combining several metaphors, he calls it not only a virus, but a pyramid, a monopoly, an industry. Junk is quantitative, measurable, the ideal product, the ultimate merchandise, since no sales talk is necessary. The more you use the less you have. "Opium is profane and quantitative like money" (xxxviii–xxxix). Small wonder that he paraphrases the words of the *Communist Manifesto*: "Paregoric Babies of the World Unite. We have nothing to lose but Our Pushers" (xlviii). But Burroughs can hardly reach the millions who live in misery and are afflicted with drug addiction in the United States and elsewhere. While the governments of the West trumpet the victory over communism, the drug scourge continues where we live, in an obscene enactment of the arguments of Engels and Marx.

Another feature of Burroughs's depiction of drugs is that of a worldwide operation in which, as many have perceived since, governments, police agencies, and secret services participate. "Junk is a big industry," and an American is quoted as wanting to perpetuate its epidemic in Mexico (xl). Bradley the Buyer, once the "best narcotics agent in the industry," has to be eliminated because he has become "a menace to the narcotics industry on all levels" (15–18). Benway, that "manipulator and coordinator of symbol systems, an expert on all phases of interrogation, brainwashing and control," views drugs as "an essential tool of the interrogator in his assault on the subject's personal identity" (21, 25).

This passage, together with many others on brainwashing and thought control, epitomizes the Orwellian strain that has always been recognized in *Naked Lunch*. It again indicates how the drug virus permeates everything, governments included. The good government-evil criminal dichotomy is dissolved. More fundamentally, as with many of the writers treated in this study, the moral antinomy is absolutely challenged, here through the notion of drug dependence. "The face of 'evil' is always the face of total need," and the answer to the question, "*Wouldn't you?*" is always yes (xxxix).

Curiously, when in the "Atrophied Preface" Burroughs speaks in the form of his two given names, William Seward, he promises to "cowboy [murder] the white whale," "reduce Satan to Automatic Obedience, and sublimate subsidiary fiends," eliminate the genitally invasive candiru, and "issue a bull on Immaculate Birth Control. . . ." (226). Here the writer assumes attributes opposed to his typical stance. Popelike, he will issue instructions not for conception, since homosexuality cannot produce it, but for birth control, and he will reduce various forms of satanic revolt to absolute obedience. Drugs, conceptions and practices of sexuality, governments, and religions all seek to subdue us, somewhat as in the "Fast-Fish and Loose-Fish" chapter in *Moby-Dick*. Most threateningly here, the rebellious writer seems to participate.

This last note parallels a feature suggested earlier, the substantial apparent correctness of Benway's views. It is he in fact who furnishes one of the most horrible visions of what drug addiction is: "Squatting on old bones and excrement and rusty iron, in a white blaze of heat, a panorama of naked idiots stretches to the horizon." No sound, since speech centers have been destroyed, singed flesh from electrodes applied to spines. "A group of children have tied an idiot to a post with barbed wire and built a fire between his legs and stand watching with bestial curiosity as the flames lick his thighs. His flesh jerks in the fire with insect agony" (25). For Benway this is a digression, but despite the troubling link between him and his creator, for Burroughs it is what we should see on the end of our *Naked Lunch* fork.

Drugs furnish another element in *Naked Lunch*: they contribute to its worldwide scope. An early passage (6–7) introduces features that will resonate later: "Sometimes you can see maybe fifty ratty-looking junkies [. . . .]" This is followed by a varied enumeration of persons and places in New York City, then this: "The world network of junkies, tuned on a cord of rancid jissom, tying up in furnished rooms, shivering in the junk-sick morning [. . . .] In Yemen, Paris, New Orleans, Mexico City and Istanbul — shivering under the air hammers. . . . Istanbul is being torn down and rebuilt, especially shabby junk quarters. Istanbul has more heroin junkies than NYC." Granted, sex is not absent from this wasted scene, but it is essentially junk that reconstitutes in degraded fashion the worldwide geography of the visionary tradition.

The movement between New York, recalling London and Paris in the works earlier, and that distant geography corresponds to the dual history, American and global. As for the United States, near the end "the tiresome old prophet" points us forward in "space-time direction" to the hair, shit, and blood spurting out on the wall in 1963, the year President Kennedy was to be assassinated (226). In the "futuristic" portions, as the name Islam Inc. indicates, the history of the Middle East, source of mystic revelation in earlier works, is again, often farcically, at issue. The agitation by A. J. for the destruction of Israel is dismissed as a cover story. Whereas Clem and Jody are supposed to be boosting the value of their Venezuelan oil holdings, they are really Russian agents out to embarrass the United States. "Morbid crowds follow them about hoping to witness some superlative American outrage" — for example, "their plan to kidnap the Black Stone with a helicopter and substitute a hog pen" (158–60).

Just about everyone's commitments or sensitivities, religious and patriotic, take a beating here, not least Arab religious and political movements. It is stated later (230) that "the Inscrutable East need a heap of salt to get it down." So much for exoticism. And the narrator describes the rank and file of Islam Inc. as a "rout of Mullahs and Muftis and Musseins and Caids and Glaouis and Sheiks and Sultans and Holy Men and representatives of every conceivable Arab party." At their meetings people are burned or shot to death, "Nationalist martyrs with grenades up the ass mingle with the assembled conferents and suddenly explode," and the British prime minister is sodomized, "the spectacle being televised to the entire Arab world" (145–46). The work's anal obsession persists, and no one would argue that Arab religious and political aspirations are given sympathetic expression. What is? But in its antic way, the passage is historically prescient of events since 1959.

An earlier sequence (37–45), the revolt of the inmates of the Reconditioning Center in Freeland, is longer, carnivalesque but also not without historical suggestiveness.[21] Inmates in various grotesque states, the unreal fauna of Burroughs's world, Latahs and simopaths, are not nearly so unsettling as the rampant bores who besiege us with their stories. Arab rioters mingle with obscenely dancing boys and women; horrible scenes of rape and castration unfold.

Astonishingly, something like the history of AIDS[22] is eerily foreshadowed, in the passage about a venereal virus supposedly indigenous to Ethiopia (insults of course for Ethiopians and Egyptians). "So it started in Addis Ababa like the Jersey Bounce, but these are modern times, One World. Now the climactic buboes swell up in Shanghai and Esmereldas, New Orleans and Helsinki, Seattle and Capetown." Since the disease shows a predilection for blacks, white supremacists are elated, but British sailors have caught it and the white coroner of Dead Coon County, Arkansas, is burned to death because he shows its symptoms "fore and aft." Moreover, "the Mau voodoo men are said to be cooking up a real dilly of a VD for the white folks." The "One World" not only of drug addiction but of sexual disease, together with murderous racial hatred — from 1959 through the current history of AIDS Burroughs is monstrously on target.

But this sequence ends in universal farce as the narrator shows us "Rock and Roll adolescent hoodlums" storming the streets of all nations. Among other atrocities they desecrate the Mona Lisa, open zoos, chop the floor out of airplane lavatories, ram the *Queen Mary* into New York Harbor, disconnect artificial kidneys, "shit on the floor of the United Nations and wipe their ass with treaties, pacts, alliances," provoking mass flight to the borders by tourists. The inane quality, the exuberance, the multiplicity and comedy of these scenes have a strangely liberating effect, perhaps not least of all because of the desecration of the world political organization by youth and by the ever-present bodily functions.

Naked Lunch's many "expansions," some extending "levels of experience" through drugs and sex, some absurd in the extreme, are filled with ominous world history, arguably as grim now as then. Writing in 1992 I proposed the words *drugs, CIA, Bush, Noriega, Saddam,* and AIDS in support of that argument, and I see no reason to change them now, except by addition — *Bosnia, Somalia, Rwanda, Nigeria, Haiti, Cuba, Algeria* . . . The reader might add his or her list of warlords, dictators, fanatics, and politicians. Although *Naked Lunch* ends despondently ("No glot . . . C'lom Fliday"), some have been heartened by a passage reminiscent of the sixties (134–35) in praise of cooperatives, as opposed to democracy, which is viewed as cancerously spawning bureaucracy with "the complete parasitism of a virus" until "the structure of the state collapses." The trouble is that this occurs in a diatribe by Benway. As we have seen, the extent to which he resembles his creator suggests the extent to which we have also to distrust Burroughs. In particular, in this passage Benway, with the transition only of a reference to a tapeworm, begins to talk of the Arab boy who could play a flute with his ass . . .

Another passage (168–69) is to me more interesting in the bleakness with which it nevertheless asserts a hopeful perspective. Completing the description of the party of the Senders, it is stated that there is finally only one Sender, not an actual person but the Human Virus. The following lines do not make complete sense to me, but they conclude with the comprehensible definition of what Burroughs means by Master Virus — the "Deteriorated Image" of a species. There follows Burroughs's twentieth-century version of the anguish experienced by a Blake or a Nerval: "The broken image of Man moves in minute by minute and cell by cell. . . . Poverty, hatred, war, police-criminals, bureaucracy, insanity, all symptoms of The Human Virus." Inexplicably the narrator then adds, "*The Human Virus can now be isolated and treated.*" Nothing in *Naked Lunch* tells us how.

chapter seven

Visionary Women ~~
Wittig's *Guérillères* and Kincaid's
At the Bottom of the River

The preceding chapters have traced a remarkably persistent tradition of writing, though one with a variety of permutations. In one way or another, all of our authors are visionary in that they reject the apparently solid world of reality in which most of us seem to exist. Both Blake and Aragon use the word *visionary* itself to describe their effort to transcend or dissolve the perceptual experiences that we take to be true. Blake's fourfold vision and Swedenborgian "Memorable Fancies"; dreams, imagination as "magic idealism," the fantastic form of the *Märchen* in Novalis; dream, trance, and insanity in Nerval; even the antivisionary writing in *Maldoror*; the various versions of the surreal in Breton and Aragon; and finally the drug and sex transmutations to other levels of experience in *Naked Lunch* — these are the diverse means of access to the visionary. And we have seen the range of writing, of visionary "textualities" that are thereby generated and deployed. More or less violently or obsessively, too, the resistance to what is thought to be real extends to a questioning of or vehement challenge to traditional values and societal institutions — of religion, family, gender, and sexuality, not to speak of government. Sexual themes are indeed increasingly anguished throughout these works, whose potential for unmitigated rebellion against the sociopolitical order is also apparent from Blake to Burroughs.

7 Leonor Fini, *Les Apatrides,* 1994. © 1996 Artists Rights Society (ARS), New York/SPADEM, Paris.

Although my scope is wide, I am vividly aware of the partial nature of my treatment, which is largely due to the limits of my reading and linguistic competence. Another book might treat comparable writing in other European writers and languages, the literatures of the Americas, and the languages of the Middle East as well as North African francophone writing.[1] And, although it might be tempting to view recrudescences of apocalyptic writing as an anticipation of our oncoming millennium, it seems to me more likely that the persistence of such works throughout the two hundred years since the French Revolution and the Terror has a more directly pertinent historical suggestiveness. Some very talented writers have wanted to show us that what we take to be *real* is illusory, have given eloquent, if often horrendous, testimony to the oppression imposed by religious, societal, and sexual beliefs and forms.

However oppositional in the terms summarized above, this tradition nonetheless cries out for a feminist critique, in that on the issue of sexuality these works differ from the mainstream of modern Western literature only in being more obsessively male-oriented. "Masculinist" at the least in Blake and Novalis, deriving from an anguished experience of sexuality in Nerval, blatantly sexist in the surrealists, and homosexual in a horrible way in Lautréamont and Burroughs, the "visionary" is troubling in its subjection, utilization, brutalization of the female, and notably of the female body. Think of Blake's sexual symbolism, the sacrifice of the mother in *Heinrich*, Nerval's dismembered female bodies, the rape of women, as well as the murder of boys, in *Maldoror*, the exploitation of the female form in surrealist iconography, and Burroughs's not at all funny scorn for all that is female. Early on I suggested that feminist interpretations of Blake's later sexual symbolism, in *Milton*, show it perhaps to be emblematic in simultaneously making sex the key to the visionary and also presenting the body, with its multiple potential for "perversions," as the source of evil. The "visionary" thus almost literally embodies a recurrent, two-century-long anguish of sexuality, from the passage concerning the monkeys in Blake's *Marriage* to the repugnant images of *Maldoror* and *Naked Lunch*.

The consideration of two women writers, Monique Wittig and Jamaica Kincaid, the one an avowed lesbian living in virtual exile from her native France, the other a native of Antigua who published the account of her personal pains and anger only after having achieved notoriety as a successful *New Yorker* writer, will not dissipate these contradictions of the sexual. But it will introduce a female corrective and perspective.[2]

Among the many women writers who might have been treated, Wittig is appropriate in that she follows upon the French surrealists and yet presents an impressive refutation of the sexism of Western thought.[3] *Les Guérillères*, my primary text here, is a celebration of the female body as opposed to the obsession with the male in Lautréamont and Burroughs; her *Corps lesbien* can be read as a lesbian counterpart of *Naked Lunch* and Burroughs's later writing.[4] But *Les Guérillères* goes beyond the fixation on the female body. Relatively pale as visionary writing, it nonetheless contains passages of ecstatic intensity and mythic beauty and is reminiscent of the millennial in Novalis in its suggestion of an ultimate reconciliation of men and women. This is not to imply that *Les Guérillères* is better, or more acceptable, than Wittig's later books, from which men are entirely absent. Indeed, the most incisive feminist interpretations of *Le corps lesbien* and other later Wittig texts emphasize both their wholly positive view of female homosexuality and their potential to be "truly the subversive discourse of The Body Politic."[5]

Jamaica Kincaid can be linked to Wittig through the resemblances between Wittig's first book, *L'Oppoponax*, and passages in *At the Bottom of the River* and elsewhere that dramatize the formation of the submissive female self through the influence of mother and school. On the other hand, Kincaid's obsession with the theme of motherhood, so different from the lesbian and amazonian motifs in Wittig, has lent itself to explanation in Freudian and Lacanian terms,[6] so much so that the contrast between Wittig and Hélène Cixous, expressed as that between amazons and mothers, might be reformulated in terms of Wittig and Kincaid. Lesbian notes are not lacking in Kincaid's work, however, and they should lead us to temper the absoluteness of this opposition. Most of all, though, I am interested in Kincaid's frightening and beautiful writing because its visionary qualities largely derive from sources other than those seen in the earlier writers. In her work visionary writing is nonbiblical, not essentially derived from the traditions of the Middle East, but rather Caribbean and perhaps sub-Sahara African, as well as strikingly female. Indeed, in an interview with Selwyn R. Cudjoe, Kincaid stressed the influence of her mother, voodoo magic, an awareness of a higher reality beyond the normal sense world, and the inseparability of waking and dream states.[7]

Published in 1969, in the immediate aftermath of the most recent failed upheaval (with delusive revolutionary potential) in the history of late Western capitalism, *Les Guérillères*, which appeared in translation in England and the United States within a few years, became one of "the most widely read and frequently cited non-American feminist" works of our times. It also contributed, along with other Wittig criticisms of Cixous's "essentialism," to the "splintering" of the French feminist movement in subsequent years.[8] From our perspective, then, *Les Guérillères*, like the *Marriage* and *Heinrich*, *Aurélia* and the surrealist texts, appears as a visionary work produced in what was believed to be a revolutionary setting, expressive of utopian hopes for the transformation of society and the renovation of human sexuality.[9]

Hence *Les Guérillères*'s antinovelistic form begins and (nearly) ends with a poem or litany of phrases evoking female violence and all action as overthrow: "TOUT GESTE EST RENVERSEMENT" (5, 143).[10] Amid its discontinuous segments, statements of what "the women say" ("Elles disent"), lists of women's names providing a basis for a new female mythology,[11] sensuous descriptions of items presumably expressive of female experience (spices, fruits, vegetables, birds — see 9, 11, 18, 122–23, and similar writing in Kincaid),[12] and intrusions of the letter O (emblematic of female anatomy as well as of women's ability to elude male discourse and systems and even to imprison and overthrow men, 14, 114) — amid all of this Wittig's text repeatedly depicts female warfare against these same systems.

We recognize familiar feminist-socialist-Marxist-Leninist-Maoist phrasing: attacks on proprietors and possessors, allusions to Flora Tristan, a hundred flowers blooming, and power at the end of a rifle (76, 85, 102, 114, 131, 141). In a systematic disorder, various phases of the war (beginning, progress, defeat, ultimate victory) are evoked.

Certain of these deliberately nonsequential passages include a questioning by the women: "What was the beginning?" (30). Elsewhere, from some distant moment in the future they examine photographs of women's strikes and demonstrations (39), but later in the text they seem to be involved in an intermediate phase of flight and the establishment of a colony (49–50). Evocations of defeat and victory in battle (76–78, 104, 108, 115) frame their vision, in a surreal setting, of a new world order (86). Interestingly, they imagine themselves as "already in possession of the industrial complexes" (95). But earlier in our reading (73), after the nonspecific notation "Things being in this state," we had read a passage in which domestic, textile, secretarial, and industrial machinery are burned by the women, leading to a bacchantic dance. From the debris they reassemble and paint "grotesque grandiose abracadabrant compositions to which they give names." This reminds us of efforts by poets from Rimbaud to Breton and trade unionists from Marx to French factory workers to subvert the industrial system and its products.[13]

Toward the end of the work there is an increasing interplay between passages describing battle and reconciliation. Young men and women gather to bury the dead and solemnly celebrate peace (124), but on the following page the battle rages on; the two sexes vow that they have ended the last war in history (127–28), but the next segment shows the women on a grueling long march early in the conflict. Late in the text (130) the women proclaim hellish anger and, in a passage recalling Burroughs, minus the humor, they promise violence to "theatres national assemblies to museums libraries prisons psychiatric hospitals factories old and new from which they free the slaves."

After the last sequence of alternating moments of sexual strife and peace the concluding paragraph of the work, unique in its use of the formal past tense (*passé simple*) and of the plural *we*, evokes what appears to be the final end of the war and an opening to the future, but perhaps in terms too familiar for us to accept:

Moved by a common impulse, we all stood to seek gropingly the even flow, the exultant unity of the Internationale. An aged grizzled woman soldier sobbed like a child. Alexandra Ollontaï could hardly restrain her tears. The great song filled the hall, burst through doors and windows and rose to the calm sky. The war is over, the war is over, said a young working woman next to me. Her face shone. And when it was finished and we remained there in a kind of embarrassed silence, a woman at the end of the hall cried, Comrades, let us remember the women who died for liberty. And then we intoned the Funeral March, a slow, melancholy and yet triumphant air.

The closing sense of triumph, the feeling of collective sacrifice by women of the working class, the references to the Internationale and to pre-Stalinist Russian socialist feminism and the comradeship of discredited parties: all of this produces in historical hindsight a terrible sadness, and not because one accepts United States State Department propaganda about "the end of history." As with all utopias, historical events overtake the desiring imagination. But here as in her later work, Wittig again brings to mind Blake as a lonely figure continuing to pursue the visionary path, and not without agonizing relevance to contemporary historical events. Let us think of persistent antigay sentiment in the United States and of the systematic use of rape of women in what for a time was Yugoslavia.

Or perhaps the best way to gauge the continuing importance of Wittig's message is to quote the passage in which she ascribes to her women the role of utter resistance expressed differently in Breton and Burroughs:

They say that they foster disorder in all its forms. Confusion troubles violent debates disarray upsets disturbances incoherences irregularities divergences complications disagreements discords clashes polemics discussions contentions brawls disputes conflicts routs débâcles cataclysms disturbances quarrels agitation turbulence conflagrations chaos anarchy. (93)

Or again, in fiery female-Blakean terms:

They say, compare yourself to a slow fire. They say, let your breast be a furnace, let your blood become heated like metal that is about to melt. They say, let your eye be fiery, your breath burning. They say, you will realize your strength, arms in hand. They say, put your legendary resistance to the test in battle. They say, you who are invincible, be invincible. They say, go, spread over the entire surface of the earth. They say, does the weapon exist that can prevail against you? (136–37)

Having noted the recurrence of the link between visionary writing and the fearful grasp of history, as well as the appetite suggested above for continuing resistance to that grasp, we come to an even more important issue, the reclaiming of the female. *Les Guérillères* is a signal expression, amid the exuberant debates of feminists in France and the United States, of the reappropriation of the female from the oppressive male order so clearly enshrined (even!) in the "oppositional" texts that we have been studying.

Inevitably there is much violence directed against men. The women do battle with bared breasts (100), and in the first female state men are emasculated (114–15). Those who, like the Lemnian women, slaughtered men are celebrated (112). Recognizable and not-so-recognizable myths represent powerful women and exhort them to be bloodthirsty (85, 119, 120, 127). Scenes of submission of men (98) give way to mockery of the penis and feminization of the male body (106). Paroxysms of rage (116–18) accompany descriptions of torture and slaughter (110, 118); in one of these, which features exhibition of the dried skins of the victims, the historical resonances are unbearable. But the following, reminiscent of passages in *Milton*, reminds us of the sadistic component that seems inevitably to accompany the drive toward visionary sexual liberation:

Then the women reach their prey at a bound and, giving the signal,
joined at once by the others, they begin to dance while uttering cries,
swaying to and fro, while their victim writhes on the ground, shaken by
spasms and groaning. (120)

But, as mentioned above, elsewhere the women renounce violence against men (99). There is even a passage in which heterosexual lovers seem to escape lesbian persecution (123). Then, almost in a permanently realized version of Charlotte Perkins Gilman's *Herland*, toward the end the men admire the women warriors' horticultural expertise and the mildness of their climate (137–38). This is followed by mighty embraces in which the defeated men transfer to the women their most treasured attributes, celebrating them as "thrice-great, woman trismegista" (142), a female appropriation of the epithet of the divinity of occult sciences.

But this reconciliation in no way implies submission to accepted sexual arrangements, namely marriage (108) and the prescribed role of procreation: "They say, take an example from the wild birds who, even if they mate with the males to relieve their boredom, refuse to reproduce so long as they are not at liberty" (135). This last explains the rejection of the defeated male's claim to be necessary as the source of sperm (as well as all work, government, and writing, 97), together with the presence of numerous girl children and the pride in the vulva as "emblem of fecundity and the reproductive force in nature" (31). Birth thus becomes the capture of a child by a warrior — not enjoyable but heroic: "The women look over Emily Norton's shoulders at the effigies of women with mouths wide open, screaming, squatting, the child's head between their thighs" (72). As we shall see, this is anything but an acceptance of the Freudian argument that the child is a replacement for the absent penis.

On the contrary, there is an emphatic celebration of the female body amid recurrent scenes of collective lesbian sex (9, 15), often bacchantic in intensity (19–20, 60–61, 70–71). Although in the background there are reminders of male prejudice, for example, the stench emanating from various bodies of water (10, 16, 20), numerous passages evoke and detail the labia (9, 31) and every aspect of the vulva (22–23, 48–49). These very beautiful passages serve as a corrective to the obsession with the male body in texts from *Moby-Dick* to *Naked Lunch*. The vulva becomes an instrument of navigation (10) and — exposed — a mirror reflecting the sun, with a Medusa-like effect (19); elsewhere it serves to hide the fire that the women have stolen (45).

We should also note the function of analogy in the passages on the female organs. They are compared to many things, from the spider's web and quicksilver to flowers, moons, butterflies, birds, fruits, coral, shells, eyes, mouths, geometric figures, rings, jewels, treasures, and gems. But they are also compared to "traps vices pincers" (19, 23, 31, 32, 44, 48). These last, familiar threats or fears, explain why at a certain point (49) the women decide that the "feminaries have fulfilled their function," that indeed they are "indoctrinated" with ancient (male) texts. The feminaries are texts from which the young girls learn, and, together with female storytelling and female myth, as well as the recurrent "Elles disent," they indicate the link between the body and writing, even if, *pace* Cixous, Wittig never identifies the two.[14] For, having sufficiently exalted their sexual organs, the women realize that it is no longer useful, in symbols and conventional figures, to see the vulva as the center of the universe (61, 66).

Refusing any longer to be prisoners of their own ideology in exalting one part of the body "on the grounds that it was formerly a forbidden object," the women "perceive their bodies in their entirety" (57). Rephrased, this argument, that "any symbol that exalts the fragmented body is transient, must disappear," allows the women, confident in "the integrity of the body," to march "together into another world" (72). Recalling Blake and Rimbaud,[15] this culminates the process by which female sexual anatomy is rediscovered as a prelude to a utopian opening to the future as "another world."

Similarly, Wittig's celebrated subversion of traditional myths and creation of new feminist ones are also seen, early on in the unfolding of the text, as "no longer in order" (30). In keeping with that I will for the moment have little to say of this feature of *Les Guérillères*. Instead I will give attention here to passages that, in vigorous intellectual terms, confront the patriarchal ideology underlying the view of the female body and its accompanying mythology.

These passages correspond to philosophical or doctrinal pronouncements seen in the earlier writers, with the exception of the passages' feminist stance, which, despite differences noted above, Wittig shares with Cixous as well as with Luce Irigaray, Julia Kristeva, and many American feminists. Hence, first of all, the (negative) elements with which women are associated are denounced as the products of "mechanistic reasoning," the systematic relation of "opposite terms." Like Blake refusing such simplistic separation of contraries, jokingly playing with the myth of Scylla and Charybdis, the women proclaim such thinking "no longer valid" (78–80). Male-female opposition, seen as "essential difference" through "biological variation," is also denounced and linked to similarly untenable biological arguments for the inferiority of nonwhites. Behind it all lurk "domination and appropriation," "the same domineering oppressors who sleep crouched over their money-bags" (100–101).

The feminist-Marxist thrust expands to include as targets Freud, Lacan, and Lévi-Strauss, among others. The women first seem to doubt that they can spit on the phallus, stop speaking men's language, burn their currency, effigies, art, and symbols. But immediately they add, "I refuse to mumble after them the words lack of penis lack of money lack of insignia lack of name." They refuse the category of possession, for if they are to take over the world it is in order to dispossess themselves of it immediately, "to forge new links between myself and the world" (106–7). Similarly, echoing phrases of Freud and Lévi-Strauss ("Has he not indeed written, power and the possession of women, leisure and the enjoyment of women? He writes that you are currency, an item of exchange"), the women prefer death to submission (115–16). Elsewhere, as already mentioned, men's monopoly of the symbolic order is subverted (112–14). And, in a rewriting of the ultimate patriarchal myth, that of the earthly paradise, the women, realizing that "he has invented your history," threaten to crush men as serpents under their heels, crying "Paradise exists in the shadow of the sword" (110–11). Here the inversion of values seen as early as Blake takes on a new and differently threatening but liberating aspect.

As suggested earlier, in the pursuit of freeing the female, *Les Guérillères* is not so much a visionary work, transforming the physical world before our eyes, as it is a utopian allegory, revealing what needs to be destroyed and suggesting what needs to be discovered. Nonetheless, it is already clear that the work hardly reads like a realistic novel. In addition to nonrealistic elements already noted there are a variety of surreal and futuristic features, all finally in the service of an experience that provides a female version of myth and collective ecstasy.

Early on, one of the women asserts that that which is is, adding that that which is not also is (14). This refusal of the principle of noncontradiction fits well with the evocation of strange animals, some Burroughs-like (22, 57), incomprehensible machines and unvisualizable geometric figures (26, 69), impossible but supremely deadly weapons (103–4, 118–19, 120), combatants with insect eyes, and women from whose orifices spinning glands produce wings, causing them to resemble giant bats (108, 132).

As in a number of the earlier writers, a strange architecture is sometimes involved. In one of these scenes (88) we "see" hundreds of thousands of gem-studded spherical habitations, some transparent, some floating in air, some attached to tall pylons, all of great height among the heavenly spheres. A Rimbaud-like pseudoperspective ("It is not possible at this distance to determine what allows the inhabitants to gain access to their houses") does not produce the sense of unreality characteristic of some of his prose poems. Instead the fantastic setting becomes the locus of the women's armed rebellion, as from all points they march on the city, singing warlike songs. Another structure, only initially and superficially recalling Blake, evokes hundreds of thousands of cell-like receptacles hollowed out of a rock face in which the naked women sleep. Comparisons of each cell to an egg, a sarcophagus, an *O*, and the indication that in one's cell one is out of contact with all the others, mix suggestions of female sexuality and gestation but also of isolation — and death. But not this: "It is a place of privileged sanctuary ("refuge") though not sealed off." Finally at nightfall voices are heard, at first confused, then distinct: "This order must be changed, forcefully repeated by a thousand voices" (86). In still another passage (90–91) the women's critical discussion of accepted logic about progressions, cycles, and myths leads them to a laughter so powerful as to destroy the edifice in which they find themselves. Bricks, gilded paneling, mosaics fall, and the women destroy the remaining statues, continuing to laugh even as they evacuate those *not* wounded, until the building is totally destroyed. "Then they lie down and fall asleep."

So the quite individual visionary architecture in *Les Guérillères* leads where everything else leads: toward the millennial battle. As for transformed consciousness, that is also represented, by a series of passages concerning drunkenness and trance. In one of these (60–61) narcotics and aphrodisiacs produce delirium and nightlong dance but also incoherence on the part of some, which is criticized by others of the women. Succeeding passages (62, 64) represent the trance state in brutal, frightening terms, with

eyes, spitting mouths, bleeding gums, but also with song. Else-
3) there is a more stately version of the bacchantic state:

that they leap like the young horses beside the Eurotas. Stamping
d they speed their movements. They shake their hair like the bac-
cnantes who love to agitate their thyrsi. They say, quickly now, fasten
your floating hair with a bandeau and stamp the ground. Stamp it like a
doe, beat out the rhythm needed for the dance, homage to warlike Mi-
nerva, the warrior, bravest of the goddesses. Begin the dance, step forward
lightly, move in a circle, hold each other by the hand, let everyone observe
the rhythm of the dance. Spring forward [Paraissez en avant] lightly. The
ring of dancers must revolve so that their glance lights everywhere.

Particularly in a work that has warned us about the danger of traditional
myth and that is filled with non-European female versions ranging from
Mexican warrior and sun goddesses to Asian women who have fought off in-
vaders and others who have pursued the sun and saved the universe (26, 27,
65, 74, 80–81),[16] it is a delicate question which passages should be chosen for
analysis. Here indeed a familiar Greek setting and divinities are evoked.
But, despite the presence of the thyrsi, Dionysus makes no appearance, and
the goddess of wisdom is also goddess of war. Moreover, Wittig's text
differs in crucial ways from the quintessential modern poetic expression of
the theme, Coleridge's "Kubla Khan." In that poem, as noted in the
previous chapter, the element of war is only mentioned, as opposed to the
consistent allegory of Les Guérillères. In Coleridge too, an isolated male
speaker can only imagine the ecstatic state, provoked by the loss of a music-
playing "damsel." Here, on the contrary, female expression is foregrounded
— "Elles disent," as always. Moreover, the experience is collective. And the
rhythms, not yet frenzied but stately, as I have said, produce not an obscuring of consciousness but an enlarged horizon of vision: "Il faut que le cercle
des danseuses fasse sa révolution et qu'elles portent leurs yeux de toutes
parts." The translation obscures much that is subtly meaningful here: the
circle and the female dancers that are so resonant throughout the work, the
activity by which they lucidly cast their eyes in every direction, the turning
that is also revolution.

I will close my discussion of Les Guérillères with another beautiful passage (52–53) that conflates and transforms traditional myth in the interest
of superior female knowledge, once again leading to the collective bacchantic dance: "Dans la légende de Sophie Ménade, il est question d'un verger
planté d'arbres de toutes les couleurs. Une femme nue y marche. Son beau
corps est noir et brillant."[17] Too long to quote in its entirety, the passage

may be summarized as follows. A woman named Sophie Ménade recounts a legend about a magically colored orchard where walks a beautiful naked black woman, whose hair is made of snakes, the favorite called Orpheus. Orpheus advises her about what fruit to eat and predicts that she will grow until her forehead touches the stars and she acquires knowledge.

Treated critically in a passage mentioned earlier, the Garden of Eden motif returns, as does the figure of the snake, which exercises much fascination elsewhere (74). Medusa is there too, and explicitly Orpheus, with the danger that his counseling and advising role (the snakes make up the woman's "chevelure conseillère") may perpetuate the dominant role of the male poet. But he is merely the woman's favorite snake, and Sophie Ménade's name, fusing wisdom and bacchantic ecstasy, implies a superior unity of faculties and experiences. Moreover, the snakes produce music with every movement the woman makes. Most of all, it is not Orpheus but Sophie who recounts the legend, producing pressing questions from the other women.

To the first questions Sophie responds that the woman in the orchard "will have a clear understanding of the solar myth that all texts have deliberately obscured." What our male writers sought, Wittig's alter ego says, women shall possess. To their further questions Sophie responds with an incantation: "soleil qui épouvantes et ravis / insecte multicolore, châtoyant / tu te consumes dans la mémoire nocturne / sexe qui flamboie / le cercle est ton symbole / de toute éternité tu es / de toute éternité tu seras." Here we have a glimpse of eternity, which unites opposites (fearful and ravishing, nocturnal but flaming) and repeats the fundamental female symbols: sun, insect, sex, circle. In response the women begin a circular dance, stamping the ground and clapping their hands, giving voice to a song, "un chant dont il ne sort pas une phrase logique." "Phrase" may mean "musical phrase," as the translation suggests, but also "sentence"; other than "coherent," "logique" of course literally means "logical." Once again, woman's discourse, transforming traditional myth, leads to a collective female knowledge bordering on ecstasy, together with a glimpse of a form of expression that transcends the known limits of language.

The beautiful black shining woman in the multicolored garden of Sophie Ménade's legend fits well with the vivid writing of Jamaica Kincaid, writing that has occasional links with earlier authors as well as Wittig but that is nonetheless highly original. Caribbean and perhaps African magic and myth in the colonial and postcolonial setting, an exacerbated mother-daughter love-hate relationship, the quest for the female self amid visionary voids and expansions: these are the themes we shall pursue, first selectively in the opening "stories," with brief excursions to other works by

Kincaid, then more fully in the concluding three pieces of *At the Bottom of the River*, "Blackness," "My Mother," and the long title story.[18]

Less than three pages long, "Girl" (3–5) sets the tone for Kincaid's marvelously concise writing. One can think of it as a condensed version of Wittig's demonstration of the formation of the young female self, except that the field of action is not that of the school, as in *L'Oppoponax*, but the home. In a rapid-fire series of imperatives, directions, and questions, the mother tells the girl everything she should know about domestic skills ("Wash the white clothes on Monday"), bodily cleanliness and future sexual behavior ("on Sundays try to walk like a lady and not like the slut you are so bent on becoming"), feminine comportment and class awareness ("you mustn't speak to the wharf-rat boys, not even to give directions"; "don't squat down to play marbles — you are not a boy, you know"). References to religion (Sunday school), the supernatural ("don't throw stones at blackbirds, because it might not be a blackbird at all"), and the secrets of folk medicine ("this is how to make a good medicine to throw away a child before it even becomes a child") are not lacking. The girl barely gets to protest, but the overall tone, while domineering, is also affectionate and empowering, particularly regarding men, who are entirely marginal to the intense mother-daughter relationship. There are father's clothes to be ironed, a lover to be bullied, a child to be avoided, a baker to be cajoled: "you mean to say that after all you are really going to be the kind of woman who the baker won't let near the bread?"

But Kincaid does not neglect the oppressiveness of the school experience, deftly evoked (as in Wittig) and the source, one imagines, of the French writer's later oppositional stance and of the anger expressed in Kincaid's *Annie John* and particularly *A Small Place*.[19] In the former we see the heroine reading *Roman Britain* and *A History of the West Indies* and being punished by having to copy out the first two books of *Paradise Lost*. But if her teacher is reading *The Tempest*, we may recall Aimé Césaire's *Une Tempête*, just as the girl's favorite book, *Jane Eyre*, recalls Jean Rhys and *Wide Sargasso Sea*. Most of all, her reaction to a picture of Columbus in chains leads her to think that he got what he deserved (39, 73, 77, 82, 92).

A Small Place is infinitely more angry, detailing the horrors of conquest and the slave trade. These include the number of black slaves swallowed by the ocean, the "English maritime criminal, Horatio Nelson," the beginnings of Barclays Bank in the slave trade, the Northern Irish teacher who tells the children to stop acting like monkeys, the Condrington family, specialists in breeding blacks for slavery, the irony that to commemorate their independence Antiguans "go to church and thank God, a British God," the fury at having been deprived of a tongue, at having to write in "the language of the criminal." In the corruption of independence local politicians are not spared, but neither are the Syrian and Lebanese drug dealers and landowners who exploit the population of former slaves. The Middle East, source of so much inspiration and violence, even here seems inescapable! But the tourists who are attacked from the outset are mainly *us*, and if as readers we resist that accusation[20] we cannot ignore the threat of American power in the reference to the invasion of Grenada and the fear that it could occur again in Antigua (9, 11, 14, 24, 26, 29, 31, 41–46, 51, 58, 61–62, 72–74, 80).

In *River* these themes are fleeting but not less significant. Aside from various articles imported from England and glasses commemorating a coronation, as well as suggestions of later travel to various regions of the United States (7, 10, 13, 32–35), in "Wingless" we see small children reading simple words and sentences, producing beautiful penmanship, learning the English calendar and system of money and weights. The book they read from is Charles Kingsley's *The Water Babies*, with its finally un-Blakean chimney sweeps and apparent prettification of child labor: " 'You, of course, would have been very cold sitting there on a September night, without the least bit of clothes on your wet back; but Tom was a water-baby, and therefore felt cold no more than a fish' " (20–21).[21] Later the visionary sequences of "What I Have Been Doing Lately" are initiated when the speaker steps outdoors into a drizzle or damp dust tasting "like government school ink." This small notation speaks volumes and is related to the following vision of beautiful black and shiny people, which, however, is quickly negated: "All around me was black mud and the people all looked as if they had been made up out of the black mud" (40, 44). Only later will the racial shame engendered by an oppressive education be eradicated.

But the mother-daughter obsession is more traumatic, and is the source as well of many fantastic passages. The second piece in the collection, "In the Night" (6–12), is a Caribbean version of dream experience. The narrator, a child who wets her bed and dreams of a baby being born, nonetheless projects a temporal distance: "my mother, who is still young, and still beautiful." Supernatural presences loom — the spirit of a murdered woman, the dead Mr. Gishard standing under a tree, the eery night-soil men, a woman who removes her skin, drinks the blood of her enemies, and is said to be reasonable in admiring honeybees and the hibiscus but who also brays like a donkey. "Magic realism,"[22] perhaps, but particularly inflected by the figure of the mother, who describes the "jablesse" (presumably a deformation of *diablesse* — the mother in *Annie John* speaks a French patois): a person who can turn into anything, whose eyes shine like lamps, and who looks like a beautiful woman. But the mother is a beautiful woman! Moreover, the positive father figure in this story is a night-soil man, whose lack of substance is stressed by the fact that he is introduced as a negation: "No one has ever said to me, 'My father, a night-soil man, is very nice and very kind.' "

At the end of "In the Night," beginning "Now I am a girl," the narrator dreams of marrying a red-skinned woman with black bramblebush hair in whose lap she can bury her head. Together they would lead a childlike existence, throwing hardened cow dung at people they don't like, stealing green figs, and being forever "completely happy." In another pointed historical note, they also frighten little children with John Bull masks. This is the phase of utter identification with the mother, but the inevitability of future separation is threatened by pictures of good-byes on a jetty, like the end of *Annie John*.

The separation is painfully dramatized in the two parts of the following piece, "At Last" (13–19), whose title stresses the temporal dimension of anticipation and fulfillment. The fulfillment is the anguished meeting between aged mother and grown daughter, now immeasurably apart: "So I was loved?" "Yes." A man appears briefly, only to die, whereupon a worm crawls out of his leg. The mother recalls acting like a jablesse, shining in the dark, appearing as a man or a hoofed animal.

The second part apparently represents the reflections of the daughter on children and on the passage of time: "Children are so quick"; "A pirate's trunk. A fisherman's catch. A tree, bearing fruits. A bullying boy's marbles. All that used to be is alive here." But the reflection on time opens up to the nonhuman, a little as in Blake, to reflections on the life of ants, oranges, frogs, chickens:

Unusually large berries, red, gold, and indigo, sliced open and embedded in soft mud. The duck's bill, hard and sharp and shiny; the duck itself, driven and ruthless. The heat, in waves, coiling and uncoiling until everything seeks shelter in the shade.

Sensing the danger, the spotted beetle pauses, then retraces its primitive crawl. Red fluid rock was deposited here, and now the soil is rich in minerals. On the vines, the ripening vegetables.

But what is a beetle? What is one fly? What is one day? What is anything after it is dead and gone? (19)

Here the recurrent mother-daughter thematic engenders a Blake-like[23] reflection, recalling "The Argument" and passages in *Milton*, on the relationship between concretely existing creatures and a vast geological time frame, on the now-existing and the now-about-to-die.

The following four pieces, some aspects of which have been mentioned, ring various changes on the mother-daughter, temporal-visionary motifs.

Among the school children in "Wingless" (20–28), the narrator can distance herself in the reiterated "But I swim in a shaft of light, upside down, and I can see myself clearly, through and through, from every angle." Older than the girl in the opening story, this "I" has emotions of desire, competition, vulnerability in relation to the mother: "That woman over there. Is she cruel? Does she love me? And if not, can I make her?" Substitute female objects of attraction begin to emerge in the repeated claim to have "humped" other girls.[24] Nonetheless she feels defenseless and small, and there are a couple of sharp dialogues, mean versions of "Girl." At one point she follows the woman she loves, who walks on water and magically slays a man who emerges: "Then, instead of removing her cutlass from the folds of her big and beautiful skirt and cutting the man in two at the waist, she only smiled — a red, red smile — and like a fly he dropped dead." The girl's desire for this castrating mother produces another reflection on the nonhuman, the animal and the insect world, before mysteriously regressing to the childhood state, "now, even now, so still in bed, in sleep."

"Holidays" is on the whole a happy piece, but even so the narrator thinks of the superstitious belief that "if you sit with your hands on your head, you will kill your mother" (31). Its last segment is rare in that it presents the vacation laughter of a family complete with handsome man, beautiful woman, and happy children (35–36). But in "The Letter from Home" (37–39), a woman, well prepared (one may feel) by "Girl," recounts in singsong fashion the numerous domestic tasks that she performs. A marital situation emerges, with husband and children, but he is whiny and sick, about to be taken off to the hospital. At the same time, the magical returns as the narrative "I" sheds her skin, and the closing encounter with a man is deathly and refusing: "I saw a man, He was in a shroud, I sat in a rowboat, He whistled sweetly to me, I narrowed my eyes, He beckoned to me, Come now; I turned and rowed away, as if I didn't know what I was doing." Previous to that, the domestic frame had abruptly veered to the geological and the religious: "the angiosperms prospered, the mammal-like reptiles vanished (Is the Heaven to be above? Is the Hell below? Does the Lamb still lie meek? Does the Lion roar? Will the streams all run clear? Will we kiss each other deeply?)." Blake, Novalis, and Nerval come to mind, with the exception that the human equivalent to cosmic and supernatural issues, the kiss between lovers, has the baleful end that I have already cited.

The title "What I Have Been Doing Lately" (40–45), and that piece's initial situation, "I was lying in bed and the doorbell rang," resemble the preceding in their quotidian tone. The quest for the mother persists, too, as the speaker goes on a strange journey at the end of which she finally encounters a lone figure. At first she is sure it is her mother, then realizes it is not, although she is not frightened since she can "see that it was a woman." She imagines sarcastic responses to the woman's question about what she has been doing lately, but instead begins the story again: "I was lying in bed." The action recurs with differences, including the encounter with the beautiful black people who turn into mud, and concludes with another memory of childhood and motherly care, concluding, "And I went back to lying in bed, just before the doorbell rang." Differing somewhat from earlier stories dramatizing one or another phase of the mother-daughter relationship, this piece implies the perpetual possibility of reenacting the loss, the search, the regression. And another kind of visionary movement and landscape is engendered by the mother-daughter relationship — an endless journey, a large body of water to be crossed, years of waiting, a hole into which the narrator falls, glimpsing unreadable foreign writing. Recalling Alice as well as the visionary writers, the "I" here exerts unusual power in reversing her fall and in ordering the hole to close up: "You can close up now, and it did."[25]

So we repeatedly encounter in these pieces visionary openings that recall some of our earlier writers but that are strikingly original due to the Caribbean, and thus racial, component as well as the female orientation — domination of the mother and elimination, sometimes gruesome, of the male. The three last stories, progressively longer (seven, nine, and twenty pages), explore these concerns more fully, through anguish providing resolution of the racial, mother-daughter, and visionary motifs. The titles, "Blackness," "My Mother," "At the Bottom of the River" (Kincaid's final visionary setting), correspond.

These "stories" are so magical as to merit close attention. The opening sentence of the first (46–52) illustrates Kincaid's verbal felicity in the language of the criminal: "How soft is the blackness as it falls."[26] This first part (there are two others, the second shockingly political, the third concerning the speaker's child, for the "girl" here is again a mother in her own right) describes a dissolution of self occasioned by the falling of darkness. "The blackness is visible and yet it is invisible, for I see that I cannot see it. The blackness fills up a small room, a large field, an island, my own being." This is different from, say, Nerval's treatment of vision and the impossibility of vision. The familiar Antiguan scenery dissolves, but the blackness is interior also, and not only in a racial sense. It flows through her veins, entering her "many-tiered spaces," so that significant words and events vanish. What we might describe as a materialist-mystical experience follows, as she is annihilated, becomes formless, "absorbed into a vastness of free-flowing matter." She is erased, can no longer say her name or point to her "I," "swallowed up in the darkness so that I am one with it."

The speaker tries to retain small flashes of experience in her daily life, clinging to common and familiar objects, but surprisingly discovers her own foot as separate from herself. Her question "What is my nature, then?" she answers with reflections on evolution, evoking familiar images of "a miner seeking veins of treasure," of stark mountains turned to meadow, with "a spring of clear water, its origins a mystery." But the concluding sentence of this part seems uniquely female, uniquely characteristic of the woman who changed her name to Jamaica Kincaid:[27] "And again and again, the heart — buried deeply as ever in the human breast, its four chambers exposed to love and joy and pain and the small shafts that fall with desperation in between."

In shocking contrast, illustrating the continuing presence of destructive history that the visionary text can never ignore, in the second part the woman dreams of a band of guerrillas who pass between the sun and the earth, so that "they blotted out the daylight and night fell immediately and permanently." No one can persuade me that Kincaid is ignorant of the apocalyptic-political significance of such symbolism in the tradition treated in this book. In the last decade of the twentieth century the reader might think of guerrillas and death squads and dictators in Caribbean states and of long-term United States responsibility therein.[28] The narrator's immediate reaction is more specific to her life: "No longer could I see the blooming trefoils, their overpowering perfume a constant giddy delight to me," nor the domesticated animals, wild beasts, hunter and prey, "the smith moving cautiously in a swirl of hot sparks or bent over anvil and bellows." The men scorch flowers with their breath and with bare hands destroy the marble columns of the woman's house. Then she watches "their backs until they were just a small spot on the horizon."

Frightful as this evocation is, then, it is passing, giving way in the last part to evocation of the woman's child. First there is an extraordinarily positive and satisfying sense of maternity as she observes the girl and remembers having chewed food for her when she was weak: "This is my child!" Harmful notes are not avoided as she describes the girl's hyperbolic cruelty to a hunchback boy. Her arms grow to incredible lengths, her whisper shatters his eardrum, and with his sense of direction destroyed she builds him a hut on the edge of a cliff, daily observing his nearness to "a fate which he knows and yet cannot truly know until the moment it consumes him."

The girl now experiences the metaphysical awareness first expressed by her mother, tracing all things back to their beginnings, moving from dark to light, from death to death. In the fleeting existence that her mother gave her, "she embraces time as it passes in numbing sameness, bearing in its wake a multitude of great sadnesses." This nonetheless allows the mother to accept the annihilation of self that blackness first threatened. She shrugs off conflict, hatred, and despair, and in love stands "inside the silent voice," enfolded by it so that "even in memory the blackness is erased." Prehistoric motifs return, as "lions roam the continents, the continents are not separated." The woman is no longer "I"; she is "at peace," "erased."

Having achieved maternity and reconciliation with the loss of self in the context of destructive history and at the cost of a compensatory brutalization of the male, in "My Mother" the woman narrator finally, and very movingly, achieves reunion with her mother. This may be thought to redeem the sadness of the break with the mother in *Annie John*, corresponding to the dedication, in part, of *At the Bottom of the River* to Kincaid's mother.

"My Mother" (53–61) unfolds in nine sequences containing familiar themes and transformations. The first concerns guilt over the desire to kill the mother, the latter's suffocating forgiveness, and the girl's growing of breasts on which to rest her head and hence comfort herself, culminating in a concretization of hypocritical poses that recalls Blake. With the tears she has cried the girl makes a pond between them, a poisonous pond filled with unnameable invertebrates: "My mother and I now watched each other carefully, always making sure to shower the other with words and deeds of love and affection." Back in a more familiar setting, in the second part the girl sits in the dark on her mother's bed, "trying to get a good look at myself." The effort of achieving self-identity under the influence of the mother is clear, particularly since the mother first lights then extinguishes candles, so that at the end the daughter is still on the bed, "trying to get a good look at myself."

The next four parts involve monstrous transformations as the two turn into reptiles, then journey across a valley into a cave, where they stay for years, the girl growing a special lens to see in the darkness and a special coat to keep warm. Along the way they visit the Garden of Fruits, leaving in their wake as they depart "small colonies of worms." The daughter tries to accomplish her desire to kill the mother by building a floorless house over a hole, but her mother again walks miraculously, this time on air, before vanishing. The daughter then grows to monstrous height, but the mother is three times as tall so that sometimes she "cannot see from her breasts on up." Once again, although there is nothing like the elaborate attention to the female body found in Wittig, the breasts reappear as symbol of physical maturity and separation from the mother. Furious anger then gives way to sleep, "the only dreamless sleep I have ever had."

At this point the mother decides on a journey of departure, the jetty of *Annie John* reappearing. But this time the separation is positive, as the daughter encounters on a new island a woman with a different face but feet completely like her own, in whom she recognizes her mother. Peace descends on her, and in a different house she and her mother grow together, eating from the same bowl, sleeping on the same pillow. In passing we note another dead youth as well as a domineering father. In the concluding part, men appear only as servants of the reunited mother and daughter, in a magically regressive mode of writing:

> The fishermen are coming in from sea; their catch is bountiful, my mother has seen to that. As the waves plop, plop against each other, the fishermen are happy that the sea is calm. My mother points out the fishermen to me, their contentment is a source of my contentment. I am sitting in my mother's enormous lap. Sometimes I sit on a mat she has made for me from her hair. The lime trees are weighed down with limes — I have already perfumed myself with their blossoms. A hummingbird has nested on my stomach, a sign of my fertileness. My mother and I live in a bower made from flowers whose petals are imperishable. There is the silvery blue of the sea, crisscrossed with sharp darts of light, there is the warm rain falling on the clumps of castor bush, there is the small lamb bounding across the pasture, there is the soft ground welcoming the soles of my pink feet. It is in this way my mother and I have lived for a long time now. (60–61)

The mother's power and the subservient role of men, the imperishable lushness and bounty of nature, the pastoral symbol of innocence, the child's body rediscovered together with a mature fertileness requiring no immediate male presence — one would think that all of this would conclude the work. But there is more: "This, then, is the terrain." Another deft sentence, a simplified alliterative and rhythmic pattern, deictically calls our attention to the scene, the terrain of vision in "At the Bottom of the River" (62–82), with the word *then* having temporal and logical dimensions (the ultimate time, the conclusion which all that has preceded has prepared).

The first section of "At the Bottom of the River" describes this terrain, then, unusually, the lives of two men. The scene — steepest mountains, sharp rocks posing greatest danger, perilously flowing stream that from babbling brook swells to a thundering waterfall, ruthlessly conquering the plain, then after a gorge creating a basin and a pool — reminds us of both the opening of *Heinrich* and of "Kubla Khan." But there is no sexualized element, just a comparison to a small boy playfully dragging a toy and the suggestion that only the "most deeply arched of human feet," surely a female reference, can venture here. At the end of the description, indeed, the scene "awaits the eye, the hand, the foot that shall then give all this a meaning."

The innocent boy (how rare) allows the introduction of two male figures, neither of whom will be able to tread the visionary terrain. The first exists in autistic solitude, incapable of appreciating nature, the world of work and commerce, family life, emotions, the turbulence of human history. "He sits in nothing, in nothing, in nothing." The second man, like the father in *Annie John*, instead appreciates all of the above: "Look! A man steps out of bed, a good half hour after his wife, and washes himself." This passage is the only "happy" evocation of conventional domestic life. Like the father in *Annie John*, the man here is a gifted carpenter and builder, achieving satisfaction from his creations as well as from his appreciation of ordinary events and the beauty of nature. There is love but submission on the part of mother and daughter. But when leaving the house for work he in turn is paralyzed by geological-metaphysical reflections, images of subterranean veins of gold, "bubbling sulfurous fountains, the mountains covered with hot lava; at the bottom of some caves lies the black dust, and below that rich clay sediment, and trapped between the layers are filaments of winged beasts and remnants of invertebrates." " 'And where shall I be?' asks this man" (67). Like the first, he too at the end of the first section confronts nothing: "For stretching out before him is a silence so dreadful, a vastness, its length and breadth and depth immeasurable. Nothing" (68).

Amid images of death ("The branches were dead; a fly hung dead on the branches, its fragile body fluttering in the wind as if it were remnants of a beautiful gown; a beetle had fed on the body of the fly but now lay dead, too. Death on death on death," 68), an older woman, reflecting in the first person, recalls now-grown children and the bitterness of her awareness of mortality. Repeatedly a "you" (could we imagine a husband here?) reminds her that death is natural, life an intrusion. Discovering a spot that marks the disappearance of a small creature, she "divines" its life, once again in terms recalling Blake's range from the minute to the cosmic — its male and female existence, its broadly striped and colorful body, the delicious pain it felt in the sting of a honeybee, its "deep, dark memory unspeakable." In terms of its experience, the creature "lived so in a length of time that may be measured to be no less than the blink of an eye, or no more than one hundred millenniums." Yet it too vanished, provoking the mocking, and, we feel more and more sure, male reaction: "Death is natural." The passage ends with a sequence of deaths — the miserable form of a worm, eaten by a majestic bird, who however will be killed by the again more destructive boy. "And what of the boy? His ends are numberless. I glean again the death in life."

Then the "I" recalls again her childhood and her loving mother, wishing to return to the time of the glorious aspects of nature "from which I had no trouble tearing myself away, since their end was unknown to me." Most positively, though, she remembers seeing her mother's face, whose negroid beauty is now celebrated:

the lips like a moon in its first and last quarter, a nose with a bony bridge and wide nostrils that flared out and trembled visibly in excitement, ears the lobes of which were large and soft and silk-like; and what pleasure it gave me to press them between my thumb and forefinger. How I worshipped this beauty, and in my childish heart I would always say to it, "Yes, yes, yes." (73)

Now comes the time for the female narrator to immerse herself in the visionary river, the one evoked at the outset, presumably, but now having reached the sea: "I walked to the mouth of the river, and it was then still in the old place near the lime tree grove. The water was clear and still. I looked in, and at the bottom of the river I could see a house, and it was a house of only one room, with an A-shaped roof." Coleridge may once more be in the background,[29] but the domestic Caribbean setting is suggested by the house, the setting for so many interactions between mother and daughter. The return in time is patent, too, since the river is said to be still in the same place. But the house, like certain visions in Novalis and Nerval, though apparently fully real, is uncanny. There is no life or movement or sound, only a strange light in which "nothing cast a shadow."

A woman now appears at the door, a naked black woman whose hair stands out in a straight line, her insteps high from climbing mountains, her brown clay skin like that of a statue, liquid and gleaming. She presents a second positive and powerful image of black female beauty. The woman looks at something that finally the narrator is able to see, a world not of passing appearances but of benevolence and purpose, "unquestionable truth and purpose and beauty." Although this world is inhabited by creatures, it is not yet divided, examined, numbered, not yet dead: "I longed to go there."

This vision of a world that all the "facts" of normal experience deny produces for the narrating female "I" a wonderful discovery of self:

I stood above the land and the sea and looked back up at myself as I stood on the bank of the mouth of the river. I saw that my face was round in shape, that my irises took up almost all the space in my eyes, and that my eyes were brown, with yellow-colored and black-colored flecks; that my mouth was large and closed; that my nose, too, was large and my nostrils broken circles; my arms were long, my hands large, the veins pushing up against my skin; my legs were long, and, judging from the shape of them, I was used to running long distances. I saw that my hair grew out long from my head and in a disorderly way, as if I were a strange tree, with many branches. I saw my skin, and it was red. It was the red of flames when a fire is properly fed, the red of flames when a fire burns alone in a darkened place, and not the red of flames when a fire is burning in a cozy room. I saw myself clearly, as if I were looking through a pane of glass. (78–79)

Pace Lacan, this is no mirror stage but rather a stage of adult superior self-awareness. Standing above the land and the sea, the speaker nonetheless looks back up at herself, thus reversing the normal perspective, and her self-vision at the end has the clarity of one looking *through* a window. She details her facial, particularly racial, features. Strong, unsubmissive, undomestic, she has the fiery redness of a female Orc. This self-vision is set "on the bank of the mouth of the river." In the next paragraph she discovers a self superior to the body and made of will and dominion: whereupon "I entered the sea then" (another portentous "then"). Evoking again familiar motifs, her immersion seems to be in "freshly spilled blood." Then she moves through deep caverns, crosses great ridges, reaches bottom, perceives a vast crystal plane, and finally sits like a child on the edge of a basin. But the self she now experiences has been stripped of every terrestrial attribute; she has no name for it, exists beyond pain and pleasure, has no sense of "real or not real."

Yet, as she discovers, "how beautiful I became." Still this beauty "was not in the way" of known realities — ancient cities, women and men in stereotypical pursuits, or a child or an apple or tiny beads of water after rain, "or the sound the hummingbird makes with its wings as it propels itself through the earthly air." In a manner wholly different from Lautréamont's or Aragon's analogy games, this negative evocation of the unearthly beauty that she has found paradoxically materializes and visualizes the concrete beauties of our here-and-now world.

This prepares the brief final section of the work, where the here-and-now world is rejoined. This reentry proceeds first by questions ("Yet what was that light in which I stood?"), then by possibilities: "For now a door might suddenly be pushed open and the morning light might rush in, revealing to me creation and a force whose nature is implacable, unmindful of any of the individual needs of existence, and without knowledge of future or past." This leads to the possibility of a belief in a superior being "whose impartiality I cannot know or ever fully understand and accept," as well as to a coveting of the mute state of rocks and mountains. Nonetheless, emerging from her pit in a movement recalling the end of *Milton* and *Auré-lia*, she now steps into a room and sees lamp, chair, table, pen — she is a writer, after all — fruit, milk, flute, "the clothes that I will wear." Seeing these perishable things, she faces mutability and yet the knowledge that she is bound "to all that is human endeavor." Then, in an enactment that no amount of theorizing, French or Anglo-Saxon, can match, she comes to full self-awareness: "I claim these things then — mine — and now feel myself grow solid and complete, my name filling up my mouth." The physical self, the sense of identity with an authentic name, the gift of utterance — such are the accomplishments of the female at the term of the visionary expansions and voids of *At the Bottom of the River*.

Conclusion ✌

After the intensities of vision and the annihilations in geological time, Jamaica Kincaid brings us, along with her narrator-protagonist, down to earth. This is somewhat like earlier works that, despite persistent indeterminacy, return to the present and make an attempt at resolution and integration — Nerval's narrator amid his books and souvenirs, Aragon's explanatory letter to Soupault, Blake's awakening in his garden, in his wife's presence, at the end of *Milton*. There is, of course, too the important difference that the satisfactions of Kincaid's and of Wittig's work include their reversal of the male sexism of earlier texts, their vindication and celebration of female and black self, body, name, writing.

Back to earth after various strange and exalting excursions, in the interest of summarizing the essence of myriad features encountered and of reflecting on questions raised in the introduction, what do we "conclude"? Most surprising, for the unsuspecting reader, at least, is the fact that these fantastic, dreamlike, and even "insane" works are so insistently historical, not only in general scope but in specific detail, and sometimes more so than novels centered in the realist line. In Kincaid the postcolonial details — the reading in Kingsley, the drizzle tasting like government school ink, the (momentarily!) apocalyptic passage of the guerrillas — are slight but readily understandable, and powerful. More explicitly and massively, Wittig draws on and attacks numerous political and other authors and sources in projecting her utopian warfare against the male-dominated capitalist system.

Without repeating all that has gone before, it is nonetheless important to stress the ways in which the other writers studied here constitute what my subtitle correctly calls an apocalyptic tradition in the postrevolutionary age, extending from 1789 into the present moment with its imminent historical future. Blake and Novalis write in immediate response to the French Revolution. Whereas the one is sympathetic to the overthrow of the ancien régime, the other to enlightened monarchy, and whereas these tendencies produce mystical and apocalyptic visions in the first, millennial dreams of universal nuptial bliss in the second, we have seen that both are directly historical and critical. This is no surprise in the case of the explosive Blake, with his broadsides against church, state, educational system, and ideological controls. But we observed too how the mystic Novalis includes some poetry that might be read as ambiguously revolutionary, how he treats the economic system, not to speak of the family, how he condemns the monstrousness of war in the case of the Crusades.

The next two works frame the repressive Second Empire in France, and hence are characterized by disguise: Nerval's is muted, Ducasse/Lautréamont's coded but immeasurably virulent. We saw how in the first the narrative of the protagonist's "madness" allows for an evocation of the upheavals and repressions of French history (1789, 1815, 1830, 1848, 1851) so that the black sun and bloody globe over the Tuileries are political as well as apocalyptic. The ongoing Crimean War is the subject of pacifist longing, and, with even greater anguish than in Novalis, the Arab-Western conflict that convulses medieval and modern and current history is foregrounded. As for Maldoror, his murderousness, following a few early hints, in the closing "novel" leads to a chilling allegory, prophetic in fact, of class retribution and destruction, played out among the historically relevant sites and monuments of Paris. But we noted the irony that *Maldoror*'s allegory is "backward," that the workers' government of the Commune and thousands upon thousands of its supporters were the ones crushed, slaughtered, executed in May 1871.

Despite the threat of opprobrium and trial, disguise is not much practiced by Aragon and Breton, whose works, once again situated in the politically charged geography of Paris, are flagrantly oppositional. We sketched the courageous and dubious positions of both, constituting an epitome of the dilemmas and terrors of our century, and noted even in their surrealist "novels" their premonitions of those monstrosities, in the names of the streets on the Buttes-Chaumont, echoed in Aragon's Resistance poetry, in the conflagration of the Manoir D'Ango. As for Burroughs, critics have acutely compared him to Swift, interpreting his work not as futuristic but as an enraged, therefore nearly insane, depiction of present reality as it truly exists. *Naked Lunch*, including in its sordid "expansions," is overwhelmingly disturbing, not only sexually but in its evocation of Middle Eastern terrorism, mind control and state-sponsored intelligence operations, and especially the worldwide drug industry.

For Americans the burden is heavy, since Burroughs sees us as deeply evil. The scene in which his narrator obscenely furnishes the president with drugs conveys this scorn in a way that makes us cringe. We recall that Kincaid presents Antigua as suffering not only from the past depredations of the English but also from present exploitation by Arabs, not to mention the nightmare of an American Grenada-style invasion. Throughout we have noted the ominous relevance of all of these references to the current and future historical scene, including the unification of Germany, the dislocation of the Soviet Union, the warfare in eastern Europe, slaughter in Africa, and again dictators and mass suffering in the Caribbean.

Despite being given to writing that may be variously characterized as apocalyptic, regressive, millennial, orientalist, utopian, and despite their appeals to sometimes contradictory, sometimes other-worldly sources and traditions, our writers turn out to be obsessed with the real history that human beings have lived and continue to live. Moreover, with the exception of Novalis, they are oppositional, although more or less flagrantly so depending on temperament and circumstances. Read as a group, these "visionary" works constitute a powerful condemnation of the modern history of the West in a worldwide perspective.

Here we may begin to get some understanding, if not "the" answer, concerning a question raised at the outset: Why this persistence of apocalyptic texts that are also oppositional? Why is the visionary subversive? In one sense the connection is obvious: if you want the world to end it must be because you think the world pretty awful. Beyond that, these apocalypses extend from the immediate post-Revolution era to the present, so *postrevolutionary* here has to include the achievements and failures of all subsequent revolutions, including those of the twentieth century. And, as I have suggested throughout, both historical events and also the anguish and atrocities in the works studied are arguably progressively *worse*. To repeat an idea expressed in the introduction, the immense "visionary fiction" of the French Revolution inaugurated a long and horrible period of history in which apocalyptic and millennial expectations have been raised, followed by disastrous events on an increasingly global scale. If O'Leary is right in claiming that the preaching of apocalypse is an uninterrupted textual tradition, in the literary field — and *literary* will rapidly need nuancing — there is a marked increase in, and perpetuation of, visionary apocalypse in the "postrevolutionary" period.[1]

To understand these features I have invoked ideas from Marx, Nietzsche, and Freud, hinted at here and developed systematically in my earlier books. There is Nietzsche's disconcerting genealogy of traditional morality, his arguments about the illusoriness of the self and about the instability of meanings. Despite the opposition between the fantastic or uncanny and the reality principle, Freud's insights concerning sexuality, desire, repression, dream, and social existence have a relevance that extends far beyond surrealism. And Marx: it is he who argues that our all-encompassing "mode of production" produces crippling alienations in every sphere. Despite propaganda to the contrary, his ideas on class conflict, the denaturing of human (including family and sexual) relations, and the obscuring function of national myth and other "ideology," all in a global as well as a local framework, will simply not go away. Indeed, contemporary world events might be interpreted not as disproving Marx's theories but as illustrating his prediction of enormously protracted and violent conflict, ongoing and to come.[2] Such arguments make a work like *Naked Lunch* appear even more prescient.

But — and this is our second point of reflection, suggested at the beginning and illustrated throughout — our primary authors, as compelling as any philosopher or theorist, are oppositional not only in terms of particular regimes or events but in relation to the entire "personal-societal" system. This almost certainly explains why they have been quite systematically submitted to forms of censorship. In this connection we should keep in mind the explicit irony of certain formulations by Novalis, Nerval's evasion of censorship laws, the threats of government actions against figures like Blake and Aragon, Burroughs's trial, the solitude and/or ostracism to which some have been submitted, from Blake to Wittig, and the recurrent charge of insanity, as a label for Blake and Ducasse and as the diagnosis of Nerval and Burroughs, not to mention Nadja.

Simultaneously one grasps the usefulness, for disguise and revelation, of various visionary tactics. Recalling that even some of the most vehemently subversive resort to disguise (Ducasse's *Poésies*, Burroughs's "scientific" articles on drugs and pretense of writing tracts against capital punishment), it is clear how such tactics may allow a visionary-oppositional writer, say Nerval, to survive, at least for a time. Then too there are the possibilities of enhanced revelation generated by the functions of burlesque and satire (Blake, Lautréamont, Burroughs), distancing (Novalis, Wittig), displacement (Nerval), radically changed perspective (Blake, Aragon), and distortion or magnification (Blake, Lautréamont, Burroughs).

Indeed, through such devices of disguise and amplification, the visionary writers undermine the ideological value system of our civilization, including not only government but also religion, morality, family, sexuality, and the discourses that support these entities, structures, and values. Despite the smoke screen of Ducasse's *Poésies*, despite the lapses of a Breton, in the tradition that stretches from Blake to Lautréamont, the surrealists, Burroughs, and Wittig we encounter a stance of all-inclusive resistance and attack. Kincaid is more focused on colonialism, slavery, sexual and racial oppression, but is no less firm. Revealingly, the least revolutionary, Novalis and Nerval, furnish some of the most damaging "evidence" on family, sexuality, and religion.

With Sade and *Faust* in the background (where, because of their sexism, they belong), it was rather Nietzsche who came to mind in relation to Blake's much earlier reversal of values, "evil" henceforth designating the creative forces of energy and liberated sexuality. But Blake, we saw, forces us to be honest in contemplating this satisfying freedom from restraint. "Exuberance is Beauty" is one thing, "Sooner murder an infant in its cradle than nurse unacted desires" another, or rather precisely *not* another. In his gruesome way Lautréamont enacts this proposition for us by instructing us in how to flay a child with our bare hands, so that one wonders what is wrong with the reader who continues beyond this point in *Maldoror*. Other fearful examples include the "compensatory" antimale violence in Wittig and Kincaid, the answer we know the addict must give to Burroughs's reiterated question: *"Wouldn't you?"*

But there is something to Ducasse's claim in *Poésies* that in *Maldoror* he wanted to provoke an ethical counterresponse from the reader. Also, despite a supposedly absolute rejection of morality, the ultimate surrealist act being that of senseless murder, Breton later adopted certain principled oppositions to communism and in *Arcane 17* analyzed the rise of fascism in moral terms. Perhaps Blake's doctrine of contraries may be brought to bear most usefully here. If no ethical principle is absolute, rather than being dispensed from ethical choice we are obliged at every point freely to decide and act. On morality the modern visionary tradition is enormously unsettling, in denying fixed principles and hence in obliging us to involve ourselves continually in choice. Jean-Paul Sartre too *avant la lettre*.

I stressed in the introduction corresponding ambiguities concerning religion. Breton has his troubles defending against the accusation of mysticism, and the differences between Blake's *Marriage* and *Milton*, but also the continuities, are apparent. There is no hesitation, however, in the attack on religion in Burroughs, and Blake himself never stops arguing that God is a human being, that "Prisons are built with stones of Law, Brothels with bricks of Religion." African and Caribbean religion contributes to the visionary imagination in Kincaid's writing but should not escape scrutiny for all that. More appalling is Lautréamont's hatred: the child's revolt, the resistance to sleep, during which God usurps our independence, God in the brothel and as a pederast, Goya-like devouring human beings. But as suggested above, perhaps most telling of all is what appears in the writing of Novalis and Nerval: in the one the reiterated sacrifice of women, in the other the fractured family, overvaluation of woman, and guilt-ridden male sexuality, together with the phallic threat and Jesus as double, mounted between protagonist and beloved. Could Blake or Nietzsche have argued more convincingly that our forms of religion destroy sexuality?

Here we confront the paradox of visionary literature turning against the religious sources of its most dazzling motifs, already visible in Blake's parody of the Apocalypse in the *Marriage*, outrageously amplified in *Maldoror*. It appears from this literature, and this is not new in view of Nietzchean arguments about the death of God, that the modern postrevolutionary period is also one of utter revolt against absolute sources of authoritative truth, that is, against all religions. Blake is on the historical cusp here, writing immediately after the French Revolution, celebrating liberation from political *and* religious repression, attacking priesthood as a perversion of poetic inspiration, claiming the last great preceding visionary writer, Milton, as being unconsciously of the devil's party.

Blake's rejection of the mills of industry and preference for the preindustrial method of etching is also illustrative of his historically liminal position among our writers. But just as this recalls Benjamin, Nerval's struggle against insanity reminds us of arguments in Deleuze and Guattari and Foucault.[3] Other characteristic features and forms of the postrevolutionary era — the novel, photography, and film — are stressed in Lautréamont, Breton, and Burroughs, while Burroughs's thematics and verbal texture correspond to the ideological conflicts, international drug markets, intelligence services, and mind control of the late twentieth century. In accord with another well-known argument, this one from a Marxist perspective, the earlier writers, Blake, Novalis, and Nerval, tend to hopeful conclusions. After 1848, 1851, the Second Empire, and the succeeding world wars, the visions are radically more distraught. In summarizing this second concluding point we may say that our visionary writers, while reflecting and subverting the dominant modes of thought and expression of the modern postrevolutionary period, utterly reject its most cherished values and beliefs, including the religions from which many visionary motifs derive.

A third point concerns the paradox of the body, sex, and inevitably also family, also mentioned at the outset and pursued throughout. The undermining of the idealized view of the family is indeed persistent, from the death of the mother in *Heinrich* and the anguished familial thematics in *Aurélia* to the vicious nuclear unit in Blake, Maldoror's crusade against families, surrealist and homosexual refusals in Aragon, Breton, Burroughs, and Wittig, and the obsession with the mother in Kincaid. Sexuality itself fares even worse in relation to religion. The simian and cannibalistic version that Blake draws from the Bible finds many expansions in Lautréamont and Burroughs. Murderous strife between and within the sexes occurs without limit: dismembered giant females in Nerval, reiterated torture and slaughter in Lautréamont and Burroughs, banal versions in Breton, mistreatment of men and warfare against them in Wittig and Kincaid.

Nonetheless the body, and primarily in its sexual aspect, is consistently presented as the privileged source of the visionary. If for the considerably unrepressed Blake the genitals *are* Beauty, then the "improvement of sensual enjoyment" is indeed the key to eternity. We have seen abundant, if unappetizing, illustration of the proposition in male homosexual terms in Burroughs. In more or less idealized or degraded ways the other writers propose a similar theme in the figure of a concluding, perhaps apocalyptic union. This is apparent in Blake's title and in the variously glorious and anguished endings of Klingsohr's tale and of both parts of *Aurélia*. *Maldoror* provides a parody of the myth, whereas in Aragon and Breton it seems to occur in real life, as both surrealist works end with the encounter with a newly beloved woman.

All of these may be considered refigurings of the ancient myth of the Androgyne, present in numerous traditions and holding forth the goal of a reunified, hence multiple and complete sexuality. Clearly the Androgyne has no attraction for Burroughs, Kincaid, or Wittig.[4] For example, critics have seen in *Le corps lesbien* an exclusively female Song of Songs. But we recall the passage on the Androgyne in *Maldoror*, with its touch of irony but also its pervasive tone of tenderness and sadness, so unique in that work, a tone deriving from a devastating sense of sexual inadaptation.

Also inescapably relevant is the conclusion of *Milton*, criticized as sexist by some feminists, seen by others to combine regressive and enlightened attitudes. Minus its undeniable portion of sexism, minus any necessarily heterosexual preference, it could be understood as a promising effort to integrate a range of experiences, including homosexual-sadistic-ecstatic ones, into a fuller, superior, visionary sexuality. And let no one claim that the promise and the horror of sex, in Blake and the others, have no bearing on "real" life, since divorce, abuse, pornography, rape loom so large in the domestic and, we have seen in Bosnia, historical spheres. Hence the "Song of Liberty" announcing revolution and apocalypse at the end of the *Marriage* concludes with a "Chorus" concerning sex and religion, that is, an attack against religious repression of desire: "Nor pale religious letchery call that virginity, that wishes but acts not!"

Blake cannot be made to speak for all, but there is a consistent tendency to make sexual energy central to the visionary and apocalyptic, with, as we have seen, constant attention to history. This recalls another opening point in the introduction, namely my belief and, I think, demonstration that hardly a one of the writers treated here would conceive of his or her writing as a work of "idealism" unrelated to social and political reality. Neither, on the other hand, are their works mere disguised political allegories. On the contrary, one of the strongest protests against an oppressive "reality system" is to make it go away, to realize before our eyes another realm, threatening and exciting. I have on this point dismissed the "vulgar" Marxist argument. And, although we shall return to the question of the fundamental inefficacy of visionary writing, I have disputed the too-simple Freudian opposition between the reality and the pleasure principles. There is plenty of unpleasant reality in the works studied. And the paradox of the sexual body, as means to ecstasy, apocalypse, terror, remains.

Freud, used and misused by Breton and introduced by me to explain the curiously convincing impact of Lautréamont's "antivisionary" writing, allows a further concluding reflection, on the confusing array of sources and the powerful vitality of forms in the visionary writers. The Old and New Testaments, numerous esoteric traditions, Neoplatonic, Catholic, and Protestant mystics, the lore of the East (with its danger of "Orientalism," turned sordid and deflated by the time we reach twentieth-century authors), idealist philosophers (Berkeley, Kant, Fichte, Hegel, and others are variously brought into play), romantic science and philosophical-scientific debates about the nature of physical sight, and Freud himself, not to speak of Engels and Marx, are principal "sources." This in part condenses long lists provided by Nerval and Breton. Although I have noted Breton's not-always-successful balancing act, I think such a criticism unjustified for Blake, or Burroughs, or Wittig. Worrying about how these strands fit together is a Scribe-like enterprise anyway, to which there are several responses, all of which reject the split between mental and external realms: Breton at his best arguing that Rimbaud and Marx send the same message; Blake's attack against the dichotomy between body and soul; Marx's refusal in *Theses on Feuerbach* to accept the opposition of active idealism and passive materialism, arguing that human imagination and activity are material *and* creative. We have also seen that, whereas the tradition from Blake to Breton thus aims at what I would call a subversive syncretism, Wittig takes the system

conclusion

167

apart and appropriates elements of it for feminist purposes, and Kincaid largely ignores it.

The visionary is a highly self-conscious tradition, which explains the combination of "family resemblance" and high originality that we have encountered, in terms of both what the visionary "is" and the forms in which it is presented to us. Since it comes from a realm other than the one in which we normally function, it is often elusive, fragmentary, or disordered, as in the preface to "Kubla Khan," the temporal dislocations of Wittig's narrative, Kincaid's initially unrelated "stories." In the cases of Novalis and Nerval death imposes a fragmentariness that is starker. The format of direct transcription of heightened experience is recurrent in Nerval, Breton, Burroughs, and Coleridge and Sartre. But we have noted unifying features too: framing devices in Nerval, Breton, and Burroughs as well as in Coleridge; visions alternating with manifestos in Blake, Aragon, and Burroughs; and concluding unifications — Blake in his garden, Nerval's protagonist among his possessions, the essential "theorem" in Lautréamont's thirty-page novel, Aragon's letter to Soupault, even the progression of Kincaid's stories, which recount a life.

Despite the latter, the works we have studied are more heavily characterized by dazzling mixtures of forms. Blake's *Marriage* incorporates poetry, argument, proverb, song, chorus, and vision, Novalis's *Heinrich* novel, dream, myth, and poetry, not to mention the abrupt switches, amalgamations of myth, and dreamlike absurdities of Klingsohr's tale. Like his two predecessors, Nerval synthesizes universal myth, and *Aurélia* is a dense texture of dreams, hallucinations, fragmentary letters, jottings, and Mémorables. Parodies of the novel form increasingly characterize succeeding writing. Many of these writers could say with Burroughs "I am not American Express." His book burlesques detective and futuristic fiction, whereas Aragon's *Paysan* plays with the reader's novelistic expectations more successfully than Breton in *Nadja*. But the diabolical predecessor here is the "textual terrorism" of *Maldoror*, which, preceded by Blake's contraries, disrupts possibilities of stable meaning.

Despite a high degree of individual creativity, there are therefore many family resemblances: dreams, visions, myths, "out of the body" experiences, trances, cosmic flights, terrestrial voyages, projections of the human brain as global geology, combats, temporal and spatial switches, metamorphoses, arduous movement through the natural, and the architectural and urban "geography" of the visionary — altars, houses, casinos, halls and stairways, mountains, fountains, and rivers, with eery silence and preternatural luminosity. Hence we discover echoes of Blake, Novalis, Coleridge, and Nerval in Kincaid, despite her generally Caribbean imagery. Parody and transformation of the tradition are also widespread: Blake on the Bible, his and Nerval's use of a Swedenborgian form for different effects, "Memorable Fancies," and Mémorables. There are Klingsohr's amalgamations and Wittig's differently subversive combinations, Burroughs's tawdry evocations, Aragon's modernization of myth, Nerval's adoption of the discourse of psychiatry. In all of these we see what the Russian formalists and Northrup Frye have stressed in parody, its potential for exuberant, productive creativity.[5] *Maldoror* is perhaps most fascinating in its shrill attack on the targets of the visionary tradition, precisely through outlandish burlesque of visionary conventions, which nonetheless produce a powerfully oneiric impact on the reader. The narrator in that work indeed wants to paralyze, cretinize the reader in inescapably hypnotic fashion.

Here we return for a concluding reflection on the most flagrant feature of visionary writing, namely, its supraliterary reality claim, more absolute than that in fantastic literature. This indeed involves questions about the reader that I have raised since the outset; it can also be seen to be usefully related to "poststructuralist" positions that I have evoked along the way as pertinent for particular authors. It involves as well what I have called the "antivisionary."

For the antivisionary in *Maldoror*, in which visionary motifs are parodied yet appear to the reader with powerful intensity, can be seen to exacerbate the issue of the reality of what the visionary text proffers. We recall attitudes from doubt to denigration to denial in Heinrich's father's distrust of dreams, Nerval's and Burroughs's medical diagnoses, the discrepancy between Breton's claims and his drawing back from Nadja as she becomes insane, Aragon's humorous vision of surrealism's ultimate defeat at the hands of conventional society. On the other hand, we remember the arrogantly confident stances variously adopted by Blake, Lautréamont, Aragon, and Burroughs, their domination of the reader, their claim to make us see impossible things. For Blake truth cannot be told properly without belief immediately following. For Nerval everything imagined is true in some world. Lautréamont's and Aragon's epistemological subtleties and absurdities coincide with their imposition on the reader of what they describe, a realization of the program expressed by the very word *surrealism*. And *Naked Lunch* aspires literally to extend our levels of experience.

These positions and their literary realizations seem to me more powerful not only than those of the fantastic but also than certain poststructuralist concepts, which they of course on the whole predate. As suggested earlier in relation to Barthes and Derrida, our works constitute a very varied antimimetic kind of writing. Similarly, recalling but in more vigorous fashion Barthes, Derrida, and Foucault, most of them obliterate the distinction between author, narrator, and protagonist that guarantees the fictionality, that is, the unreality, of most literature. Think in this regard of the texts by Blake, Nerval, Lautréamont, the surrealists, and Burroughs that we have studied.

And, as for the fading or dissolution of the subject announced in various ways by Barthes, Foucault, Lévi-Strauss, Deleuze and Guattari,[6] and others, there are more powerful realizations of such themes in the visionary writers: Blake's out-of-the-body experiences, the eternal/infinite transcendences of space-time in him and Nerval, the dreams and visions in Novalis and Nerval, the collective trance in Wittig, the jarring dislocations of space and time, body and mind in Burroughs, the headless human being transformed into a constellation in Aragon. At the extremes of such states, or scenes, the world is transfigured, as are body and self, bringing us to the brink of an annihilation aptly stressed by Aragon, Burroughs, and Kincaid. Such anguish, such exaltation, are produced by the various visionary textualities that we have observed.

Perhaps Blake's printing house in hell, with its amazing images and transitions, all contained in books on library shelves, most aptly epitomizes the relation between visionary text and the reader's experience. It will be recalled that at the beginning, and later in relation to specific authors and passages, I raised questions about the reaction of the reader, and it is important to return to that issue, in terms not only of individual readers but also of the paradoxes of the readership or public for visionary literature. On the first count, if we enjoy these writers, are stimulated by these texts, why? They must speak to some sense of deep dissatisfaction, some appetite for rebellion against constraints, some joy in magical transformations, some refusal to separate the imagination, considered as a productive power, from the social order. But they must also speak to some ability to confront pain, what I still want to call evil, personal annihilation. As this indicates, and as already suggested, considering such reactions regressive is much too simple. Perhaps, again at his best, Breton's belief in the resolution of dream and waking states in a superior surreality, although utopian, is still more to the point.

But who are the readers who may be thought to respond in these ways? In other terms, what readerships have these oppositional works created? Blake, solitary for most of his life, has thanks to scholarship and teaching been experienced by what by now must be millions of readers and viewers, but to a great extent, I believe, within that academic framework. Millions may read a writer without his or her becoming a mainstream phenomenon. Lautréamont and Burroughs have also been very widely read, but as noted in regard to the latter this is itself troubling, since they have become virtually canonical writers in cultlike traditions.

The avant-garde tactic pursued by the surrealists allowed that large group of talented writers and artists to have an enormous impact.[7] We could not avoid noticing, however, their troublesome sexism and Breton's and Aragon's sometimes self-protective, sometimes mendacious behavior. And I think it fair to say that surrealism has essentially been generalized as an enormously profitable commercial enterprise, in art, decor, film, photography, fashion, many kinds of verbal expression, and much else. Trends of other sorts affect the women writers treated. Having attracted a large early following, Wittig is not now much heard of, either in France or in the United States. Kincaid, after a very unhappy initial experience in this country, has succeeded within the hothouse *New Yorker* environment but has since experienced some vicissitudes.

In contrast, when one wants to teach *Heinrich von Ofterdingen* or *Aurélia* in translation, one will likely not find an English edition in print. Somewhat similarly, and symptomatically, the third volume of the Pléiade edition of Nerval's works was greeted by an article in *Le Nouvel Observateur* in which Jacques Drillon situates Nerval somewhat unfavorably in relation to the more philosophical and rational poet Paul Valéry, nonetheless concluding with the exhortation, "Let's read him!"[8]

The sadness of this appeal, and by extension of this remarkably persistent and corrosive tradition of writing, has to do with such limitations of readership. Some writers have been largely ignored, if not condemned as insane; others have become the preserve of scholars; still others have been co-opted in commercial fashion by well-to-do society or by youth and other cults. Surrealism is by far the most pervasively successful of visionary movements, but in the finally not very subversive way suggested above.

Despite rejecting "vulgar" Freudian and Marxist reductions, one thus cannot escape what I have called the fundamental inefficacy of visionary writing. On occasion we might argue that the fault lies in some tactic or stance of the author, or in some deficiency in scholarship about the writer. But it is more absolutely the case that society remains impermeable, that the late capitalist system retains its extraordinary ability to censor, marginalize, and finally absorb and exploit resistant elements.

No Apocalypse has occurred, nor will it, I believe, occur in the year 2000, despite the preparation for that event by certain believers. Since it would be hard to imagine any of our writers identifying with the fanaticism of some of these believers, it is once more clear that to the extent that the visionary is religious it is not at all so in conventional terms. In contrast, Burroughs's conflation of American evangelicals and Arab preachers retains its hilarious and deadly point. Nonetheless, Blake and others of our writers require of us a fundamental act of belief . . .

And revolution, arguably more productive than destructive in its republican forms, has in its totalitarian versions produced immeasurable harm. Consequently we face the truly horrible problems, in Western society and throughout the world, that I surmise from my reading of events and of my texts may be progressively worsening. Here we may nonetheless note another strong point of the works I treat: they are not "visionary" (or "utopian") in the other sense, which I have avoided using, that of inventing a model of future society. Despite their timid or outrageous self-confidence they are too shrewd for that; they know that history dwarfs writing, even visionary writing.

Recognizing this awareness should also make us acknowledge their courage, their audacity in displaying the evils of history and the societal system and in proposing exhilarating if frightening transcendences. One wants to keep in mind the tactics that they have had to employ, remembering Burroughs's effort to "extend levels of experience," Nerval's struggle against the diagnosis of insanity, Breton's attack on Stalinism, Wittig's demolition of the sexist intellectual tradition, and Blake's preface to *Milton*, his attack on the "Hirelings in the Camp, the Court, & the University: who would if they could, for ever depress Mental & prolong Corporeal War." Nor can we forget the brilliant textualities in which our imaginations are challenged to believe in the reality of the scenes that open before us, as a gage of opposition, indignation, denunciation, vision, and affirmation.

introduction

1 Edward Ahearn, *Rimbaud: Visions and Habitations* (Berkeley: University of California Press, 1983); *Marx and Modern Fiction* (New Haven: Yale University Press, 1989). Having written extensively on Rimbaud and Marx, I will not elaborate on references to them in this book, but instead refer the reader throughout to my earlier work.

2 Stephen D. O'Leary, *Arguing the Apocalypse: A Theory of Millennial Rhetoric* (New York: Oxford University Press, 1994), 4–6, 215. O'Leary studies the "continuous textual tradition" (10) not of literature but of apocalyptic preaching, emphasizing Palestine and the early church and the early nineteenth and late twentieth century in the United States. A useful and beautifully illustrated source is Georges Jean, *Voyages en Utopie*, Découvertes (Paris: Gallimard, 1994).

3 In Richard and Fernande DeGeorge, eds., *The Structuralists from Marx to Levi-Strauss* (Garden City, N.Y.: Doubleday Anchor, 1972), 155–67, esp. 155, 167; Lucien Goldmann, *Pour une sociologie du roman*, Collection Idées (Paris: Gallimard, 1964); Ian Watt, *The Rise of the Novel: Studies in Defoe, Richardson, and Fielding* (Berkeley: University of California Press, 1957).

4 From the poem "With happiness stretched across the hills" in the letter to Thomas Butts, 22 November 1802, in David V. Erdman, ed. (with commentary by Harold Bloom), *The Complete Poetry and Prose of William Blake*, rev. ed. (New York: Doubleday Anchor, 1988), 722. Further quotations from this edition.

5 See the philosophically and scientifically informative article by the neurologist Oliver Sacks, "To See and Not to See," *The New Yorker*, May 10, 1993, 59–73, esp. 65. In the case studied by Sachs, and in the three-hundred-year history of such cases, the almost complete majority of blind-from-birth individuals whose organic defect is corrected by an operation cannot learn to see. The classic study is by Marius von Senden, *Raum- und gestaltauffassung bei operierten blindgeborenen vor und nach der operation* (Leipzig: J. A. Barth, 1932).

6 *Milton*, ch. I, pl. 28, ll. 17–20:

> The Microscope knows not of this nor the Telescope. they alter
> The ratio of the Spectators Organs but leave Objects untouchd
> For every Space larger than a red Globule of Mans blood.
> Is visionary

7 See Roland Fischer, "A Cartography of the Ecstatic and Meditative States," *Science* 174 (1971): 897–904, and "Cartography of Inner Space," in *Altered States of Consciousness: Current Views and Research Problems* (Washington: Drug Abuse Council, 1975), 1–57.

8 As his title indicates, Edwin Arthur Burtt subtly analyzes the epistemological complexities of early modern science from Copernicus to Descartes and Newton, using Bishop Berkeley and Alfred North Whitehead among others to counter excessively positivistic positions, in *The Metaphysical Foundations of Modern Physical Science: A Historical and Critical Essay*, rev. ed. (London: Routledge and Kegan Paul, 1932). For idealist philosophy and romantic science, primarily in Germany, see Georges Gusdorf, *Le Romantisme*, 2 vols. (Paris: Payot et Rivages, 1993), esp. 1:197 ff.; 1:257–58, 370–74, 381; 2:228–46, 399 ff., 459 ff., 489 ff., 529 ff., 593. Although noting that the attack on Newton, already visible in a quotation from Blake, typically ignores the religious strain of that scientist's thought, Gusdorf concludes with "Apologie pour la Naturphilosophie" of Schelling and other romantic figures (1:197 ff., 2:669 ff.).

9 In addition to Burtt's *Metaphysical Foundations*, see Ernst Cassirer, *The Philosophy of the Enlightenment*, trans. Fritz C. A. Koelln and James P. Pettegrove (Boston: Beacon, 1964), 93–133, and more recently, and in less detail, Martin Jay, *Downcast Eyes: The Denigration of Vision in Twentieth-Century French Thought* (Berkeley: University of California Press, 1993), 98–103. It should be noted that Berkeley's correct prediction that an operation to correct blindness from birth would not result immediately in sight was interpreted by many (e.g., Voltaire) in *anti*-idealist fashion.

10 In addition to the canonical biblical texts I first cited, for mystical, occult, and other traditions see Gusdorf, *Romantisme*, 1:80–83, 329–30, 386–87, 575, 632–34, 727–28, 764 ff., and 2:84, 115, 139, 200–21, 210 ff., 327–28, 339–40. See also Gwendolyn Bays, *The Orphic Vision: Seer Poets from Novalis to Rimbaud* (Lincoln: University of Nebraska Press, 1964); Albert Béguin, *L'Ame romantique et le rêve: Essai sur le romantisme allemand et la poésie française* (Marseilles: Editions des Cahiers du Sud, 1937); Henri Corbin, *Avicenne et le récit visionnaire* (Paris: Berg International, 1979), and *Face de Dieu, face de l'homme, Herméneutique et Soufisme* (Paris: Flammarion, 1983); Jean-Paul Corsetti, *Histoire de l'ésotérisme et des sciences occultes* (Paris: Larousse, 1992), containing glossary and extensive bibliography; Mircea Eliade, *Méphistophélès et l'Androgyne* (Paris: Gallimard, 1962); Alethea Hayter, *Opium and the Romantic Imagination* (Berkeley: University of California Press, 1968); Brian Juden, *Traditions orphiques et tendances mystiques dans le romantisme français (1800–1855)* (Paris: Klincksieck, 1971); Jacques Roos, *Aspects littéraires du mysticisme philosophique et l'influence de Boehme et de Swédenborg au début du romantisme: William Blake, Novalis, Ballanche* (Strasbourg: P. H. Heitz, 1951); A. Viatte, *Les sources occultes du romantisme: Illuminisme, théosophie* (Paris: Champion, 1928). For ecstatic states see Chapter 2 and notes in my *Rimbaud*.

11 In *Ragtime* Doctorow has J. P. Morgan tell Henry Ford about the seventeenth-century Rosicrucians, Giordano Bruno, Greek translations of the Egyptian priest Hermes Trismegistus, and the occult knowledge of the Hermetica, adding complaints about the "conspiracy" of the mechanistic science of Newton and Descartes. Ford responds that he long ago learned it all in a 25-cent book, *An Eastern Fakir's Eternal Wisdom*, concluding, "Reincarnation is the only belief I hold" (New York: Fawcett Crest Ballantine Books, 1991), 155–58.

12 Edward Said, *Orientalism* (New York: Vintage, 1978).

13 Northrup Frye, *The Anatomy of Criticism: Four Essays* (Princeton: Princeton University Press, 1957).

14 Tzvetan Todorov, *Introduction à la littérature fantastique* (Paris: Seuil, 1970), 28–45. Todorov draws on Pierre-Georges Castex, *Le conte fantastique en France de Nodier à Maupassant* (Paris: José Corti, 1951 and 1987), and Roger Caillois, *Au coeur du fantastique* (Paris: Gallimard, 1965). The difficulty of radically differentiating *fantastic* and *visionary* is seen in the fact that whereas Todorov distinguishes between the fantastic and other categories (e.g., the supernatural), he illustrates the fantastic by Nerval's *Aurélia*, which I treat as visionary. See also Joël Malrieu, *Le Fantastique* (Paris: Hachette, 1992), and Eric Rabkin, *The Fantastic in Literature* (Princeton: Princeton University Press, 1976). For the relation between the fantastic and science fiction, see Roger Bozzetto, *L'Obscur objet d'un savoir: Fantastique et science fiction* (Aix-en-Provence: Publications de l'Université de Provence, 1992), and Eric Rabkin and Robert Scholes, *Science Fiction: History, Science, Vision* (New York: Oxford University Press, 1977). Dagmar Barnou covers a lot of ground in *Die versuchte Realität oder von der Möglichkeit, glucklichere Welten zu denken: Utopischer Diskurs von Thomas Morus zur feministischen Science Fiction* (Meitigen: Corian Verlag Heinrich Wimmer, 1985).

15 Sigmund Freud, "The 'Uncanny,'" first published in 1919 in *Imago*, in *On Creativity and the Unconscious: Papers on the Psychology of Art, Literature, Love, Religion*, ed. Benjamin Nelson (New York: Harper Torchbacks, 1958, this essay translated by Alix Strachey), 122–161, esp. 147–53.

16 I am indebted to Priscilla Parkhurst Ferguson for this idea. For artistic responses to the French Revolution, including the topos of apocalypse but much more from Burke to Goya, see Ronald Paulson, *Representations of Revolution (1789–1820)* (New Haven: Yale University Press, 1983).

17 And the large field of visionary poetry in general, say by Hölderlin and Hugo, to which I devote considerable attention in my *Rimbaud*, is not treated here.

chapter 1

1 See the late E. P. Thompson's *Witness Against the Beast: William Blake and the Moral Law* (New York: New Press, 1994) for a survey of dissenting religions, for an argument that Blake belonged to a sect called the Muggletonians, and for much excellent historical and political commentary.

2 "ALL RELIGIONS are ONE," "THERE is NO NATURAL RELIGION," and annotations of Berkeley's *Siris, The Complete Poetry and Prose of William Blake*, rev. ed., ed. David V. Erdman (New York: Doubleday Anchor, 1988), 1–3, 664. This edition retains Blake's somewhat idiosyncratic punctuation. Hereafter cited as *CPP*.

3 Los, the embodiment of poetic imagination, in *Jerusalem*, ch. I, pl. 10, l. 20; *CPP*, 153.

4 *CPP*, 801. Nelson Hilton traces the history of responses to Blake from the nineteenth century to recent studies: "Blake and the Apocalypse of the Canon," *Modern Language Studies* 18 (1988): 134–40. See Dan Miller, "Contrary Revelation: *The Marriage of Heaven and Hell*," *Studies in Romanticism* 24 (1985): 491–509, for a survey of major criticism to that date on the centrality of the *Marriage* to the Blake "canon," followed by an analysis of the features in the work that resist univocal interpretation. A similar division of emphasis is visible in two anthologies of Blake criticism, the first more traditional, the second emphasizing recent feminist, poststructuralist, and deconstructionist approaches: see Harold Bloom, ed., *William Blake: Modern Critical Views* (New York: Chelsea House, 1985), and Nelson Hilton, ed., *Essential Articles for the Study of Blake* (Hamden, Conn.: Archon Books, 1986).

5 There is a large critical literature on his relation to mystical, esoteric, biblical, and non-Western traditions. See Roos, *Aspects littéraires du mysticisme philosophique et l'influence de Boehme et de Swédenborg au début du romantisme: William Blake, Novalis, Ballanche*; Kathleen Raine, *Blake and Tradition* (Princeton: Princeton University Press, 1968), and *Blake*

and the New Age (London: Allen & Unwin, 1979); Leslie Tannenbaum, *Biblical Tradition in Blake's Early Prophecies: The Great Code in Art* (Princeton: Princeton University Press, 1982). Although he frames his argument in terms of the history of language theory and presents himself as Derridean, Robert N. Essick in *William Blake and the Language of Adam* (Oxford: Clarendon Press, 1989) correctly argues for what I would term a sacred interpretation of Blake's work, in which the artist "asks us to believe in the literal existence of his trope of the Last Judgment and to refuse its conversion into trope" (99). The *Essential Articles* anthology proposes two studies of how Blake transforms his "sources": Stuart Curran, "Blake and the Gnostic Hyle: A Double Negative," and Florence Sandler, "The Iconoclastic Enterprise: Blake's Critique of 'Milton's Religion.' " In *Angel of Apocalypse: Blake's Idea of Milton* (Madison: University of Wisconsin Press, 1975), Joseph Anthony Wittreich Jr. subtly discriminates influence and tradition in Blake's relation to Milton as mediator of apocalyptic traditions. For readers wishing to go beyond the inevitably brief sketch of the relations between the two poets in this chapter, Wittreich's book is essential.

6 Not to speak of the illustrations. Blake's writing as disparate, based on the opposition of contraries, and radically unamenable to univocal interpretation, is appreciated by recent critics influenced, sometimes uncritically, by deconstructionist theories. See W. J. T. Mitchell, "Dangerous Blake," *Studies in Romanticism* 21 (1982): 410–16; see also, in *Essential Articles*, V. A. De Luca, "Semantic Structures and the Temporal Mode of Blake's Prophetic Verse," Steven Shaviro, " 'Striving with Systems': Blake and the Politics of Difference," and the Santa Cruz Blake Study Group, "What Type of Blake?"; Nelson Hilton and Thomas A. Vogler, eds., *Unnam'd Forms: Blake and Textuality* (Berkeley: University of California Press, 1986), esp. Gavin Edwards on Blake's aphorisms, "Repeating the Same Dull Round," and Vogler's "Re:Naming MIL/TON." The latter anthology also contains studies emphasizing the "radical variability" resulting from Blake's method of producing books (186), in studies by Leo Carr, "Illuminated Printing: Toward a Logic of Difference," and Robert Essick, "How Blake's Body Means" — Essick there proposes a "media-oriented hermeneutics" (216). Essick's *William Blake, Printmaker* (Princeton: Princeton University Press, 1980) and *William Blake and the Language of Adam*; David Bindman, *Blake as an Artist* (Oxford: Phaidon, New York: Dutton, 1977) and *William Blake: His Art and Times* (New Haven: Yale Center for British Art, 1982); David Erdman, *The Illuminated Blake: All of William Blake's Illuminated Works with a Plate-by-Plate Commentary* (Garden City, N.Y.: Doubleday Anchor, 1974); and Joseph Viscomi, *Blake and the Image of the Book* (Princeton: Princeton University Press, 1993) are essential studies.

7 In *Principii d'una scienza nuova* (1725), Giambattista Vico derives the intellectual disciplines from primal imagination and poetic discourse but concludes by justifying revealed Catholic religion.

8 Treating only the sexual dimension of the body, Alicia Ostriker delineates four different, and not all compatible, views throughout the range of Blake's work in "Desire Gratified and Ungratified: William Blake and Sexuality," *Blake: An Illustrated Quarterly* 16 (1982–83): 156–65, hereafter cited as *BIQ*. On the centrality of the body in Blake's visionary project, see Thomas R. Frosch, *The Awakening of Albion: The Renovation of the Body in the Poetry of William Blake* (Ithaca: Cornell University Press, 1974). Although Blake is sometimes viewed as a Gnostic, my sense is that he is not in any simple way a Gnostic regarding the body, that the positions he takes in the *Marriage* substantially persist in later works — see the discussion of *Milton* below.

9 See *Europe*, pl. 9, ll. 1–5, and *Milton*, I, 10, ll. 6–7: "The nature of Female Space is this: it shrinks the Organs / Of Life till they become Finite & Itself seems Infinite." See also Susan Fox, "The Female as Metaphor in William Blake's Poetry," *Critical Inquiry* 3 (1977): 507–19, and her *Poetic Form in Blake's* Milton (Princeton: Princeton University Press, 1976); Anne K. Mellor, "Blake's Portrayal of Women," *BIQ* 16 (1982–83): 148–55; Jean H. Hagstrum's defense of Blake in *The Romantic Body: Love and Sexuality in Keats,*

Wordsworth, and Blake (Knoxville: University of Tennessee Press, 1985); Ostriker, "Desire Gratified and Ungratified."

10 Mills, for example the "dark Satanic Mills" evoked in the poem included in the preface to *Milton*, have biblical and also industrial resonances.

11 See Jacques Derrida, *Of Grammatology*, trans. Gayatri Spivak (Baltimore: Johns Hopkins University Press, 1976). The editors of *Unnam'd Forms* indeed "displace Jacques Derrida's description of Hegel onto Blake, seeing in him the last poet of the Book and the first poet of writing" (4). As my mildly invidious reference to Derrida suggests, this does not necessarily do Blake a service, a position that may be epitomized by V. A. De Luca's claim in "A Wall of Words: The Sublime as Text" that "heaven is a form of text" (*Unnam'd Forms*, 238). Dan Miller's extensive review of *Unnam'd Forms* demonstrates the consistent misreading of Derrida in these articles, some of which draw also on Barthes, Kristeva, and Lacan, as well as the problems presented for a Derridean reading of Blake by the poet's religious beliefs and his concern for history. See *BIQ* 22 (1987–88): 116–24.

12 Blake's provocation of the reader is designed ultimately to produce the community of belief that Essick evokes (*Language of Adam*, 26, 54–55, 97, 185). See also the arguments about the creation of community between poet and audience in Blake and other romantics in Clifford Siskin, *The Historicity of Romantic Discourse* (New York and Oxford: Oxford University Press, 1988). Paul Mann throws doubt on the realization of such community in "Apocalypse and Recuperation: Blake and the Maw of Commerce," *ELH* 52 (1985): 1–32. For an overview, see Jon P. Klancher, *The Making of English Reading Audiences 1790–1832* (Madison: University of Wisconsin Press, 1987).

13 Reference to Novalis and Hegel, and the latter as corrected by Marx, for all the differences among the four authors, will suggest that Blake is not alone here. For Marx's oft-repeated reversal of Hegel's idealism, see especially "The Method of Political Economy" in *Foundations of the Critique of Political Economy*; for his use of technology to exemplify human psychology, see *Economic and Philosophic Manuscripts of 1844*, in Robert C. Tucker, ed., *The Marx-Engels Reader*, 2nd ed. (New York: Norton, 1978), 237–38, 89–90. See also Blake's annotations on Wordsworth, notably "Natural Objects always did & now do weaken, deaden & obliterate Imagination in me. Wordsworth must know that what he Writes Valuable is Not to be found in Nature" (*CPP*, 665). Along with the exalted celebration of nature in *The Disciples at Sais*, there are many subtle reflections by Novalis in that work and in *Pollens* (e.g., nos. 24, 25, 28, 45) on the relations between inner and outer, poetic intuition and scientific investigation of nature, and so on. For references in Novalis see notes to the next chapter.

14 According to Erdman, 1857 was also the date announced by Swedenborg for the "new dispensation" (*CPP*, 801).

15 See chapter 1 on "London" in William Chapman Sharpe's *Unreal Cities: Urban Figuration in Wordsworth, Baudelaire, Whitman, Eliot, and Williams* (Baltimore: Johns Hopkins University Press, 1990), and my review indicative of some of its limitations, *Modern Philology* 91 (1993): 116–18.

16 Another figure, Urthona, is named in the song.

17 See a similar argument concerning the *Marriage* and to a degree later works in Jerome J. McGann, *The Romantic Ideology: A Critical Investigation* (Chicago: University of Chicago Press, 1983), 108. On the contrary, drawing on Michael Ferber's *The Social Vision of William Blake* (Princeton: Princeton University Press, 1985), 174, Michael Ackland argues, in the case of Blake, against the standard view of an uncritical acceptance of the French Revolution followed by disillusionment after the Terror: "Ingrained Ideology: Blake, Rousseau, Voltaire and the Cult of Reason," in *Literature and Revolution*, ed. David Bevan (Amsterdam: Rodolpi, 1989), 7–18, esp. 8. For the specific context of Blake in relation to the English Swedenborgians, see Michael Scrivener, "A Swedenborgian Visionary and *The Marriage of Heaven and Hell*," *BIQ* 21 (1987–88): 102–04. The standard treatment of Blake in relation to history and politics is David Erdman, *Blake: Prophet Against Empire* (Princeton: Princeton University Press, 1954); on the *Marriage* see 160–81. Mark Schorer,

William Blake: The Politics of Vision (New York: Holt, 1946), is also fine. For marxist emphases see David Punter, *Blake, Hegel, and Dialectic* (Atlantic Highlands, N.J.: Humanities Press, 1982); Stewart Crehan, *Blake in Context* (Atlantic Highlands, N.J.: Humanities Press, 1984).

18 For the complex textual history of this fragmentary poem, see CPP, 874.

19 For example, Leopold Damrosch Jr., *Symbol and Truth in Blake's Myth* (Princeton: Princeton University Press, 1980), 168.

20 Ostriker, "Desire Gratified and Ungratified," 164. Following Webster's *Blake's Prophetic Psychology*, Anne Mellor more censoriously diagnoses Blake's supposed desire, guilt, and ambivalence toward homosexuality, anal and oral intercourse, and aggressive female sexuality in her negative review of Hagstrum's *Romantic Body: BIQ* 21 (1987): 17–19; see also his response. For a wide-ranging argument, from Plato to contemporary feminist discussion, that the figure of the androgyne primarily serves oppressive patriarchal ends, see Kari Weil, *Androgyny and the Denial of Difference* (Charlottesville: University Press of Virginia, 1992). I am grateful to Claudia Moscovici for this reference.

chapter 2

1 The English version, *Henry von Ofterdingen, A Novel*, trans. Palmer Hilty (New York: Frederick Unger, 1972), is sound save for some vagueness in the interspersed poems. For the German I cite *Heinrich von Ofterdingen*, "Universal-Bibliothek," rev. ed., ed. Wolfgang Früwald (Stuttgart: Reclam, 1987). This edition gives the text together with Novalis's and his poet friend Ludwig Tieck's notes for its intended conclusion. For the complete works, see *Novalis, Schriften: Die Werke Friedrich von Hardenbergs*, ed. Paul Kluckhohn and Richard Samuel, 5 vols. (Stuttgart: Kohlhammer, 1960–88), hereafter cited as *Schriften*. I am grateful to my colleague and friend William Crossgrove for both bibliographical and substantive suggestions regarding *Heinrich*.

   For Novalis's positions as sketched in this paragraph, see on religion *Die Christenheit oder Europa* (*Christianity or Europe*) and *Blüthenstaub* (*Pollens*), nos. 74, 77; on history and government, *Glauben und Liebe oder Der König und die Königen* (*Faith and Love or the King and the Queen*); on nature chapter 2 of *Die Lehrlinge zu Saïs* (*The Disciples at Sais*) — all in *Schriften*. Novalis's reflections are both idealistic and ambiguous. The first four entries in *Glauben und Liebe*, in which he says that he will speak indirectly and by analogy for the initiated, do not exclude the possibility of irony in his reflections on monarchy. At the least, the distance between his idealism and the government of Friedrich-Wilhelm III, who came to the Prussian throne in 1797, was considerable. On politics in general, see Hans W. Kuhn, *Der Apokalyptiker und die Politik: Studien zur Staatsphilosophie des Novalis* (Freiburg: Rombach, 1961); Hermann Kurzke, *Romantik und Konservatismus: das "politische" Werk Friedrich von Hardenbergs (Novalis) im Horizont seiner Wirkungsgeschichte* (Munich: W. Fink, 1983). For a forcefully argued view that the conservative image of Novalis projected after his death is a false one, that he was critical of religion and politically revolutionary, see W. Arctander O'Brien, *Novalis: Signs of Revolution* (Durham, N.C.: Duke University Press, 1995).

2 *Schriften*, 4:262–64, 506–10. For these letters, and for a comprehensive treatment of many of the themes summarized in the following paragraphs, see Georges Gusdorf, *Le Romantisme*, 2 vols. (Paris: Payot, 1993), esp. 1:67, 257–58, 338–41, 355–60, 370–74, 381–90, 399, 441–53, 588; 2:48, 122–33, 228–46, 338–41. More specialized critical materials on individual features will be given in later notes in direct relation to *Heinrich*.

3 See several of Blake's shorter prophetic books, notably *The [First] Book of Urizen* and *The Book of Los*, as well as Nerval's *Aurélia*.

4 For an extensive survey of many branches of romantic science and pseudoscience, including biology, geology, electricity, and galvanism (and F. W. J. von Schelling's *Naturphilosophie*), see Gusdorf, *Romantisme*, 2:359–668.

5 See *Schriften*, 2:459 (*Blüthenstaub*, 107), 3:646.

6 Compare Burghart Wachinger, *Sängerkrieg: Untersuchen zur Spruch-dichtung des 13.*

Jahrhunderts (Munich: C. H. Beck, 1973), as well as the same author's entries on Heinrich and Klingsohr in *Die deutsche Literatur des Mittelalters: Verfasserlexikon*, 2nd ed., ed. Kurt Ruh et al. (Berlin: De Gruyter, 1978), vol. 4 (1983), 855, 1220–21.

7 As already noted, *Heinrich* is fragmentary because it was incomplete when Novalis died. But see Jean-Pierre Etienne, "Novalis ou le double discours: *Heinrich von Ofterdingen*," *Romantisme* 8 (1978): 61–68; Alice Kuzniar, *Delayed Endings: Nonclosure in Novalis and Hölderlin* (Athens: University of Georgia Press, 1987); Eugene E. Reed, "*Heinrich von Ofterdingen* as 'Gesamtkunstwerk," *Philological Quarterly* 33 (1954):200–211; Oskar Walzel, "Die Formkunst von Hardenbergs *Heinrich von Ofterdingen*," *Germanisch-Romanische Monatsschrift* 7 (1915–19):403–44, 465–79.

8 In addition to Béguin's classic study *L'Ame romantique et le rêve* (Marseilles: Editions des Cahiers du Sud, 1937), see Louis Wiesmann, "Die Wiederentdeckung des Traums in der Romantik: Novalis, Hoffman, Eichendorff," in *Traum und Träumen: Traumanalysen in Wissenschaft, Religion und Kunst*, ed. Therese Wagner-Simon and Gaetano Benedetti (Göttingen: Vanderhoeck & Ruprecht, 1984), 102–12.

9 For Western sources in addition to Roos see Walter Feilchenfeld, *Der Einfluß Jacob Böhmes auf Novalis* (Berlin: Nendeln, Krauss, 1922; reprint 1967); William A. O'Brien, "Twilight in Atlantis: Novalis' *Heinrich von Ofterdingen* and Plato's *Republic*," *MLN* 95 (1980): 1292–1332; Carl Paschek, "Novalis und Böhme: Böhmenlektüre für die Dichtung des späten Novalis," *Jahrbuch des Freien Deutschen Hochstefts* (1976): 138–67. For a comparative study see Joachim J. Scholz, *Blake and Novalis: A Comparison of Romanticism's High Arguments* (Frankfurt: Lang, 1978).

10 "We seek everywhere for the unconditioned, and find always only things." Note the play on words, since "unconditioned" translates "Unbedingte," literally "unthinged." Other words quoted above similarly carry philosophical, religious, and poetic resonances. "Verkehrte" (in "astrologers in reverse") is a verb used by Hegel to signal fundamental oppositions/parallelisms. "Bild" (variously "image," "formation," "symbol") is widely employed in a variety of discourses and is a favorite word for suggesting correspondences between the phenomenal and the noumenal. For other Nerval-like expressions concerning mystic origins, the primeval human race, the search for the lost sacred language, and the role of myth, memory, and poetry, see *The Disciples at Sais* and *Pollens*, nos. 2, 101, 109.

11 The original Klingsohr is supposed, among much else, to have studied with Mohammed and Merlin. For his discussion of poetry, external nature, and subjective emotion, see 107–10. See also Dennis F. Mahoney, *Die Poetisierung der Natur bei Novalis: Beweggründe, Gestaltung, Folgen* (Bonn: Bouvier, 1980); Alfred Schlagdenhauffen, "Klingsohr — Goethe?", in *Un dialogue des nations: Albert Fuchs zum 70. Geburtstag*, ed. Maurice Colleville (Paris: Klincksieck, 1967), 121–30.

12 See Luitgard Albrecht, *Der magische Idealismus in Novalis' Märchentheorie und Märchendichtung* (Hamburg: Hansischer Gildenverlag, 1948); Gordon Birrell, *The Boundless Present: Space and Time in the Literary Fairy Tales of Novalis and Tieck* (Chapel Hill: University of North Carolina Press, 1979); Max Dietz, "Metapher und Märchengestalt. III. Novalis und das allegorische Märchen," *PMLA* 48 (1933): 488–507; Friedrich Hiebel, "Goethe's *Märchen* in the Light of Novalis," *PMLA* 63 (1948): 918–34; Walter D. Wetzels, "Klingsohrs Märchen als Science Fiction," *Monatshefte für deutschen Unterricht, deutsche Sprache und Literatur* 65 (1973): 167–75.

13 See Hans-Joachim Mähl, *Die Idee des goldenen Zeitalters im Werk des Novalis: Studien zur Wesensbestimmung der früromantischen Utopie und zu ihren ideengeschichtlichen Voraussetzungen* (Heidelberg: C. Winter, 1965); Eberhard Haufe, "Die Aufhebung der Zeit im *Heinrich von Ofterdingen*," in *Gestaltung, Umgestaltung: Festschrift zum 75. Geburtstag von Hermann August Korf*, ed. Joachim Müller (Leipzig: Koehler and Amelang, 1957), 178–88; Heinz J. Schueler, "Cosmology and Quest in Novalis' *Klingsohrs Märchen*," *Germanic Review* 49 (1974): 259–66; Eleonore M. Zimmermann, "*Heinrich von Ofterdingen*: A Striving Towards Unity," *Germanic Review* 31 (1956): 269–75.

14 For a feminist reading, see Alice Kuzniar, "Hearing Women's Voices in *Heinrich von Of-terdingen*," *PMLA* 107 (1992): 1196–1207, including her bibliography, esp. Friedrich A. Kittler, "Die Irrwege des Eros und die 'absolute Familie': Psychoanalytischer und diskur-sanalytischer Kommentar zu Klingsohrs Märchen in Novalis' *Heinrich von Ofterdingen*," in *Psychoanalytische und psychopathologische Literaturinterpretation*, ed. Bernd Urban and Winfried Kudszus (Darmstadt: Wissenschaftliche Buchgesellschaft, 1981), 421–70.

15 See Werner J. Fries, "Ginnistan und Eros: Ein Beitrag zur Symbolik in *Heinrich von Of-terdingen*," *Neophilologus* 3 (1954): 23–36; Ernst-Georg Gade, *Eros und Identität: Zur Grundstruktur der Dichtungen Friedrich von Hardenbergs (Novalis)* (Marburg: Elwert, 1974).

16 See *Faith and Love*, nos. 29, 30, 37, 41. The last speaks of a coming golden age. The refer-ence to Marx below is to the first part of *The German Ideology*, in Tucker, 147 ff. For No-valis and Fichte, see Richard W. Hannah, *The Fichtean Dynamic of Novalis' Poetics* (Bern: Peter Lang, 1981); Géza von Molnar, *Novalis' "Fichte Studies": The Foundations of His Aes-thetics* (The Hague: Mouton, 1970).

17 Subsequently (1815) Lusatia was divided between Saxony and Prussia and subjected to an intensive Germanification, much to the detriment to its Slav population.

18 See Wolfgang Kloppmann, "Eine materialistische Lektüre des Bergmann-Kapitels im *Of-terdingen*," in *Romantische Utopie, Utopische Romantik*, ed. Gisela Dischner and Richard Faber (Hildesheim: Gerstenberg, 1979), 222–39; Anthony Phelan, " 'Das Centrum das Symbol des Goldes': Analogy and Money in *Heinrich von Ofterdingen*," *German Life and Letters* 37 (1983/84): 307–21.

19 See Fredric Jameson, *The Political Unconscious: Narrative as a Socially Symbolic Act* (Ithaca: Cornell University Press, 1981), for an argument that literary works may project the union through marriage of conflicting class elements. On the basis of these passages, together with others on the family, objects, the city, trade, mining, money, profit, the feu-dal system, conquest and partition of regions, and conflict with the Middle East, treated above and in what follows, one could argue that *Heinrich* concerns the modern world much more than is initially apparent. Note *Pollens* 67, in which the noble spirit of commerce in the Middle Ages, including the Fuggers and the Medicis, is contrasted with the low com-mercial spirit of Novalis's period.

20 See Edward Said, *Orientalism* (New York: Vintage, 1978), and a contrasting view in Den-nis Porter, *Haunted Journeys: Desire and Transgression in European Travel Writing* (Prince-ton: Princeton University Press, 1991).

chapter 3

1 Ross Chambers, *Room for Maneuver: Reading (the) Oppositional (in) Narrative* (Chicago: University of Chicago Press, 1991): 103–43; *Mélancolie et opposition: Les débuts du mod-ernisme en France* (Paris: José Corti, 1987), 71–129. Chambers views Nerval as oppositional in his commitment to utopian and early socialist enthusiasms of the 1840s, bloodily re-pressed in 1848, and shows how he eludes censorship laws in the early years of the Second Empire. Kari Lokke's presentation of Nerval as socialist and republican in *Gérard de Ner-val: The Poet as Social Visionary* (Lexington, Ky.: French Forum, 1987), is viewed as ex-cessive by Susan Dunn, *French Review* 62 (1989): 1074–75.

2 See Ross Chambers, "Duplicité du pouvoir, pouvoir de la duplicité dans *Léo Burckart*," in *Nerval: Une poétique du rêve*, ed. Jacques Huré et al. (Paris: Champion, 1989), 89–98.

3 Gérard de Nerval, *Oeuvres*, Classiques Garnier, 2 vols., ed. Henri Lemaitre (Paris: Gar-nier, 1958), 1:319, 400, 503 (hereafter cited as *CG*). For the translation of *Aurélia* I cite *Se-lected Writings of Gérard de Nerval*, trans. Geoffrey Wagner (New York: Grove Press, 1957), 111–78, and for the French text *Les filles du feu, La Pandora, Aurélia*, Folio, ed. Béa-trice Didier (Paris: Gallimard, 1972), 289–354. For the extremely unstable, not to say im-possible, status of the text of *Aurélia*, the second part of which was published after the au-thor's suicide, see the apparatus in the last volume of the authoritative edition, *Oeuvres complètes*, Bibliothèque de la Pléiade, 3 vols., ed. Jean Guillaume et al. (Paris: Gallimard,

1993). Other works by Nerval that I cite by title only are contained in both *CG* and Pléiade editions.

4 Gilles Deleuze and Félix Guattari, *Anti-Oedipus: Capitalism and Schizophrenia*, trans. Robert Hurley, Mark Seem, and Helen R. Lane (Minneapolis: University of Minnesota Press, 1983).

5 Baudelaire's correspondence contains only two brief notes to Nerval. But as his editors remark, in a letter to Auguste Poulet-Mallassis (20 March 1861?) he expressed the fear of a sickness "à la Gérard," the inability to think or write a single line. Since Nerval experienced such fear but never expressed it in published works, this implies a greater closeness between the two than generally supposed: *Correspondance*, ed. Claude Pichot and Jean Ziegler, 2 vols., Bibliothèque de la Pléiade (Paris: Gallimard, 1973), 1:164, 165; 2:135–36, 717.

6 The second-century author of a Latin romance, *The Golden Ass*, which among much else contains material on Eastern religions, including the cult of Isis and Osiris. In this passage Nerval, recalling Blake, notes that Swedenborg called his visions *Memorabilia*. The *Mémorables* at the end of *Aurélia* are Nerval's version of the form.

7 See *Les Chimères*, "Artémis."

8 *Des métaphores obsédantes au mythe personnel: Introduction à la psychocritique* (Paris: José Corti, 1963). See also Shoshana Felman, "Gérard de Nerval: Writing Living, or Madness and Autobiography," in *Writing and Madness (Literature/Philosophy/Psychoanalysis)*, trans. Martha Noel Evans and the author (Ithaca: Cornell University Press, 1989), 59–77; Michel Jeanneret, *La lettre perdue: Ecriture et folie dans l'oeuvre de Nerval* (Paris: Flammarion, 1978).

9 Chambers, *Room*, 134: "small-scale and large-scale parataxis."

10 On the cabalistic materials here and the readings evoked in the second synthesizing passage treated below there are also Nerval's own references, scattered throughout *Le voyage en Orient*, as well as his systematic summaries of authors and readings in the second section of the chapter on Cazotte and the first of that on Cagliostro in *Les Illuminés*. But an older tendency to explain all in Nerval in reference to esoteric doctrine, exemplified by Jean Richer, especially in *Gérard de Nerval et les doctrines ésotériques* (Paris: Editions du Griffon d'or, 1947), is no longer widely shared.

11 Nerval's *Voyage en Orient* must be one of the works least subject to this criticism, since it deromanticizes attitudes toward the Middle East, explaining misconceptions (in particular stressing Eastern traditions of religious tolerance) and contrasting the allure of Oriental women with the narrator's self-referential humor and sometimes self-ridiculing behavior. Here again we recall Novalis, especially chapter 4 of *Heinrich*. In personal, political, and religious terms, the very long *Voyage* is at virtually every point acute.

12 Wagner translation, p. 157 n.

13 Chambers, *Mélancholie*, 167–86; Edward Ahearn, "Marx's Relevance for Second Empire Literature: Baudelaire's 'Le Cygne,' " *Nineteenth-Century French Studies* 14 (1986): 269–77.

14 See *Les filles du feu, La Pandora*, the first chapter of *Petits châteaux de Bohème*, and *Aurélia*, 431.

15 See *Les nuits d'octobre* (1852) for melancholy (but not frantic) evocations of the same itinerary. The nocturnal wanderings in *Aurélia* are filled with historically resonant references to streets, churches, and monuments, too detailed to be exhausted here, but that may be explored in the appropriate entries in Jacques Hillairet's superb *Dictionnaire historique des rues de Paris*, 2 vols. (Paris: Minuit, 1985). In addition to the implicit history I sketch here, the narrator directly evokes events of the Hundred Years' War and the reign of Napoleon.

16 Chambers (*Room*, 134) somewhat differently sees the Mémorables as a "series of discrete dreams following an internal order of succession that is without apparent logic." My analysis suggests an indirect logic concerning religion, sexuality, and history and linking the Mémorables to the rest of the work. See Michel Jeanneret, "La folie est un rêve: Nerval et le docteur Moreau de Tours," *Romantisme* 27 (1980): 59–75, for an emphasis on the work

as a "discours incertain," and Frank Bowman's contrary emphasis on coherence: " 'Mémorables' d'*Aurélia*: Signification et situation générique," *French Forum* 11, 2 (May 1986): 169–81, now available in English in Bowman's *French Romanticism: Intertextual and Interdisciplinary Readings. Parallax Re-visions of Culture and Society* (Baltimore: Johns Hopkins University Press, 1990). For other aspects of form, see Jeanneret, *La lettre perdue*; Léon Cellier, *De "Sylvie" à "Aurélia": Structure close et structure ouverte* (Paris: Lettres Modernes, 1971); Jacques Bony, *Le Récit nervalien* (Paris: Corti, 1990) — and the negative review of the last by Bruno Tritsmans, summarizing an array of scholarship in *Nineteenth-Century French Studies* 20 (1991–92): 228–31.

17 *CG* 1:818 n. 1.

18 See Nerval's subversion of the biblical story of Solomon and Sheba in the *Voyage*: "Histoire de la reine du matin et de Soliman prince des génies" (esp. *CG* 2:585–88, 610, 654, 658). Elsewhere the *huppe* is noted as sacred to Soliman, and Adonis is identified as a Syrian divinity (*CG* 1:155, 335).

19 *Libération*, 24 Jan. 1992, 16–17.

chapter 4

1 A most useful edition is Isidore Ducasse, le comte de Lautréamont, *Les chants de Maldoror, Poésies I et II, Correspondance*, "GF," ed. Jean-Luc Steinmetz (Paris: Flammarion, 1990), so comprehensive in notes and bibliography that occasionally I will refer without specific notation to Steinmetz's information on a particular passage or theme, or even take it for granted without mention (e.g., in the critical discussion concerning the relation between *Maldoror* and *Poésies*). When specific pages are given, they will be preceded by *GF*. The best, though not a perfect, English translation is by Alexis Lykiard, *Lautréamont's "Maldoror"* (London: Allison & Busby, 1983). I will refer parenthetically to *chants* (or cantos), strophes (which are not numbered in Lykiard's translation), and pages in that translation by roman capital, roman lower case, and arabic numbers (I, i, 1–2). As I will remind the reader later, the "novel" in the concluding canto contains chapters divided by capital roman numerals in both French and English editions.

2 For satanic and sadistic elements see Maurice Blanchot, *Lautréamont et Sade* (Paris: Minuit, 1949); for the fantastic see Pierre-Georges Castex, *Le conte fantastique en France de Nodier à Maupassant* (Paris: Corti, 1951), 315–44 — subsequently withdrawn on the grounds that the *Chants* are not fantastic (*GF* 471).

3 See Gaston Bachelard, *Lautréamont* (Paris: Corti, 1939); Marcel Jean and Arpad Mezei, *Maldoror* (Paris: Pavois, 1947).

4 *GF*, 14; Bruno Guitard, "Tendresse de Lautréamont," *Europe* (Aug.-Sept. 1987):68–77. Steinmetz (following Steve Murphy) correctly points out that "infundibuliforme" (shaped like a funnel) was the term used in the medical report on Verlaine after he wounded Rimbaud in July 1873 (*GF* 416).

5 Whereas the male divinity evoked in Rimbaud's "Génie" is in no way parodic.

6 See *GF* 27–30, Steinmetz's references to discussions of aspects of form throughout, e.g., Raymond Jean on the conflict between "récit" (narrative) and interrupting "discours" in *Lectures du désir* (Paris: Seuil, 1986); Philippe Sollers on the subversion of representation in *Logiques* (Paris: Seuil, 1968), 250–301; Julia Kristeva on the mobile subject and metalinguistic function in *La Révolution du langage poétique* (Paris: Seuil, 1974); Ora Avni, *Tics, tics et tics: Figures, syllogismes, récits dans "Les Chants de Maldoror"* (Lexington, Ky.: French Forum, 1984).

7 Tzvetan Todorov, *Introduction à la littérature fantastique* (Paris: Seuil, 1970), 28–45.

8 Steinmetz aptly speaks of "production onirique insomniaque," *GF* 36. See also J. M. G. Le Clézio, "Le Rêve de Maldoror," in *Lautréamont*, collective edition (Paris: Complexe, 1987), 65–134.

9 A passage in *Poésies II* (*GF* 348), with what degree of irony it is difficult to judge, claims, along with much else, that poetry is not involved with political events. And from a com-

ment about anarchy in literature Steinmetz argues against Ducasse as revolutionary (*GF*, 338, 432). But see Raoul Vaneigem, "Isidore Ducasse et le comte de Lautréamont," *Poésies, Synthèses* (Dec. 1958):243–49; Marcelin Pleynet, "Lautréamont politique," *Tel Quel* 45 (spring 1971):23–45; and especially Lucienne Rochon, "Le trajet de Mervyn, ou le roman parodique de lui-même," *Littérature* 16 (Dec. 1974): 67–87. For the argument in what follows about the historical and political aspects of streets, neighborhoods, and monuments see Priscilla Parkhurst Ferguson, "Reading Revolutionary Paris," in Philippe Desan, Priscilla Parkhurst Ferguson, and Wendy Griswold, eds., *Literature and Social Practice* (Chicago: University of Chicago Press, 1989), 46–68; as well as her book, Priscilla Parkhurst Clark, *Literary France: The Making of a Culture* (Berkeley: University of California Press, 1991), 1–7.

10 An extensive literature on the chiffonnier is cited in Richard D. E. Burton's excellent *Baudelaire and the Revolution of 1848: The Making of the Wine Poems*, published by the author at the University of Sussex, Brighton, England in 1984. See particularly Victor Fournel, *Ce qu'on voit dans les rues de Paris* (Paris: Adolphe Delahays, 1858), esp. 326–29; H.-A. Fréguier, *Des classes dangereuses de la société dans les grandes villes* (Paris: J. B. Baillière, 1840). I am indebted to Ross Chambers for this reference. The ragman was widely viewed as the lowest of the poor in Paris. In the initial euphoria of 1848, he represented a vague republican fraternalism, but, like Daumier's Ratapoil, soon embodied the *Lumpenproletariat* who supported Louis-Bonaparte. Since he literally handled every kind of refuse, he recalls the castrating décrotteur, which suggests contradiction (simultaneously protective and murderous), both in sexual-scatological themes and in terms of class.

11 This Parisian geography, which closely overlaps that in *Aurélia*, is again filled with historical meaning, as a perusal of Hillairet's *Dictionnaire* shows. Two examples: the rue Vivienne, dating from the seventeenth century and associated with Colbert, Mazarin, and Richelieu, passes behind the Bibliothèque Nationale and within sight of the Bourse; in the nineteenth century it was the site of theaters, luxurious restaurants, and some of the first shopping malls and *grands magasins*. Mervyn's family lives on a street built under Charles X and named for that monarch until he was overthrown in 1830, whereupon it acquired the name it has retained, rue de La Fayette!

12 Edward Ahearn, *Marx and Modern Fiction* (New Haven: Yale University Press, 1989), 201, on Marx's *Eighteenth Brumaire of Louis Bonaparte*; Tucker, 617; *Moby-Dick*, ch. 35, "The Mast-Head."

13 Kristin Ross, *The Emergence of Social Space: Rimbaud and the Paris Commune* (Minneapolis: University of Minnesota Press, 1988), 3–43, discusses the relation between the toppling of the column and the poetry of Rimbaud, with reference to Lautréamont and Marx.

14 Some twenty-five thousand persons, most of them working-class, died in the fighting, more than died in the Franco-Prussian War or the Terror. See Stewart Edwards, *The Paris Commune: 1871* (Devon: Newton Abbot, 1972), 313–50; and Jacques Rougerie, *Procès des Communards* (Paris: Gallimard, 1978), cited in Ross, *The Emergence of Social Space*, 4.

chapter 5

1 I thus refer to *Manifestoes of Surrealism*, trans. Richard Seaver and Helen R. Lane, Ann Arbor Paperbacks (Ann Arbor: University of Michigan Press, 1974), containing the first and second manifestos and a number of related works. I cite Richard Howard's translation of *Nadja* (New York: Grove Press, 1960), which does not contain the 1962 preface to the revised French edition, Folio (Paris: Gallimard, 1964). I refer to the French edition of *Manifestes du surréalisme*, Folio (Paris: Gallimard, 1991), and to *L'Amour fou* (Paris: Gallimard, 1937) and *Arcane 17* (Paris: "10/18," 1965). I quote *Le paysan de Paris*, rev. ed. (Paris: Gallimard, 1953), abbreviated in notes as *PP*, translated by Frederik Brown as *Nightwalker (Le paysan de Paris)* (Englewood Cliffs, N.J.: Prentice-Hall, 1970). I refer to Aragon's *Traité du style*, Collection L'Imaginaire (1928; reprint, Paris: Gallimard 1983). See Alyson Waters's translation, *Treatise on Style* (Lincoln: University of Nebraska Press, 1991).

2 Pierre Daix, *Aragon: Une vie à changer*, rev. ed. (Paris: Flammarion, 1994), 509.

3 Feuerbach is foregrounded because of his humanistic critique of religion; Breton makes no mention of Marx's critique of Feuerbach. The problem of the relations between mental and socioeconomic realms is labored over in the second manifesto. Margaret Cohen, *Profane Illumination: Walter Benjamin and the Paris of Surrealist Revolution* (Berkeley: University of California Press, 1993), 120–39, shows Breton to be more subtle and successful in relating Engels and Marx, including the latter's *Theses on Feuerbach*, to the surrealist themes in *Les vases communicants*. In the first manifesto Breton recognizes not only Apollinaire and Nerval but Greek oracles, Shakespeare (playfully), and figures as different as Kant, Pascal, and Curie. On the nineteenth-century literature of protest, alchemy, magic, and Gnostic traditions, see the second manifesto and the much later (1953) *Du surréalisme en ses oeuvres vives* (M 152–53, 173–78, 302–04). *Prolégomènes à un troisième manifeste du surréalisme ou non* (1942), which is included in both the French and English editions of the *Manifestes* that I cite, and *Arcane 17* (1945) range as widely, from Novalis, Nerval and Hugo to Paracelsus, Swedenborg, Pythagoras, Apuleius, the Cabala and even Theresa of Avila. (Not to mention Heraclitus, Eckhart, Swift, Sade, Engels, and others). Trotsky expressed concern about Breton's other-worldly tendency, calling his concept of "le hasard objectif" a window to the "au-delà": Breton quoted in Sarane Alexandrian, *André Breton par lui-même* (Paris: Seuil, 1971), 112. But at the 1935 Congrès des écrivains Breton proclaimed, " 'Transformer le monde' a dit Marx; 'Changer la vie' a dit Rimbaud: ces deux mots d'ordre pour nous n'en font qu'un": quoted in Bernard Noël, "L'Oeil surréaliste," in *La planète affollée: Surréalisme, dispersion et influences 1938–47*, collective edition (Marseille: Flammarion, 1986), 15. Concerning idealist philosophy, Breton refers to Berkeley in *Nadja* (86) and to Hegel and Feuerbach at a number of points in the second manifesto. Aragon subtly transcends arguments in Kant, Hegel, and others in *Paysan*, particularly in "Préface à une mythologie moderne," ch. 1 of "Le sentiment de la nature aux Buttes-Chaumont," and in "Le songe du paysan." It should be noted that Aragon protests against such criticisms based on contradictions in surrealism, including reliance on the movement's predecessors (*Traité*, 197–232). For recent efforts to reconcile Freud, Marx, philosophical idealism, and esoteric thought in surrealism, see the collectively edited volume, *Surréalisme et philosophie* (Paris: Editions du Centre Pompidou, 1992).

4 Daix's book, though primarily concerned with Aragon, is wonderfully evenhanded in its treatment of the positions of the two writers. As is conveyed by its title, Cohen's *Profane Illumination: Walter Benjamin and the Paris of Surrealist Revolution* takes as its point of departure Benjamin's marxist-oriented celebration not only of *Nadja* but also of *Le paysan de Paris*. On Benjamin see esp. 9–10, 173, 188, drawing on his *Reflections*, ed. Peter Demetz, trans. Edmund Jephcott (New York: Harcourt Brace Jovanovich, 1978). As will be apparent, my evaluation of Breton is more negative than Cohen's.

5 Daix, *Aragon*, 201–15. On the identity of Nadja, Breton's love for other women (first Lise Meyer, then Suzanne Muzard), and his subsequent divorce from his wife Simone, see the Chronologie and Notice in the first volume of *Oeuvres complètes*, Bibliothèque de la Pléiade, ed. Marguerite Bonnet et al. (Paris: Gallimard, 1988), esp. 1509–17.

6 Roland Barthes, "To Write: An Intransitive Verb?," in Richard and Fernande DeGeorge, eds., *The Structuralists from Marx to Lévi-Strauss* (Garden City, N.Y.: Doubleday Anchor, 1972), 163.

7 *Nadja* is the only work revised for republication by Breton. See the Notes et variantes in the Pléiade edition.

8 For example the object that Breton photographs, then explains as an Italian device for demographic calculations (52). For more positive views on objects see Jean Baudrillard, *Le système des objets* (Paris: Gallimard, 1960), 114–20; Paule Plouvier, *Poétique de l'amour chez André Breton* (Paris: Corti, 1983), 51–53. On the photographs see J. H. Matthews, "Désir et merveilleux dans *Nadja* d'André Breton," *Symposium* 27 (1973): 258–62; Jean Arrouye, "La Photographie dans *Nadja*," *Mélusine* 4 (1983): 123–51; Dawn Ades, "Photography and the Surrealist Text," in L'Amour fou: *Photography and Surrealism*, ed. Rosalind Krauss and

Jane Livingston (New York: Abbeville Press, 1985), 165; Normand Lalonde, "L'Icono-
graphie photographique de *Nadja*," *French Review* 66 (1992): 48–58.

9 Here Breton is close to Nerval; in *L'Amour fou* he systematizes such experiences as "le
hasard objectif."

10 See especially Françoise Calin's excellent *"Le Paysan de Paris* et son 'entreprise insen-
sée,' " Degré Second: *Studies in French Literature* 9 (1985):51–65. On form in both works
see also Aleksander Ablamowicz, "Le Fonctionnement des images dans *Le Paysan de Paris*
de Louis Aragon," in *L'Ordre du descriptif*, ed. Jean Bessière (Paris: PUF, 1988), 193–208,
and "La Structure du romanesque dans *Nadja* d'André Breton," in *Signes du roman, signes
de la transition*, ed. Jean Bessière (Paris: PUF, 1986), 235–46; Franz-Josef Albersmeier,
"Collage und Montage im surrealistischen Roman: Zu Aragons *Le Paysan de Paris* und
Bretons *Nadja*," *LiLi: Zeitschrift fur Literaturwissenschaft und Linguistik* 12 (1982): 46–63;
Stamos Metzidakis, "L'Apothéose de l'erreur: Etude du jeu dans *Le Paysan de Paris*,"
Rackham Literary Studies 9 (1978): 7–13; Lawrence D. Kritzman, "For a Structural Analy-
sis of *Nadja*: A Scientific Experiment," *Rackham Literary Studies* 4 (1973): 9–23; Peter W.
Nesselroth, "Form and Meaning in *Le Paysan de Paris*," *Dada/Surrealism* 5 (1975): 20–27;
Claude Martin, "*Nadja* et le mieux-dire," *Revue de l'Histoire Littéraire de la France* 72
(1972): 274–86; René R. Hubert, "The Coherence of Breton's *Nadja*," *Contemporary Literature* 10 (1967): 241–52.

11 Roman Jakobson, "The Metaphoric and Metonymic Poles," in *Critical Theory Since Plato*,
ed. Hazard Adams (New York: Harcourt Brace Jovanovich, 1971), 1113–16.

12 It is true that I discuss the contradictions of surrealism and even later introduce a comparison with Montaigne. See *Traité*, 215 ff. But I agree strongly with Aragon's attack on the
ideologically repressive role of much journalistic and academic criticism, and with his
stress on the politically subversive role of literature.

13 See Jean Luc Steinmetz's edition of *Les Chants de Maldoror* (Paris: Flammarion, 1990), 143;
the Breton lecture is collected in *Les pas perdus*, Collection Idées (Paris: Gallimard, 1969),
148–174, esp. 163.

14 Rimbaud's famous *lettre du voyant*, 15 May 1871, and the prose poem "Solde."

15 This accounts for the relative absence of traditional visionary motifs in Aragon, who refers
to the "séduisantes erreurs" of religions encountered in a "gros livre allemand" (140), presumably Georg Friedrich Creuzer's *Symbolik und Mythologie der alten Völker*. Similarly,
Breton rejects the religious literature of the East and Scandinavia as childish (*M* 25–26).
PP humorously evokes (82) the "dormeurs éveillés des mille et une nuits," "les miraculés
et les convulsionnaires," claiming that "les haschischins modernes" have superior "pouvoir visionnaire." The reference to another Rimbaud prose poem, "Matinée d'ivresse," is
clear.

16 On the surreal city, see Peter Collier, "Surrealist City Narrative: Breton and Aragon," in
Unreal City: Urban Experience in Modern European Literature and Art, ed. Edward Timms
and Peter Collier (New York: Saint Martin's Press, 1985), 214–29; Jean Gaulmier, "Re-
marques sur le thème de Paris chez André Breton, de *Nadja* à *L'Amour fou*," *Travaux de
Linguistique et de Littérature* 9 (1971): 159–70; Nicolas Wagner, "*Nadja*: Ville de l'an-
goisse," *Travaux de Linguistique et de Littérature* 14 (1976): 221–28; and esp. Jacques Leenhardt, "Le passage comme forme d'expérience: Benjamin face à Aragon," in *Walter Benjamin et Paris* (Paris: Cerf, 1986), 163–71. Although she does not include Leenhardt in her
bibliography, Cohen, *Profane Illuminations*, 77–119, 173–259, writes extensively on the city
in Breton, Benjamin, Marx, and Baudelaire.

17 For another aspect of Aragon's visionary writing, see *Traité*, 175–80, where as "le bijoutier
des matières déchues" Aragon, like a jeweller, makes poetry out of the small and the low:
insects, bits of glass, shit, rat's hair. Analogies are to be found in Blake, Rimbaud's *Ce qu'on
dit au poète à propos de fleurs*, Sartre's *La Nausée*, Kincaid's *At the Bottom of the River*.

18 Robert Champigny, "Analyse d'une définition du surréalisme," *PMLA* 81 (1966): 139–44.

19 For an extensive and critical treatment of the surrealists see Xavière Gauthier, *Surréalisme
et sexualité*, Collection Idées (Paris: Gallimard, 1971). On *Nadja* see Susan Rubin Suleiman,

notes to pages 97–105

185

Subversive Intent: Gender, Politics, and the Avant-Garde (Cambridge, Mass.: Harvard University Press, 1990): 99–110. Although hardly blind to his faults, Cohen (*Profane Illumination*) treats the love theme in Breton's Parisian trilogy far more sympathetically.

20 Gauthier, *Surréalisme et sexualité*, 236–46 — e.g., the nocturnal visit of the three men to the park in *PP*. Aragon was the only surrealist not to express opposition to homosexuality. Daix, *Aragon*, 407, 409, 532 ff., refers to Aragon's homosexual tendency before his marriage to Elsa Triolet, her concern about it, and the flamboyant dress and coterie of young men that after her death caused him to be lampooned as a homosexual.

21 Following André Pieyre de Mandiargues, the Pléiade edition (1515–16) notes that the original text contains the name of the hotel where Nadja and Breton arrived in the middle of the night, hence making it clearer that they did have a sexual relationship.

22 The exoticism of earlier works makes up a significant portion of sexual "bad taste" in both writers. Examples in *PP* include the theater featuring naked women representing regions of the world, "cet alhambra de putain," and Breton's Gauguin-like cane, exhibiting obscene postures, including the "drôle de spectacle terrifiant un nègre barbu qui bande vers le bas" (133–34, 183).

23 Gloria Orenstien, "*Nadja* Revisited: A Feminist Approach," *Dada/Surrealism* 8 (1978): 91–106.

24 Aragon (*Traité*, 227) defends himself against a similar criticism about the discrepancy between the claims of his writing and the apparent prudence of his life. He later risked prosecution for the poem "Front rouge," and, whatever we think of the politics of both writers, we should recognize their considerable courage in pursuing them.

25 See Jean-Paul Sartre, "Qu'est-ce que la littérature?," in *Situations II* (Paris: Gallimard, 1948), 172–74, 214–25.

26 For basic information, see Maurice Nadeau, *Histoire du surréalisme* (Paris: Seuil, 1945), 202–6. Nadeau is considered anti-Breton by Breton defenders such as Alexandrian in *André Breton par lui-même*, esp. 100 ff. Pierre Daix's revised biography of Aragon provides full and objective evidence for the summary I give below. The following provide variously objective and slanted presentations: Dominique Arban, *Aragon parle avec Dominique Arban* (Paris: Seghers, 1968); Roger Garaudy, *L'Itinéraire d'Aragon* (Paris: Gallimard, 1961); C. G. Geoghegan, "Surrealism and Communism: The Hesitations of Aragon from Kharkov to the 'Affaire Front Rouge,' " *Journal of European Studies* 8 (1978): 12–33; Walter Heist, "Aragon, der seltsame Kommunist," *Frankfurter Hefte* 17 (1962): 118–25; Sylvia Kantarizis, "Surrealism, Communism and Love," *Essays in French Literature* 7 (1970): 1–17; Helena Lewis, *Dada Turns Red: The Politics of Surrealism* (Edinburgh: Edinburgh University Press, 1990); André Thirion, *Révolutionnaires sans révolution* (Paris: R. Laffont, 1972).

27 According to Daix (*Aragon*, 445–46), Aragon and Elsa Triolet were nonetheless aware of the extent of earlier communist repression. Their role in France may be judged by the fact that the accusation leading to the expulsion of the wife of Louis Althusser from the French Communist Party came from Elsa. See Michel Contat's review of Althusser's posthumous memoir, *L'Avenir dure longtemps* (Paris: Stock/IMEC, 1992), and of the first volume of Yann Moulier Boutang, *Louis Althusser: Une biographie* (Paris: Grasset, 1992), *Le Monde*, 24 April 1992, p. 31.

28 Cited in *La planète affollée*, 271. Breton's warning against communism is in *Prolégomènes à un troisième manifeste du surréalisme ou non* (1942).

29 See Françoise Calin's remarkable "Une relecture des 'faits-glissades' dans *Nadja*: Mise en ordre des hantises, déchiffrage des non-dits," *Neophilologus* 74 (1990): 44–57, which treats the portion of the work leading to this "apocalypse," with many points similar to mine, and much more, together with a full bibliography. In contrast, a canonical, apolitical interpretation, that the conflagration anticipates the tragic fate of Nadja, is presented in the Pléiade edition (1498, 1541–42), which also provides the information that the manoir was a hotel. Aragon was staying nearby, writing his *Traité de style*, and the two met repeatedly to discuss their work (1502–3). In the final edition, the passage on the destruction of the

Manoir d'Ango is unchanged from the original. Cohen, *Profane Illumination* (77–119, 217–59) remarks many historical features of Parisian literature, in Baudelaire and Marx as well as in Breton, but unlike Calin (who also does not appear in her bibliography) she evidences little awareness of Breton's contradictions.

30 In the letter to Soupault, Aragon speaks of slipping into his book "quelques propos un peu libres pour la France" (224), doubtless primarily concerning sex.

31 See Daix's reading of certain Resistance poems in which some of the same regions, then the scene of World War II battles, are evoked in disguised form, together with revolutionary echoes of texts by Baudelaire ("Le Cygne" and "Le Mauvais Vitrier"). Thus for "la Crimée": "Le crime de rêver je consens qu'on l'instaure / Si je rêve c'est bien de ce qu'on m'interdit" (*Aragon*, 392–93).

chapter 6

1 William S. Burroughs's *Naked Lunch* was first published in the United States in 1962. I cite the First Evergreen Cat edition (New York: Grove Press, 1966). Two extremely useful critical anthologies are *William S. Burroughs at the Front: Critical Reception, 1959–1989*, ed. Jennie Skerl and Robin Lydenberg (Carbondale: Southern Illinois University Press, 1991), hereafter *Front*, and the Burroughs issue of *The Review of Contemporary Fiction* 4 (1984), hereafter *Review*. See also Eric Mottram, *William Burroughs: The Algebra of Need* (London: Boyars, 1977); Michael B. Goodman, *Contemporary Literary Censorship: The Case History of Burroughs' Naked Lunch* (Metuchen, N.J.: Scarecrow, 1981). *Naked Lunch* is often presented as a trilogy along with *The Soft Machine* (1961) and *Nova Express* (1964), but *The Ticket That Exploded*, although published later, was written in 1962. For Jennie Skerl (*Front*, 189), *Naked Lunch* is a seminal work for the three others, and this is one reason why I treat it here. It is also more accessible, having by 1984 sold more than a half million copies and achieved "canonical status amongst Underground readers": David Glover, "Utopia and Fantasy in the Late 1960s: Burroughs, Moorcock, Tolkien," in *Popular Fiction and Social Change*, ed. Christopher Pawling (New York: St. Martin's Press, 1984), 194–95. Such canonical status gives one pause with respect to the validity of the visionary in Burroughs, an issue to which we will return. This theme is highlighted in Ted Morgan's biography, *Literary Outlaw: The Life and Times of William S. Burroughs* (New York: Henry Holt and Company, 1988), which also treats the writer's relations with other figures of the beat generation.

2 See Ihab Hassan's fine "The Subtracting Machine: The Work of William Burroughs" — he alludes also to Rimbaud (*Front*, 53); Marshall McLuhan ("Notes on Burroughs," *Front*, 69–73, especially 70) sees *Naked Lunch* as "the anti-Utopia of *Illuminations*."

3 See "Negative Ecstasy: Experience and Form in the 'Jardin public' Passage in *La Nausée*," in *Fiction, Form, Experience: The French Novel from Naturalism to the Present* (Essays in Honor of Albert J. Salvan), ed. Grant E. Kaiser (Montreal: Editions France-Québec, 1976), 144–153. For Sartre's attack on surrealism below see "Qu'est-ce que la littérature?" in *Situations II* (Paris: Gallimard, 1948), 172–74, 214–25.

4 In "Reading Robbe-Grillet: Sadism and Text in *Projet pour une révolution à New York*" (*Subversive Intent: Gender, Politics, and the Avant-Garde* (Cambridge, Mass: Harvard University Press, 1990), 51–71), Susan Suleiman refuses to allow *écriture* to obfuscate the sadism and misogyny in Robbe-Grillet's book. We encounter similar issues in *Naked Lunch*. Concerning the link with Sartre, we should recall the complex sexuality of his work, including bisexual notes, fascination with homosexuality, and identification of eating, excreting, sex. See George H. Bauer, "Sartre's Homo / Textuality: Eating / The Other," and Serge Doubrovsky, "Sartre's *La Nausée*: Fragment of an Analytic Reading," both in *Homosexualities and French Literature: Cultural Contexts/Critical Texts*, ed. George Stambolian and Elaine Marks (Ithaca: Cornell University Press, 1979), 312–40.

5 See Frank D. McConnell, "William Burroughs and the Literature of Addiction" (*Front*, 87–101). McConnell sees the centrality of "Kubla Khan" and links romantic poetry, as "the

packaging of experience," to both drugs and the economic. See also my "Toward a Model of Ecstatic Poetry: Coleridge's 'Kubla Khan' and Rimbaud's 'Villes I' and 'Barbare,'" *Modern Language Studies* 12 (1982): 42–58, and *Rimbaud: Visions and Habitations* (Berkeley: University of California Press, 1983), 187–92. In a letter to Richard Woodhouse (27 October 1818) Keats referred to Wordsworth as the "egotistical sublime."

6 This is not widely recognized. But see Barbara L. Estrin, "The Revelatory Connection: Inspired Poetry and *Naked Lunch*" (*Review*, 58–64), linking *Naked Lunch* to God, Moses, and Aaron in the book of Exodus.

7 Frequently Burroughs drops the *s* at end of third-person singular verbs, presumably as part of his fabled mastery of speech rhythms, which often as here becomes an intrusive mannerism.

8 McConnell ("Literature of Addiction," *Front*, 97, 99) is very good on both of these elements; in particular he correctly stresses that the futuristic in *Naked Lunch* concerns not the future but the present, that the fearsome visions making up the bulk of the book are not drug-induced hallucinations but "clarified visions of present reality made more terrible."

9 The film analogy is used at a number of points: it appears in the blue movies of the A. J. chapter and in various fadeouts, e.g. that concerning the futuristic senders and their early history: "Techniques of Sending were crude at first. Fadeout to the National Electronic Conference in Chicago" (162). Like the earlier writers Burroughs is highly "mixed-media," collaborating with artists and filmmakers: see the introduction to *Front* (10); Anne Friedberg, " 'Cut-Ups': A Syn*ema of the text*," *Front*, 169–73. Burroughs also contributed to David Cronenberg's film version of *Naked Lunch*.

10 Despite reported participation by Ginsberg, Kerouac, and others in the production of *Naked Lunch*, the book is much less marked than its successors by collaborative and chance methods such as Brion Gysin's "cut-up" method and Burroughs's "fold-in" method. (But see Nicholas Zurbrugg, "Burroughs, Grauerholz, and *Cities of the Red Night*: An Interview with James Grauerholz," *Review*, 19–32, esp. 20, 30 n. 17). Michael Leddy is suspicious of suggestions in *Naked Lunch* that the book is unfinished or innocent of authorial responsibility (" 'Departed Have Left No Address': Revelation/Concealment Presence/Absence in *Naked Lunch*," *Review*, 33–40); Robin Lydenberg presents the case for persistent contradiction and indeterminacy, supposedly making the book elusive for "humanistic" criticism ("Beyond Good and Evil: 'How-to' Read *Naked Lunch*" *Review*, 75–85). On cut-ups, fold-ins, and tape recorders, see Burroughs and Gysin's *The Third Mind* (New York: Viking, 1978); Daniel Odier, *The Job: Interviews with William S. Burroughs* (New York: Grove Press, 1969); Michael Skau, "The Central Verbal System: The Prose of William Burroughs," *Style* 15 (1981): 401–14; Olivier C. G. Harris, "Cut-Up Closure: The Return to Narrative," in *Front*, 251–61. For Burroughs in relation to écriture and "postmodernism," see Nicholas Zurbrugg, "Burroughs, Barthes, and the Limits of Intertextuality," in *Review*, 86–102; Robin Lydenberg, *Word Cultures: Radical Theory and Practice in William S. Burroughs' Fiction* (Urbana: University of Illinois Press, 1987).

11 See Anthony C. Hilfer, "Mariner and Wedding Guest in William Burroughs' *Naked Lunch*," *Criticism* 22 (1980): 252–65.

12 Gregory Stephenson, "The Gnostic Vision of William S. Burroughs," *Review*, 40–49.

13 For an opposing, and justifiably very negative, view on the body in Burroughs, see Cary Nelson, "The End of the Body: Radical Space in Burroughs," *Front*, 119–32; Wayne Pounds argues for a utopian function for anality in Burroughs, although he in no way minimizes his misogyny, in "The Postmodern Anus: Parody and Utopia in Two Recent Novels by William Burroughs," *Front*, 217–32.

14 Odier, *The Job*, 50. The same work (97) shows how Burroughs recalls the surrealists in linking notions of reality and morality: "As soon as we say that something is real then immediately things are not permitted." With the exception of Aragon, the surrealists condemned homosexuality, Breton strongly. But recall Xavière Gauthier's demonstration of pervasive homosocial or homosexual and sadomasochistic elements throughout the production of many surrealists in *Surréalisme et sexualité* (Paris: Gallimard, 1991), 230–68.

15 *Front* anthologizes the early moral debate over *Naked Lunch* and subsequent books: the Ugh review in *TLS*, David Lodge's ethical broadsides, the to me more persuasive sense of deadly relevance in Burroughs expressed by McLuhan and Mary McCarthy. Noting that Burroughs had been diagnosed by a psychiatrist as a schizophrenic paranoid, Hassan ("The Subtracting Machine," *Front*, 54) persuasively argues for the closeness of madness and moral passion, claiming that like Swift, Breughel, and Bosch, Burroughs "pushes satire toward the threshold of pathology." Robin Lydenberg's "Beyond Good and Evil" (*Review*, 75–85) cites a number of Burroughs's oppositional positions but may rely too much on Inspector Lee in *Nova Express* in expressing an ethical inactivism that needs to be examined and may wrongly assume that Burroughs is always positively motivated: "Burroughs is trying to take the thrill out of junk, just as he tries to take the thrill out of violence and sex orgy in the Blue Movie scene" (81). I think Burroughs more morally insidious than that, and in any case Lydenberg ascribes to him here a quite straightforward and conventional ethical intention. Similarly, David Glover, "Utopia and Fantasy in the Late 1960s," illustrates Burroughs's violent rejection of virtually everything in our world, including any known form of political struggle. He warns that this is "no simple liberal humanist vision" but seems insufficiently concerned about Burroughs's canonical status for underground culture — not to speak of linking him with Moorcock and Tolkien. Marxist critics soon counterattacked on ideological grounds (see note 21).

16 See *Front*, 15 n. 20, esp. Alice Jardine, *Gynesis: Configurations of Woman and Modernity* (Ithaca: Cornell University Press, 1985), and, for Burroughs's comments on his misogyny, Pounds, "The Postmodern Anus," *Front*, 224–25, 232 n. 22. Neal Oxenhandler's psychologically oriented study, "Listening to Burroughs' Voice" (*Front*, 133–47), emphasizes sadomasochism; Hassan ("The Subtracting Machine," *Front*, 55) stresses sadism, masochism, and pederasty, adding, "tenderness, love, and knowledge are absent. Sex is simply the obscene correlative of alienation. Despite the elaborate depiction of homosexuality in Burroughs' work, there is no attempt to understand or justify the homosexual."

17 Leddy (" 'Departed,' " *Review*, 36), citing Hilfer on the reader.

18 Catherine R. Stimpson, "The Beat Generation and the Trials of Homosexual Liberation," *Salmagundi* 58–59 (1982–83): 382–83.

19 Pounds ("The Postmodern Anus," *Front*, 225–26) argues that violence in Burroughs's work echoes that of mass slaughter and the death camps of World War II, and this is true of a book like *Nova Express* (although with dubious ethical impact). But it is not the case for *Naked Lunch*, whose "history" has virtually nothing to do with the Holocaust.

20 This is an obscene equivalent of Burroughs's many violent attacks on the structures and individuals that govern the world. Glover ("Utopia and Fantasy," 186) quotes Burroughs from *Rolling Stone*, 28 Feb. 1974: "why should we let these fucking newspaper politicians take over from us?" Although there is something naive in believing that the takeover has not yet occurred or is reversible, the relevance of the materials in *Naked Lunch* for American political life is inescapable.

21 Pounds, "Postmodern Anus" (*Front*, 217–32), uses Bakhtin's arguments on carnival to defend Burroughs's late fiction against marxist attacks on postmodernism. He also draws on Burroughs and Fredric Jameson to argue that Burroughs's work maps the oppressiveness of first-world society in itself and in its dominance in the third world. These propositions are relevant for the passage under discussion and for *Naked Lunch* as a whole. See Jameson, "Postmodernism, or The Cultural Logic of Late Capitalism," *New Left Review* 146 (1984): 53–92; and "Third World Literature in the Era of Multinational Capitalism," *Social Text* 15 (1986): 65–88; see also Terry Eagleton, "Capitalism, Modernism and Postmodernism," *New Left Review* 148 (1984): 116–28.

22 Burroughs discussed ignorance about AIDS and prejudice against homosexuals in an interview with David Ehrenstein, "Burroughs: On Tear Gas, Queers, *Naked Lunch*, and the Ginsberg Affair," *The Advocate* 581 (July 16, 1991): 43, cited by Lee Edelman, "The Mirror and the Tank: 'AIDS,' Subjectivity, and the Rhetoric of Activism," in *Writing* AIDS: *Gay*

Literature, Language, and Analysis, ed. Timothy F. Murphy and Suzanne Poirier (New York: Columbia University Press, 1993), 36 n. 14.

chapter 7

1 See for example the brilliant article by my colleague Réda Bensmaïa, "Poétique et androgynie: *Le livre du sang* d'Abdelkebir Khatibi," in *Poétiques croisées du Maghreb*, special number of *Itinéraires et Contacts de Cultures* 14 (1991): 99–109; David M. Bethea, *The Shape of Apocalypse in Modern Russian Fiction* (Princeton: Princeton University Press, 1989); and the papers presented at the session entitled "Visions of the Apocalypse: End of the Century, End of the World," Modern Language Association Convention, New York, N.Y., Dec. 28, 1992, in particular Evans Lansing Smith, "(Re)Figuring *Revelation*: Mann, Broch, Cortazar," and Patricia Merivale, "Sonatas of Rubble and Rust: Four Artist Parables of the Apocalypse." Although Merivale focuses on contemporary writers such as Claude Ollier and Peter Hanka, her range of reference extends from Mary Shelley's *The Last Man* (1826) to the tradition of science fiction.

2 For a wide-ranging study including Wittig, see Frances Bartkowski, *Feminist Utopias* (Lincoln: University of Nebraska Press, 1989).

3 See Cathy Linstrum, "L'Asile des femmes: Subjectivity and Femininity in Breton's *Nadja* and Wittig's *Le Corps lesbien*," *Nottingham French Studies* 27 (1988): 35–45; and especially the superb treatment of Wittig's production as a response to surrealism and other male-dominated French movements in Elaine Marks, "Lesbian Intertextuality," in *Homosexualities in French Literature: Cultural Contexts/Critical Texts*, ed. George Stambolian and Elaine Marks (Ithaca: Cornell University Press, 1979), 353–77.

4 For Burroughs's opinion that women should create a separate utopia, and for views of *The Wild Boys* and *The Cities of Red Night* as futuristic and retroactive utopias, see Jennie Skerl and Robin Lydenberg, eds., *William Burroughs at the Front* (Carbondale: Southern Illinois University Press, 1991), 190–91, 225.

5 Hélène Vivienne Wenzel, "The Text as Body/Politics: An Appreciation of Monique Wittig's Writings in Context," *Feminist Studies* 7 (1981): 264–87, esp. 282. See also E. Marks, "Lesbian Intertextuality"; Diane Griffin Crowder, "Amazons and Mothers? Monique Wittig, Hélène Cixous and Theories of Women's Writing," *Contemporary Literature* 24 (1983): 117–44; Namascar Shaktini, "Displacing the Phallic Subject: Wittig's Lesbian Writing," *Signs: Journal of Women in Culture and Society* 8 (1982): 29–44. Wenzel, 284–85, shows how Wittig's writing appropriates for the female traditional male forms — Bildungsroman, epic (*Les Guérillères*), "Song of Songs," dictionary-lexicon.

6 Among others by H. Adlai Murdoch, "Severing the (M)other Connection: The Representation of Cultural Identity in Jamaica Kincaid's *Annie John*," *Callaloo* 13 (1990): 325–40.

7 Selwyn R. Cudjoe, "Jamaica Kincaid and the Modernist Project: An Interview," in *Caribbean Women Writers: Essays from the First International Conference*, ed. Cudjoe (Wellesley, Mass.: Calaloux Publications, 1990), 215–32, esp. 218, 226, 229, 230.

8 See Wenzel, "Text as Body/Politics," 265; Crowder, "Amazons and Mothers?," 143. In addition to those articles, for the history of the conflict between Cixous and Wittig see Ann Rosalind Jones, "Writing the Body: Toward an Understanding of L'Ecriture féminine," *Feminist Studies* 7 (1981): 247–63; Cecile Lindsay, "Body/Language: French Feminist Utopias," *The French Review* 60 (1986): 46–55. Most of the articles I cite are favorable to Wittig as opposed to Cixous. In subsequent years American feminist writers have continued their attack on the "essentialism" of French feminist thought. See notably Judith Butler, *Gender Trouble: Feminism and the Subversion of Identity* (New York: Routledge, 1990). Butler mentions Cixous only once in passing, and instead focuses her critique on Wittig as well as Julia Kristeva and Luce Irigaray. For Butler, not only gender but sex and the body itself are not natural but cultural-political constructs — a pertinent but extreme position that I do not believe undermines the writing by Wittig and Kincaid treated here.

9 The sexual trauma and allegory of class murder in *Maldoror* and similar themes in *Naked Lunch* are not unrelated.

10 I quote from the translation by David Le Vay (Boston: Beacon Press, 1985); the French text was published by the Editions de Minuit (Paris, 1969). For a book-length treatment of Wittig's writing, see Erika Ostrovsky, *A Constant Journey: The Fiction of Monique Wittig* (Carbondale: Southern Illinois University Press, 1991). For aspects of form in *Les Guérillères*, see my colleague Laura G. Durand's "Heroic Feminism as Art," *Novel* 8 (1974): 71–77; Jean Duffy, "Women and Language in *Les Guérillères* by Monique Wittig," *Stanford French Review* 7 (1983): 399–412; Lawrence M. Porter, "Writing Feminism: Myth, Epic and Utopia in Monique Wittig's *Les Guérillères*," *L'Esprit Créateur* 29 (1989): 92–100; Jennifer Waelti-Walters, "Circle Games in Monique Wittig's *Les Guérillères*," *Perspectives on Contemporary Literature* 6 (1980): 59–64; and especially Marthe Rosenfeld, "Language and the Vision of a Lesbian-Feminist Utopia in Wittig's *Les Guérillères*," *Frontiers: A Journal of Women's Studies* 6 (1981): 6–9.

11 See Crowder, "Amazons and Mothers?," 126; Mary Spraggins, "Myth and Ms.: Entrapment and Liberation in Monique Wittig's *Les Guérillères*," *The International Fiction Review* 3 (1976): 47–51; and especially Winnie Woodhull, "By Myriad Constellations: Monique Wittig and the Writing of Women's Experience," in *Power, Gender, Values*, ed. Judith Genova (Alberta: Academic Printing and Publishing, 1987), 13–26.

12 Not only in *At the Bottom of the River* but in (historically and racially pointed) "floral" writing in *The New Yorker*, e.g., Oct. 5, 1992; Feb. 22 and Mar. 29, 1993 — and also in her novel *Lucy* (New York: Penguin Plume, 1991), 17–18, 28–30.

13 *Abracadabrant* recalls Rimbaud's "Le Coeur volé" and more generally his effort to see *things* in a visionary way; there are similar themes in Breton, including his preference, in *Nadja* and elsewhere, for "found" objects. See also Michel de Certeau's description of *la perruque* as practiced by French factory workers, "On the Oppositional Practices of Everyday Life," *Social Text* 3 (1980): 3–43, esp. 3–4, cited in Ross Chambers, *Room For Maneuver: Reading (the) Oppositional (in) Narrative* (Chicago: University of Chicago Press, 1991), 6–7.

14 Crowder, "Amazons and Mothers?," 119.

15 See the reunification of the fallen human being at the end of many works by Blake, and similar themes in Rimbaud, including the closing lines of *Une Saison en enfer*.

16 See Marthe Rosenfeld, "Language and the Vision," 9.

17 On this passage see Diane Griffin Crowder, "The Semiotic Functions of Ideology in Literary Discourse," in *Literature and Ideology*, special number of *The Bucknell Review*, ed. James M. Heath (East Brunswick, N.J.: Associated University Presses, 1982): 157–68. In her 1994 doctoral dissertation in comparative literature at Brown University, "Myth as Muteness, Myth as Voice: Feminism, Quest and Imperialism," Ellen H. Douglass draws on an extraordinary range of feminist theorists, theologians, and writers to develop a theory of feminist myth. Although Douglass does not treat Kincaid in the thesis, it will be seen that all of the features of her title are apt for that writer's work.

18 I quote *River*, most of which was first published in *The New Yorker*, from the Vintage Aventura edition (New York, 1985). The back cover of this book refers to the work as "stories," not (as we shall see) an adequate term. Two collections of criticism on Caribbean women writers provide background for and commentary on Kincaid: *Out of the Kumbla: Caribbean Women and Literature*, ed. Carole Boyce Davis and Elaine Savory Fido (Trenton, N.J.: Africa World Press, 1990); and *Caribbean Women Writers: Essays from the First International Conference*, ed. Selwyn R. Cudjoe (Wellesley, Mass.: Calaloux Publications, 1990). See also Murdoch, "Severing the (M)other Connection"; Patricia Ismond, "Jamaica Kincaid: 'First They Must Be Children,'" *World Literature Written in English* 28 (1988): 336–41; Wendy Dutton, "Merge and Separate: Jamaica Kincaid's Fiction," *World Literature Today* 63 (1989): 406–10. The obsession with the mother and the significance of race and of voodoo or obeah magic are stressed, though there is an unfortunate tendency to use

the semiautobiographical novel *Annie John* to "explain" the visionary moments in *River* (*Kumbla*, 5; Dutton, 406).

19 Jamaica Kincaid, *Annie John* (New York: Penguin Plume, 1985); *A Small Place* (New York: Penguin Plume, 1988).

20 Accusation systematically becomes cooperation, however, as more and more our sympathy is enlisted to understand the plight of the former slaves.

21 Among many of Kingsley's targets are the evils of class, work, and exploitation. Yet the wonderful visions in the book come about only because Tom is *dead*, and one could argue that the work is not at all ideologically liberating. In particular it must have infuriated Kincaid to see the extent to which it perpetuates English (and male) power: "Meanwhile, do you learn your lessons, and thank God that you have plenty of cold water to wash in; and wash in it too, like a true Englishman" — Charles Kingsley, *The Water Babies: A Fairy Tale for a Land-Baby*, 1st ed. (London and Cambridge: Macmillan and Company, 1863), 349.

22 I refer particularly to a classic expression of Caribbean magic realism, Alejo Carpentier's preface to *El reino de este mundo* (1949), which "rediscovers" the marvelous in Caribbean life through the influence of French surrealism (not without, may it be said, an accompanying element of sexism). Along with surrealist writers and artists, Carpentier cites Rimbaud and Lautréamont as highly representative of "literatura maravillosa." I am indebted to Ellen Douglass for this reference. See the edition prefaced by Federico Acevedo (Rio Piedras, Puerto Rico: Editorial de la Universidad de Puerto Rico, 1994), 5–11. In contrast, I remind the reader that in an interview with Selwyn R. Cudjoe reprinted in *Caribbean Women Writers*, Kincaid stresses the influence of her mother (who named her), obeah magic, including a detail reproduced in *River* (the crawling of a worm from a dead man's leg), an awareness of a higher reality beyond the normal sense world, and the inseparability of waking and dream states ("Jamaica Kincaid and the Modernist Project: An Interview," 215–32, esp. 218, 226, 229, 230).

23 Typical of some early uncomprehending journalistic reviews, Edith Milton's (!) connection between *River* and Blake is peevish: "Sometimes eccentricity works, sometimes not" (*New York Times Book Review*, Jan. 15, 1984, p. 22).

24 Like Gwen and the red girl in *Annie John*.

25 Dutton, "Merge and Separate" (408–9), evokes the Sibyl's cave in Mary Shelley's *The Last Man*. She also quotes Zora Neale Hurston on the role of women in voodoo religion in ways that indicate a closer link between Kincaid and Wittig than might otherwise be assumed:

She [the voodoo priestess] replies by throwing back her veil and revealing her sex organs. The ceremony means that this is the infinite, the ultimate truth. . . . It is considered the greatest honor for all males participating to kiss her organ of creation for Damballa, the god of gods has permitted them to come face to face with truth.
(*Tell My Horse* [Berkeley: Turtle Island, 1983], 137–38).

26 This verbal felicity includes the primarily iambic opening pattern; the hushed exclamation produced by *how* without exclamation point and the very soft sound of *soft*; the *a* and *l* sounds and the falling end rhythm of "blackness as it falls."

27 In her interview with Cudjoe ("Modernist Project," 218–20), Kincaid discusses the reason for changing her name, noting — and this is again indicative of the female, matriarchal origins of her writing — that her original name was given her by her mother.

28 See, among many news reports, Anthony Lewis' column "Fear of the Truth," *New York Times*, April 2, 1993, p. 33.

29 See the poem beginning "This lime tree bower my prison."

conclusion

1 Stephen D. O'Leary, *Arguing the Apocalypse: A Theory of Millennial Rhetoric* (New York: Oxford University Press, 1994), 10.

2 Jacques Derrida indeed argues that Marx's thought haunts the contemporary period in the way in which Marx and Engels wrote in the *Communist Manifesto* that communism haunted

Europe: *Spectres de Marx: L'Etat de la dette, le travail du deuil et la nouvelle Internationale* (Paris: Galilée, 1993).

3 In addition to works already cited, see Benjamin, "The Work of Art in the Age of Mechanical Reproduction," in *Illuminations: Essays and Reflections*, trans. Harry Zohn (New York: Schocken, 1969), 217–51; Michel Foucault, *Madness and Civilization: A History of Insanity in the Age of Reason*, trans. Richard Howard (New York: North American Library, 1971), and *The Birth of the Clinic: An Archeology of Medical Perception*, trans. A. M. Sheridan Smith (New York: Pantheon Books, 1973).

4 See, again, Kari Weil, *Androgyny and the Denial of Difference* (Charlottesville: University Press of Virginia, 1992).

5 See Northrup Frye, *The Anatomy of Criticism: Four Essays* (Princeton: Princeton University Press, 1957); Boris Eichenbaum, "The Theory of the 'Formal Method,' " in Hazard Adams, ed., *Critical Theory Since Plato* (New York: Harcourt Brace Jovanovich, 1971), 829–46, esp. 843–45.

6 In addition to works already cited, see the now-classic passages by Lévi-Strauss, Foucault, and Lacan anthologized in *The Structuralists from Marx to Lévi-Strauss*, ed. Richard T. and Fernande M. De George (Garden City: Doubleday Anchor, 1972); see also *The Foucault Reader*, ed. Paul Rabinow (New York: Pantheon, 1984). Among later theoretical writings in France, Deleuze and Guattari's *A Thousand Plateaus: Capitalism and Schizophrenia*, trans. Brian Massumi (Minneapolis: University of Minnesota Press, 1987), recalls some of our visionary writers in its fluid, even molecular conception of the self.

7 See Peter Burger, *Theory of the Avant-Garde*, trans. Michael Shaw (Minneapolis: University of Minnesota Press, 1984); Renato Poggioli, *The Theory of the Avant-Garde*, trans. Gerald Fitzgerald (Cambridge: Harvard University Press, Belknap Press, 1968); and the excellent treatment of the use of the avant-garde tactic by the surrealists to gain prominence in Beret E. Strong's doctoral thesis in comparative literature, Brown University, 1991 — forthcoming as *The Poetic Avant-Garde: The Groups of Borges, Auden and Breton* (Houston: Rice University Press, 1996).

8 *Le Nouvel Observateur*, 22–28 July 1993: 64–66.